OFF-CENTERED
LEADERSHIP

OFF-CENTERED LEADERSHIP

The DOGFISH HEAD GUIDE
to MOTIVATION,
COLLABORATION,
and SMART GROWTH

sam calagione

Cheers Joe!
NAMASTE!

WILEY

This book is dedicated to all of the leaders, past and present,
who have helped Dogfish Head grow into the strong,
off-centered company we are today;
especially Nick Benz, Todd Bollig, Mariah Calagione,
Cindy Dunson, Tim Hawn, and Neal Stewart.
Namaste!

For me, art that's alive and urgent is art that's about what it is to be a human being. And whether one is a human being in times of enormous profundity and depth and challenge, or one is trying to be a human being in times that appear to be shallow and commercial and materialistic, really isn't all that relevant to the deeper project. The deeper project is: what is it to be human?

—*David Foster Wallace*[1]

---

[1]From *Conversations with David Foster Wallace*, edited by Stephen J. Burn (Jackson, MS: University Press of Mississippi, 2012).

Contents

Introduction

But yield who will to their separation,
My object in living is to unite
My avocation and my vocation
As my two eyes make one in sight.
Only where love and need are one,
And the work is play for mortal stakes,
Is the deed ever really done
For Heaven and the future's sakes.

—*Robert Frost, "Two Tramps in Mud Time"*

Sitting in the driver's seat of my new used muscle car, paintbrush in hand, the sound of the throaty engine music to my ears, I began painting the words "Go Slowly, Go Thoughtfully" in bright-red acrylic paint on the center of my steering wheel.

ENJOY THE JOURNEY

Just before I turned 46, my grandmother Jessie passed away at the glorious age of 96. She had run a small business with her husband, Sam, and had been a great inspiration to me. As I thought about her life, I figured if my grandmother lived to the age of 96, then it was certainly reasonable to assume I could live to be, say, 92 if I started taking better care of myself,

Also featured in color photo insert

"Go slowly, go thoughtfully."

stopped stressing out so much, and stopped trying to do so many new things so quickly.

So I decided to treat my 46th birthday as my definitive midlife moment—the unofficial halfway mark of my journey along this mortal coil—and celebrate this existential milestone memorably with gusto.

I traded in my sensible used Volvo sedan for a 500-horsepower three-year-old Dodge Challenger Super Bee. This isn't just any muscle car. It's the newer iteration of my boyhood dream car that I have thought about since I was a six-year-old doodling the earlier model upon my grade school textbooks back in the late 1970s.

I bought the car on my 46th birthday and within just two months had to bring it in for service twice. The mechanic explained that the car's "big-ass engine" (mechanic's term originally, now mine as well) needed more time to warm up than normal, much smaller engines do; I couldn't just jam the car into drive and peel out.

Hence, the "go slowly" reminder. And the "go thoughtfully" part is to remind me not to check my phone for any reason while driving. To focus on the present, the task at hand, and to enjoy the journey.

Also featured in color photo insert

This is me in my new used car wearing the road-mullet wig I keep in my car to embarrass my wife when I peel out incognito.

This reminder, to go slowly and go thoughtfully, now emblazoned on my steering wheel, has also become the mantra for the thoroughly enjoyable, illuminating, and challenging personal and vocational midlife crossroads I find myself navigating. Like my engine, I am warming up to the notion that I can't move as fast and take as many risks with myself or my company as I did a couple of decades ago when we were both much younger.

CELEBRATING THE EPIPHANY

Within a few weeks of my birthday, Dogfish Head celebrated a milestone as well: our 20th anniversary as the first brewpub in the first state. I figured if I were going to treat 46 as a halfway point in my personal life, it would also make sense (at least to me) to treat the 20th anniversary of the company I founded as the halfway mark of my role within this company. Thus, I reasoned, Dogfish Head would be the only company I would ever work for. Why? Because I love what I do and I love the people I have gotten to know as coworkers and beer lovers throughout the two decades of my entrepreneurial journey. But I also realized that to be the most beneficial to the company, my role at Dogfish Head over the next 20 years needed to be different than the type of work I did during the first 20 years. In a word, I needed to *evolve*. The work priorities and habits I had relied on in those first 20 years could not sustainably remain the same for the next 20.

To commemorate, capture, and internalize this epiphany, I got a tattoo.

JOINING THE FANS

Like the famous line spoken by Blanche DuBois in the play *A Streetcar Named Desire*, I have always depended on the kindness of strangers. At the heart of Dogfish Head's exploration of goodness is our off-centered version of the golden rule—always aspire to do for others as you would want others to do for you. With the help of hundreds of amazing, talented coworkers past and present, we have succeeded in building a company focused on producing the types of beers, spirits, food, events, and spaces that we envisioned other creative, adventurous, rebellious people would want to experience, engage with, and rally around.

Also featured in color photo insert

And rally they have. Dogfish started out as the smallest brewing operation in America and is now the 13th largest craft brewery out of over 4,000. Through the years I have met, personally thanked, and high-fived tens of thousands of hardcore Dogfish fans who have acted as our evangelists, introducing their friends to our beers and helping us grow. Some of these evangelists

Just one of the Dogfish Head tattoos fans have shown me throughout the years.

are so passionate about Dogfish Head that they literally bled for us, tattoo-ing various regions of their bodies with our brand to make it part of their permanent selves.

When people would show me their tats or ask to take photos with me as they flashed their tattoos to the camera, I felt both pride and gratitude. Over time, though, as I met more and more of these bold and inked Dogfish evangelists, a third emotion would creep in—guilt.

If these people cared enough about what Dogfish stands for to literally brand themselves, the least I could do was to join them in solidarity. After all, I first sketched the Dogfish shark-and-broken-shield logo nearly 22 years ago when writing my business plan, and I have been thinking about it and obsessing about its place in the world pretty much every day since.

So now I am a 46-year-old entrepreneur with a new tattoo and a used muscle car who sometimes peels out at stop signs but doesn't break speed limits as often as he used to when he drove the more sensible Volvo. To her immense credit, my erratic driving habits embarrass my wife, Mariah, more than the muscle car or the tattoo. I have taken to wearing a mullet wig on the rare occasions she accompanies me in my car, under the pretense that I think she might be less mortified if pedestrians and other drivers in our small town don't recognize that the crazy driver she is riding with is her husband. It goes without saying that Mariah's sense of humor and patience with my shenanigans, starting when we began dating in high school in the mid-eighties, remains unflappable.

Admittedly my tat is less ornate and bold than some others I've admired, but it's pretty much identical to the sketch I first drew 22 years ago. "But it's facing the wrong way," I can almost hear you saying, if you are familiar with our logo. Nope. The image of my tattoo did not get reversed in the design phase of this book. I purposely decided to have the shark in the shield face outward on my forearm instead of inward, as it would were it a faithful representation of our company logo.

PROCEED SLOWLY, GO THOUGHTFULLY

So . . . this is how getting a tattoo, the second notable moment in my most-excellent-midlife-crossroads, ties so directly to the first notable moment of buying that used muscle car. To use a vehicular analogy, when

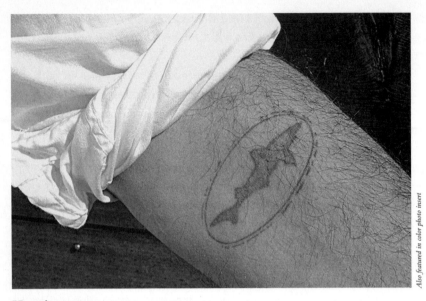

Also featured in color photo insert

Here is my tat.

Dogfish opened we were sorta like a 50cc dirt bike—simple, nimble, thrilling, and powered by a very small engine. Instead of horsepower, we originally ran on about 20 manpower if you consider our payroll the year we opened. We could bet the farm at every turn and make split-second spontaneous decisions and whimsical choices. We could all keep aware and in tune with each change of direction because all of us experienced these zigs and zags together in the same single building, the brewpub in Rehoboth Beach, where we brewed and sold our beers and cooked and sold our food.

You can risk a lot more when you have very little in totality to put at risk.

Today this company, which began pretty much as my company out of my imagination, has grown into *our* company—230 of us and counting. And our company needs to run a lot more like a very powerful, very intricate muscle car than a frisky little dirt bike.

We need to grow more slowly. And we need to go more thoughtfully.

In the last few years, we have prioritized strong growth over fast growth. We have embraced this strategy in order to carefully expand all the key components of our company in harmony: personnel, equipment, and resources. Going slowly still means going forward. Going forward means growing. And growing thoughtfully means a shift in thinking and acting at Dogfish that needs to begin with me.

It begins with me but it takes a village. This is not my leadership book. The biggest reason our company has been successful is because we have created a community of coworkers that champions strong leadership coming from many talented people within our organization. This is their book as much as it is mine; I am just telling our story. Of course, it is from my perspective, but I am hopeful that the respect I have for each of their perspectives and inputs on our journey comes through. As the leaders of Dogfish Head, over the course of 20 years, we have mostly been aligned on where the company is heading and how we will get there. Mostly, but not always.

I used to thrill in taking unplanned risks, abruptly zigging the handlebars of my dirt bike to the left when everyone (both inside and outside the company) would expect me to turn to the right. I would be thrilled when the almost-out-of-gas dashboard light would come on and my adrenaline would pump as I sped down the road without knowing if I would make it to the next fuel stop; none of that mattered because I so zealously enjoyed the risk-soaked ride.

Today, at the center of my own journey—at this midpoint in my personal and professional life—I am embracing the need for me and for our company to enter a new phase and *proceed slowly*. This evolution will occur in different ways for different coworkers, but for me it means to not act quickly or rashly, to live in the present here and now, to go deep into the moment and not spend quite so much of my time thinking about the future.

Go thoughtfully is a good working mantra as I embark on this next phase of my professional and personal journey. To think before I act, to recognize, embrace, and encourage the creative input and thoughtfulness of all of my coworkers and fellow leaders at Dogfish Head. To think less about my own personal gratification in unilaterally deciding creative and strategic direction and think more about collaboratively blending together the creativity and enthusiasm of the great people helping me run this company to decide those things. Making all this happen will certainly be challenging, but the endgame is clear. I want Dogfish to not always require my daily involvement in its running. I want the company that I started to outlive me.

In retrospect, I now see that in certain ways I spent the first 20 years of my career, for better and for worse, directing Dogfish Head as my own creative-cathartic recreation center. I have always acknowledged and I truly appreciate the incredible contributions coworkers have made to the construction and expansion of this playground. But old habits die hard. I had to be selfish in leading Dogfish when it was tiny because its potential existed more in my head than in the marketplace. In many ways, Dogfish Head has been the physical embodiment of my imagination—which is why I internalized so much of what I loved about the company and was reluctant to collaborate internally on big picture strategy for so many years.

This is no longer necessary. It's also no longer what is best for Dogfish Head if it is to continue growing—slowly and thoughtfully—in a direction that is best for the company and that allows Dogfish to have a life that is longer than my own (remember, I am pretty sure I am only going to be around for exactly 46 more years).

Now that Dogfish Head has evolved into a 230-manpower sizable machine with a "big-ass engine" that needs time to warm up, I am learning many things in all aspects of life: as an entrepreneur, as a father and a husband, as a flawed-but-committed-to-continue-learning leader. My hope in writing this book is that many of the lessons I am learning will be useful to others facing similar challenges on their own business and leadership journeys.

The narrative of this book is more of a movable feast than the first book I wrote about my entrepreneurial journey at Dogfish Head, *Brewing Up a Business*. For this book I wanted to incorporate the others who have joined me on the leadership journey within our company (like my wife, Mariah, and our CEO, Nick Benz). I also chose to include sage business and creative advice from mentors and inspiring people who don't work at our company but with whom I have forged meaningful friendships (like Nick Brayton, president of Woolrich, and the musician and actor Will Oldham). I spent a lot of writing time for this book on the road, while I was doing events and collaborative projects with many of the folks I interviewed for this book. I have written before about the importance of roaming the marketplace to get a deeper perception of your brand and your own business journey and I have done that continually during the time I have worked on this book.

As the graphic designer and professor Natalie Davis puts it in her fine essay "Sweat Equity," "Seek your inspiration in unexpected places. Expand beyond the web for research, and get out in the world—to a bookstore, library, or theater. Follow other passions you have put aside too soon. Go to the ballet, borrow your younger sister's graphic novels, and volunteer at the food bank. Take a road trip and bring along a camera and your sketchbook. Expand your life experiences and the circle of people you interact with day-to-day, and your work will become richer and deeper in meaning."

This has been true for me as my work at the company I started has continued to evolve. My role is changing. I intend to spend more of my time externalizing and sharing the creative and strategic opportunities that we, as a team, collaboratively conceive and develop together. All 230 (and growing) of us are working together to grow Dogfish Head in the right direction. I am trying to look up and look out for the best ideas instead of looking too much within—which gets me back to my midlife tattoo. As I mentioned, the shark-and-shield logo on my arm faces out. If I did the tattoo accurate to our logo, it would face in. It's facing out to remind me that I must do so as well.

A THIRD WAY FORWARD

I opened this introduction with an excerpt of a poem from one of my favorite writers, Robert Frost. When I rediscovered this particular poem awhile ago, it immediately reminded me of the happy predicament I now find myself in at Dogfish Head. While I personally enjoy creative chaos and adventurous experimentation as key components at the heart of our brand, I now know that what is best for Dogfish is for me to spend more of my time helping my coworkers organize and amplify the products and projects we have already embarked on and less of my time dreaming about new products and projects.

When you read the passage of Frost's poem, you see it's evocative and sounds conversational, anecdotal, and relaxed from the outside looking in. But from the inside looking out, it's a very complex and organized piece of art built on an organized foundation of tightly rhymed iambic tetrameter lines. I see that the contrast between external perception and internal structure is very similar to our current reality at Dogfish. It works well for us that externally Dogfish is perceived as a fun-loving, informal, experimental, whimsical company. We can be all of those things, but internally we must be focused, organized, and working from a shared and well-communicated plan if we are going to execute to the highest level of our potential.

In the poem it appears that two tramps are confronting Frost the writer and the ax wielder with an ethical binary choice. He can *either* let them chop his wood (they need the work and the pay) *or* he can continue chopping himself because he enjoys the task and finds it personally rewarding. Doing something you love as your livelihood is what I think he means when he writes about making his vocation his avocation. As I read this poem, though, I can see another way forward between the lines. Frost didn't put it on the page and I don't know if he would approve of my suggestion, but what if the narrator attempted to create a happy medium? Instead of handing his ax over to the two tramps, what if he got them their own axes? Described to them their goal in terms of number of logs split in a certain amount of time? What if he let them use their own technique and style while still sharing what he had learned from his own experiences? And what if he continued to chop away alongside them because it brings him joy? Could this collaborative approach be even more satisfying than doing what you love to do alone? I am ready to find out if this third way forward can work for me, for my fellow leaders, and for the company.

chapter 1
FROM ENTREPRENEUR TO LEADER

Since the day Dogfish Head started back in 1995, we've been lucky. That's not to say that we haven't worked hard for our success or that we haven't had to learn to roll with some punches. All in all, though, a lot of good things keep happening to Dogfish Head. We try to do good things every day. I used to believe you make your own luck. I now think that is only partially true. Karma is a close relative to luck. And as Joseph Conrad said, "It is the mark of an inexperienced man not to believe in luck."

Within the first year of launching the company, we had a consistent positive cash flow to build on at our original brewpub. Few entrepreneurs can say that. What's more, we achieved this early success in the particularly brutal world of the restaurant industry, where most new establishments don't survive past their third year. The company opened up as Dogfish Head Brewings & Eats, a pub in Rehoboth Beach, Delaware, where we brewed and sold our beer. The decision to launch as a brewpub, a brewery business within a restaurant, was a gamble, but I figured that I could reduce the risk of the brewery failing by supplementing it with revenue from the restaurant. That proved to be a good bet, but it was never a sure thing.

When I say lucky, though, I'm not talking about monetary good fortune. As I mentioned previously, "being lucky" to me means being well served by good karma, which is something we consciously try to cultivate. The hallmark of our culture, what I'm constantly emphasizing with our coworkers, is that Dogfish Head is not a company that sells beer (or food or whatever) but rather is a company that creates *high-quality, valuable, innovative experiences based on fairness and respect for our customers and community. This is our exploration of goodness.*

From day one my main goal was to satisfy beer drinkers like me, eager for an experience much more flavorful, adventurous, and satisfying than the Corporate Industrial Lager that dominated the landscape and consumer perception of American beer in the mid-nineties. I went into business more with the idealism of an artist than with ambitious financial aspirations, so I like to think that this focus on creating positive energy—enriching people's lives by making unique, authentic, off-centered beer—was my prime motivation. Not making money. Perhaps this sounds self-serving, but it's true. Money may be the fuel of a business, but at Dogfish Head it's not our soul.

We encourage free expression and nonconformity.

Another reason so many of our most valuable coworkers have stayed at Dogfish Head is the generous compensation program we implemented even as we were just getting our feet under us. Sharing the fruits of success has been our priority since our earliest days. We have a great insurance package including health and dental, a free case of beer for all brewery coworkers every paycheck, a weekly happy hour with complimentary beer and snacks for all coworkers and their families, and half-price food and drink for coworkers at our pub and brewery. The loyalties and talents of the people who have joined me to grow the company have played a tremendous role in our company's success.

By the year 2000, we had become sufficiently established so that I no longer woke up each day wondering whether Dogfish Head was going to stay in business. There had been plenty of existential doubt before then, super-stressful times when we revved hard on the revenue growth engine to buy additional equipment and brewing systems. I'd mask my concern during such moments with a confident game face and lead by example. "Sure, we're not perfect," I'd tell my coworkers, "but let's fix one small thing every day, try hard, fail forward, learn from each mistake, and we will be closer to perfect tomorrow than we are today."

In the year 2000, the production brewery we built separate from our Rehoboth location became profitable in the same way the Brewings & Eats restaurant was from the start. Profitability in our business was meager early on, so I never take it for granted. Our brand has to stay relevant to our customers; our products have to remain distinctive. But from that year forward, five years into the life of the company, I didn't have to worry about the cost side of the business. Other smart leaders at Dogfish keep costs under control, and I focus on creating new projects and products to increase revenue, competitive differentiation, and brand recognition.

We remain a frugal company, as we have been since day one. A bootstrapping mentality is hardwired into our DNA, stemming from our entrepreneurial beginnings. We still approach every project and capital expenditure with an eye toward vetting efficiencies as if we were a start-up. We're not trying to be cheap or beat up our vendors or pay less for something than it's worth, but when our business partners and our own coworkers see that we care about pennies, it makes them all sharpen their pencils. We are particularly careful and conscientious about the bidding process for our equipment and buildings. This is especially important in a bricks-and-mortar-intensive business like brewing, where the physical capital to expand capacity infrastructure can cost millions of dollars each year.

CREATIVE FREEDOM

Being freed from anxieties on the cost side allowed me the freedom to be creative. For the majority of my work hours I was unleashed to do what I most love—come up with new ideas for Dogfish Head.

My role as the founder, chairman, and majority vote holder made this creative freedom both a blessing and a curse for the company. I could launch an initiative pretty much on my own say-so, without first having to clear organizational hurdles or establish a comprehensive plan to move an idea forward. My personal vision drove our actions; strategic choices shaping the future of Dogfish Head were preeminently (and almost exclusively) mine. From my perspective as an entrepreneur, that was the good news. The bad news, from the perspective of my coworkers, was that I was always having ideas.

While often serving our goals, the result of my high-voltage energy pumping through the system could also, at times, be disruptive to the organization. As "the boss," I would announce my latest business idea, and coworkers would have to switch gears and revise schedules to prioritize it. Nobody except Mariah felt empowered to resist. And I didn't always listen to her or our CEO Nick Benz or the rest of our leadership team when they would present resistance.

After almost two decades of successful growth I was convinced that this gut-oriented approach was for the best. Sometimes it was indeed for the best, as in the case of the Choc Lobster brew we released in 2012. A brew with cocoa nibs and lobsters, it originated as part of our program to make experimental one-off batches for our beer dinners. When I tasted it, paired with chocolate lobster bisque and a white truffle lobster salad slider at the dinner, I thought it was so terrific that we brewed a scaled-up batch to offer at the pub. When I proposed rolling it out commercially, everyone internally and externally insisted it would never sell since we would have to charge so much more than the average keg price for a beer made with hundreds of pounds of lobster. I was sure the beer would be a success and rolled out production anyway. It turned out to be well received, winning a Great American Beer Festival silver medal. We went from brewing a few kegs at the pub to hundreds of kegs that we sell in states up and down the East Coast.

In other instances, though, my next great thing ended up costing us time and money without much return. Like the combination see-through visor and baseball hat I designed. I figured this hat would play off our penchant for combining beers into a new style or beverage mash ups (such as beer-wine hybrids like Sixty-One, which was conceived when I poured some red wine into a glass of 60 Minute IPA, or our Positive Contact, a hybrid of beer and cider brewed with Fuji apples, roasted farro, cayenne pepper, and fresh cilantro). In this case I wanted to do a mash up between a base-ball cap and a sun visor, with the character of Paul Bunyan featured more prominently on that hat than our logo. We must have devoted the bulk of time in 4 two-hour marketing meetings over the course of several months to this project; designers drew up a half-dozen iterations, and three different prototypes were produced. I was confident that our customers, themselves being so off-centered and fearless, were going to love it. We stocked it at the shops in our restaurant and brewery, where it died on the shelves. It is still dying on our shelves, where you can buy one very reasonably at a deeply marked-down sale price or, if you prefer, for a nominal fee on eBay.

Rather than worry about consequences of abrupt midcourse corrections, I prided myself on taking risks, learning quickly from our missteps, and changing course. Were Dogfish Head a conventional company, the seemingly erratic course I sometimes steered the organization on would not have been tolerated. But it was precisely this opportunity to boldly guide us into unexplored waters that I found so satisfying. The thrill I personally got from not knowing what would happen next was a powerful psychic reward. To me, this feeling was the essence of being an entrepreneur.

That said, I am learning that being hooked on the adrenalin of uncertainty and directing a company unilaterally by improvisation are not the hallmarks of a great leader for a company of our scale. They are important traits for an entrepreneur to have, but they need to be tempered and honed as a company grows.

Creative inspiration for me comes from traveling outside my comfort zone—outside of what I know in general life terms and, from a business perspective, outside of what already exists in our industry. I rely on this creative urge to push beyond limits when it comes to designing a new beer. As a result, we have not spent much time looking at consumer data or conventional tastes when we decide what beer to make next. Instead, our one fixed point of reference has been to seek out innovative, off-centered ways into new products and projects.

As the person who fed those creative fires for the first 20 years, I got the most satisfaction roaming around far-flung fields that interested me. I am always on the lookout for ideas, seemingly unrelated to brewing, that can inform and complement our approach to what I like to call "the soul" of Dogfish. This is probably why, as we've evolved, we have become more than a beer company, and we do our work in many industries: food, spirits, clothes. Everything we do—making a pizza, designing a shirt, brewing a beer—informs everything else we do. Each business unit collaborates with and enhances the unique stature in the marketplace of the other business units. An apt way to capture our spirit of creative roaming is the quote from *Moby Dick* I had sewn on the collar of the shirts we do in collaboration with Woolrich, America's oldest outdoor clothing company: "I am tormented with an everlasting itch for things remote, I love to sail forbidden seas and land on barbarous coasts."

YOUR COWORKERS ARE YOUR FIRST RESPONSIBILITY

There is a term in Japanese for the ultimate expression of selfless appreciation and support: *omotenashi*. There is no direct translation in English, but the best definition might be something like: the host anticipates the needs of the guest in advance and offers a pleasant experience that guests don't expect. In the context of business, this can mean that "the customer is always right." Or simply that we want to "exceed customer expectations in every way the customer interacts with our company and the things we make. " I love the concept of omotenashi, but in my journey toward leadership, I give it a different twist: the customer is secondary.

As a leader, your first responsibility is to your coworkers. You need to support them and help them to always try to do the right thing and to be as happy doing their work as possible. Going forward, I need to redirect more of my creative energy toward this end. I'm no Zen master, so there are going to be stumbles along the way. And I still intend to personally take the lead on some experimental brewing and arts projects that are dear to my heart, creatively cathartic, and marketable. Some of these projects may go into coast-to-coast distribution and some experiments may be one-time-only small-volume brews produced for events around our Delaware facility that allow me to interact with coworkers and Dogfish fans who come to visit us in our home state. But in terms of the evolving soul of Dogfish Head, my most important role is to be one among many who collectively make the important strategic and opportunity decisions facing the company. There will still be some specific functions attached to my job responsibility, particularly as majority owner, but a central component of my evolving role at Dogfish is to allow great ideas and great people to bubble up and contribute exponentially and collectively to the company we are growing together.

With my transition in the company from single-minded entrepreneur to responsible leader, my creative approach similarly needs to change. I have to make sure the vast majority of product launches and innovation are no longer driven solely by my inspirations but, rather, by the team's collective judgment of what's best for Dogfish Head. The best ideas and recommendations of my coworkers should be as important as mine in charting new directions. I fought this for years, fearing that I would get less personal satisfaction from helping other people realize their visions than I would from being the creator myself.

It has taken me a while to get comfortable with this new approach. The first big step forward in my evolution came with experiencing satisfaction in external collaborations we undertook with bands and other breweries. I had to share creative authority in navigating these projects and I found that not only did the projects succeed but I also had lots of fun learning from and working in tandem with the related external parties. The confidence I've drawn from those experiences has prepared me to collaborate better internally within our organization. I'm not naive about the difficulty in surrendering what was, before, my autonomous control. I have had to train my brain to recognize what I know and what I don't know and focus along-side my fellow leaders on identifying the talented people who have great ideas at Dogfish Head and empowering them to continue to develop and grow our business. My ongoing transition from an entrepreneur running a business to a leader inspiring a team has taken many years, lots of effort, and one particularly difficult company retreat.

THE RETREAT, FEBRUARY 2014

It was a cold day on the Chesapeake Bay when we gathered in Cambridge, a beautiful Maryland colonial town first settled in the 1680s by English tobacco planters. We were pretty much the only off-season guests, gathered together at the beautiful waterfront resort for our annual management retreat.

As I walked in, I could imagine what my coworkers on our leadership team were thinking. In recent years there was a predictable pattern to these retreats, some small victories and some growing frustrations. Every year we would go on an off-site retreat that we would call a strategic retreat but we would mostly just discuss and argue from our own perspective about the next year's brewery beer lineup and volume forecast. We would spend what was left of our time talking about how we should be better organized and how we desperately needed a longer-term strategy. Then I would get defensive, remind everyone of our track record of flying by the seat of our pants thus far, and say something like: "If we have a plan, we won't be spontaneous."

It's true; I didn't like the concept of traditional multiyear strategic business plans. This year, though, at this annual strategic off-site meeting I had made up my mind before we started that things needed to be different moving forward.

The company had been steadily growing. This growth was rewarding and exhilarating but it meant that running an increasingly large and complex group of businesses by intuition and spontaneity was no longer beneficial. In their end-of-year reviews, coworkers made it clear they needed me and our company's other leaders to communicate better. They wanted to be more involved earlier in the new products and projects we were launching. If we all participated in the conversations, they believed, the collective outcome would be that much richer. By discussing ideas together, everybody would have a much clearer vision of where we were going. In effect, they were asking me to be more accountable to them.

I couldn't disagree with the merit of their arguments.

I had always fought the standard corporate dogma that says a smart company has to develop a multiyear strategic plan through executive level consensus and then stick to it. The problem I have is that the plan is typically based on research that projects the future based on the present and past dynamics within the industry according to a comprehensive review of where a company stands in comparison to its competitors. So you are often looking sideways or backward in this process instead of forward.

Another recent experience primed me for change that day in 2014, an event that had occurred several months prior to the retreat. I was driving my secondhand Volvo with one of my best friends. The low fuel light flashed on the dashboard. I kept going. And going. Finally, as we approached a service station, my buddy nervously asked whether I intended to stop. "Not yet," I answered. "I bet we can make the next one."

I confess: I enjoy the unexpected when the gas light goes on. I like to see how far I can get on fumes. I've completely run out of gas a few times; once I had to literally coast the last quarter mile. No matter; I like tempting fate. On this occasion, though, I could see my friend was getting truly uncomfortable since there weren't many gas stations or houses or people along this particular road. He finally freaked out. "Dude, you aren't normal! This isn't fun." I was able to put myself in his seat and, riding on little more than fumes, pulled in at the next gas station.

Afterward, I got to thinking about this episode and its relevance to Dogfish Head. Maybe, in the same way that I wasn't initially sympathetic to the anxiety I caused my friend that day in the car, I was similarly insensitive to the discomfort I was causing my coworkers in the way I steered our company. They had been expressing frustration at not having a strategic road map, but I consistently dismissed their plea for a strategic plan. The best thing that could happen to us would be that we get lost. This was my belief. The need to keep finding our own way would keep us open to opportunities other companies would not encounter and inspire us to be creative. We'd be blazing trails instead of staying on the safe, beaten path. . . . What I hadn't been hearing, though, was the anxiety in their voices. They were basing their futures and the welfare of their families on the company. Dogfish Head was no longer just an entrepreneurial adventure for a few; it was now the livelihood of many. No wonder they were worried whenever they saw the company's fuel light go on.

I wasn't completely oblivious to the effect my love of risk was having at Dogfish. There was mounting frustration throughout our leadership team (including my wife, in some instances) with my management style of "ready, fire, aim." Although I still believe in the improvisational philosophy of Black Mountain College and its mantra of "We shall see what we shall see," I understood that most of my coworkers and fellow leaders were looking for more focused direction. And I knew they were growing tired of my habit of continuously imposing my will for what we should do next and my habit of being 99 percent sure about what would come after that, effectively leaving them without much space to make their own creative contributions to our agenda.

I don't have a problem with plans per se, but I believe they need to be agile and flexible. A company's longish-term strategy should be based on a foundation of the competitive landscape of its industry and where the company stands within it. Context is everything! The plan has to be grounded in the culture of the company itself, its collective soul, before grounding it as a reaction to the competitive set. You can plan a path forward, but always with the proviso that things can quickly change and necessitate a different path. You've got to always be ready to move on.

Personally, I don't particularly like paths (no surprise there, to anybody who knows me). I truly believe that "getting off paths" is at the core of Dogfish DNA; it's what our products are all about. The quotation from

Ralph Waldo Emerson that is our guiding principle, his prescription for how to pursue goodness, is an endorsement for blazing one's own trail.

> *Whoso would be a man,*
> *must be a nonconformist.*
> *He who would gather immortal palms*
> *must not be hindered*
> *by the name of goodness,*
> *but must explore if it be goodness.*
> *Nothing is at last sacred*
> *but the integrity of your own mind.*

I knew that we were getting to a point in the company's life cycle where growing strong meant empowering others to lead with me. I recognized that the other people sitting at the leadership table were talented and motived, yet another indication of the company's good luck—that we had been able to attract such individuals. The moment had come for them to be able to contribute not only their operational and technical skills but also their own creativity and opinions about our strategy. It wasn't just me letting go as an act of higher consciousness. No. As a leader, I had become increasingly aware that we needed to aggregate the maximum amount of collective creativity we could muster to fully prosper amid an increasingly competitive commercial environment. As I say, context is everything.

Walking into the retreat meeting room that brisk February morning, I had come to realize that I was ready to not only accept a strategic plan but, more importantly, embrace it and help move us forward in creating it together; to contribute to the plan but not try to direct it myself; and, the toughest challenge, to not micromanage its implementation when I got impatient or itchy for personal creative stimulation.

I began the opening session with the story about that fateful road trip with my old friend and the dashboard fuel light. It was designed as an ice-breaker to set the tone and let people know a significant change would be taking place across Dogfish Head. We would still need a couple of years to flesh out a holistic, company-wide plan, but that day the plan for the plan was hatched.

Out of that retreat would come the beginnings of a strong business plan for our main brewery business, one produced by the whole leadership team and not just me—which was a first for Dogfish Head. The cornerstone of writing that plan was formal sessions addressing Dogfish Head's Strengths, Weaknesses, Opportunities, and Threats (SWOT). I originally encountered SWOT while on the board of the Brewers Association, which uses this methodology to create its two-year plans. Simply put, the SWOT process helps an organization identify factors that are favorable and unfavorable to achieving its objectives.

Step 1 was to clarify objectives. Instead of using conventional corporate metrics like growth or profit, we chose to focus on our company's ideals. We brainstormed about the things Dogfish Head embodied, the qualities we thought made the products successful and the company special. One by one, a list accumulated on the whiteboard: Goodness, Authenticity, Valuable Differentiation, Respect, Independence, and Competitive.

At the top of our list of Strengths were such things as brand equity (off-centered, innovative, quality) and our speed in developing products and projects. In retrospect, I think the most important item on the list was our people: "right asses in most seats" was the exact phrase. The biggest gap in the org chart at that time was a director of marketing. The company had reached the size where Mariah and I couldn't do it alone anymore; we needed a full-time marketer. We also were on the lookout for a strong operations leader to add to our team.

Hiring is perhaps the toughest and most exacting thing we do at Dogfish Head, so getting those right asses in the right seats is no small accomplishment. We take executive recruitment very seriously, which perhaps explains why we are so painfully slow at it. Personal fit is particularly important to us, given the unique culture of the company. But we also need to be confident that the candidate (and family) will be comfortable living in small-town rural Delaware.

In the interviewing process we use a shorthand phrase to summarize if the potential coworkers will be able to contribute positively to the company we want to be. When we think a person is a fit, we say: "she gets It." Having It at Dogfish is a two-way street; ours is a unique culture that simply doesn't work for some folks. There are lots of super-talented, motivated people who would be more successful in a different environment.

We've never officially defined "It," but here's my take.

People who get It are generally nice, talented, and hard-working; they use their powers for good. I'm reminded of Google's corporate motto, "Don't be evil." As I tell my children again and again (they're probably sick of hearing it), I believe we all have different superpowers but we all share the ability to use our unique powers for good or for evil. And the best teams of superheroes are those that have complementary powers that they use to do the right things in every instance where a choice can be made—from obeying a stop sign to saying "thank you" when someone does something nice, to making choices that benefit others instead of yourself. We are not saints at Dogfish Head, but as a culture, we strive to opt for the choices most filled with goodness.

When we consider candidates for hire, we are looking for people with the humility to know they must first learn why we do things the way we do before they try to use the skills and experience they have to make Dogfish better. We want them to devote their talents to improving the company; we are open to ideas from anyone. But we expect newcomers to first bend toward Dogfish before they ask Dogfish to bend toward them. As Nick often says, "We don't want new people coming in and waving the wand of change before they even fully get Dogfish."

We also want people who love people, even though this sounds like a cheesy yacht-rock lyric. Some corporate cultures thrive on internal competition (think of Jack Welch's General Electric) but not us. Our objective is to grow a great company, which takes fewer rock stars and more band members. Being a good person doesn't mean playing only support roles. The company needs its brightest and its best to be internal leaders. Getting It means you understand that at Dogfish you don't advance by stepping on your coworkers but, rather, by helping them and the company as a whole move forward.

I, myself, had to get better at humility despite my unique position at Dogfish of being not just the majority owner but also the face and analog voice of the company. (Mariah is the digital voice through social media, which she does really well.) After 20 years in the small but growing craft beer community, I'm a well-known figure because I have been involved with some high-visibility projects and because of my role in conceiving most of our high-profile beers. This fills me with mixed feelings. On the one hand, being recognizable affords real benefits to me and the company. This is particularly true if either (or both) of my children eventually chooses to work at Dogfish; there will be continuity when this family-controlled and family-led company transitions from first- to second-generation leadership.

In our emerging collaborative management model, however, my coworkers need to see me as one of many creative voices, not the sole creative voice. Internally and externally, we have a culture of sharing due credit with our coworkers and celebrating their achievements. When somebody stops me on the street or calls out to me at an event to say "I love your beer" or "I love Dogfish," I always try to say something like "On behalf of the 230 of us, I thank you for the kind words and support." In thanking a fan, I am also actively and honestly thanking my coworkers for their contributions. It may sound forced or folksy, but it comes from the heart. A big part of my job description will continue to be saying "Thank you for your support" to our customers, retailers, and distributors and taking the time to hear from them on what they would like to see more of from Dogfish Head.

The Weakness quadrant in the SWOT matrix confirmed my conviction that Dogfish Head had hit a point of inflection. The list of what we needed to fix was a collective plea for more orderly stability. Here are some of the weak points we shared in this quadrant: "Too short-term oriented," "Entire management must find equilibrium," "Too many ideas and not enough resources to maintain," "Operational accountability and systems," "Scheduling."

As I stared at this list I had to admit to myself nearly all of our weaknesses stemmed from a lack of planning, a lack of communication, and a lack of follow-through: all issues that could be addressed in a multiyear strategic plan. I was fully converted. I stopped regarding a strategic plan as a betrayal of conscience and started thinking of it as a road map for opportunity. If Dogfish Head were going to continue to be bold, it was imperative that all of us—including me—move in the same direction. Our energies and resources had to be better marshaled if we were to seize forthcoming opportunities and overcome challenges. To fail to do so, I now knew, meant that a whole lot of faithful, talented people might end up going over a cliff at my personal behest. With the help of other leaders at our company, the entrepreneur was becoming a better leader.

INTERVIEW

Nick Benz, CEO, Dogfish Head

Nick Benz is one of the most astute financial- and operational-minded business people I've ever met. He received a degree in chemical engineering, then went on to earn his MBA. His career arc at Dogfish from CFO to COO to CEO speaks for itself in terms of his capabilities. But what his resume doesn't show is how he has grown personally over that period. Along with his business acumen, his sense of humor, honesty, and deep understanding about what makes Dogfish Head stand apart from traditional business models are what have made him so integral to the leadership of our company.

What Distinguishes the Dogfish Way?

SAM: First question, Nick. Which skill honed through your engineering background has proven to be most valuable to your career path and your contributions to Dogfish Head?

NICK: I don't think I've ever answered that before. It is probably problem solving. That is what engineers really train to do in those four years is to

Nick and Sam

Also featured in color photo insert

solve problems and look at things in three ways: what do you have at your disposal—what is given; what are you trying to find; and what is the solution. You have to understand what you are working with, the given; what you are searching for; and how you put that all together to find a solution. You can take large, complex things and find a way, find a commonality, and find the core uniting things that make them all link together and work in harmony. In that regard, a brewery is just one giant conundrum where you are figuring out pumps, compressors, tanks, pipes, and control systems. It is similar to a gas or a chemical plant.

When you are trying to solve problems that are related to people, or money, or banking relationships, or sales trends, although there is not a mechanical solution involved, the approach is exactly the same. You start by identifying what you know—you start with a list of what is working. That ultimately leads to questions. At the intersection of all the questions you ask about why something is not working is the root cause—the heart of what really is at issue. Once you identify that root cause, you can begin wrapping solutions around that core thing.

In the early days, we—you and I—would have to do that. Now there are other people skilled in each area who are doing that. That has been a big transformation for us. Our roles are morphing from the people who come up with the solution at a very detailed level, to being the people who oversee the process of continually evolving and continual improvement. That is just a different type of role, a different challenge.

SAM: It is inspiring and managing people.

NICK: It is inspiring and managing people. We are not managing numbers, brands, consumers, and decision making anymore. We are managing people who manage all those things. That is where you go from being a manager to being a leader. We cannot be in those trenches anymore, even though that may be where it is more fun and that may be what was familiar for so long while Dogfish was still a small entrepreneurial company. It is just not that way anymore.

SAM: You went back to school and received an MBA after you had worked as an engineer for a few years. Do you feel like your MBA education prepared you in different ways for Dogfish Head?

NICK: Engineering as a discipline is very much like mathematics in that at a very young age, you learn basic principles, one plus one equals two. Then you start introducing things like variables where X is an unknown. You search for a value for it through formulaic approaches. Then you bring in geometry. The point is you start at this very broad, simple foundation. You start layering on top of that simple foundation of mathematics, more and more complex stuff, kind of like a pyramid works.

All business school did was expand the possibility of problems that needed to be solved from operational, factory-type things to broader business concepts that can be just as difficult to figure out. Instead of just being pure mechanical systems, now it can be finance, accounting, HR, IT, fill in the blank, any kind of production or operations stuff. In terms of finance and accounting, business is very similar to mechanical engineering. Building the brand is different; it brings more subjectivity and human emotion and psychology to it than pure mechanics.

I have been at Dogfish for over a decade now, and I spent the lion's share of my time at Dogfish focused on the production and operations side of the business. More recently, I've been diving deep into the sales side of the business.

SAM: Because we had been without a VP of sales for a long time.

NICK: Right, our last VP of sales left last year. And it took us eight months to find the ideal candidate to fill that role. Sales are a foreign thing to me, so it's been a big learning curve to determine what the right questions are. Where is the right data? How do you start educating yourself about the sales process? The problem-solving process begins with the same analysis as I would apply to an engineering problem-solving exercise: in this case, the core is a consumer walking into a store and buying beer. It gets more complex when you take into consideration all of the levers that are at play to get that beer to the marketplace and at the right price and how it should be promoted. It has been a brand new challenge to think about. I am sure there is another challenge right around the corner.

SAM: So you've found the core problem-solving skills that you learned in engineering could still be applied, just more broadly across business concepts.

NICK: Yes, that is true. Then the second biggest skill I've had to develop is the people leadership stuff. In engineering school, you do not spend any time talking about the "how" required to get something done, which really speaks to the cultural component. Sure as hell, MBA programs do not teach you cultural components. They prepare you to go to large banking institutions and huge corporations where you are one of 50,000 people.

Leaving business school, I knew that was not the world that was going to excite me. That was the world I was leaving, the gas and chemical industry, a world of huge multinational companies where you are one of tens and tens and tens of thousands of people. I wanted to work somewhere more personal, where you love going to work every day because you love the people that you do it with.

SAM: You certainly did get to a company like that! In the early days, we both had to roll up our sleeves and do a lot more ourselves. The "what" and the "how," the emphasis on each, changed as the company got bigger. How about your approach to management? How has it changed since you first arrived at Dogfish as the CFO, then COO and now CEO?

NICK: I came into a world that was very survival mode. It was super entrepreneurial. It was bootstrap. Everyone wore 20 different hats. There was no time to sit down and think through, "Hey, is there a better way to do this? Is there a more efficient way? Is there a safer way? Is there some whatever better or however you define better?" It was just all hands on deck, get the damn stuff done. We did not have the money to hire highly educated, highly experienced really good thinkers. We hired people who could do a job and get a job done. Along the way, there were some folks that surprised us. They really did have a brain and while doing it, they were thinking about a faster, cheaper, safer—

SAM: Better.

NICK: Better way of doing it. Those are the people we prioritized keeping and putting in positions where they could not only get a job done but use their skills to get us to the best outcome.

I had to navigate the waters of not being the corporate douche in those first few years. I had to roll up my sleeves and needed literally to be on the floor doing the work while still building models to represent a better way of doing it. I knew that if I went out there with models and documents and paperwork and said, "Look at page 4 of the flow diagram of whether it would be better to add our dry hopping at this point of the process instead of that point in the process," people probably would have punched me in the face. They wouldn't have said, "Shut up, Nick"; I would have been punched.

I had to learn how to be sophisticated in my own head with new concepts and approaches, but not come off as being slick in my engagements with people. I had to learn the beer production process from absolute beginning to absolute end, every aspect of it without them really knowing that they were teaching me, so that I could then turn around and help think through better ways for them to do their jobs. When they looked at me as one of them, then it was easier to go in and say, "You know, we have been doing it this way for so long. If we did it this way, it would be easier for both of us." The first few little experiments were hard. People were always skeptical.

SAM: "Who's this new guy telling us what to do?!"

NICK: "We have always done it that way. Why do it different?" But after you got two or three or four successes under your belt, people realize, "Wow, he really is here to help us." Each victory brought a little bit more confidence and a little bit more trust and a little bit more mutual respect. When you have enough successes so people can really see the new ideas might be better, folks start working hand-in-hand with you instead of still seeing that "douche who came from the MBA program."

SAM: You led by example. You proved that you were genuinely interested in what people were doing, earned their trust and respect by understanding their jobs and helping them figure out how everyone could do their jobs easier. We made great strides with that. Back in the days when it was management next to the workers. Now that the company has evolved into less management next to the workers, how has your management style evolved?

NICK: I expect every new hire, even to this day, who comes in to higher executive roles, managers and division managers and even VPs, to meaningfully connect to each person that is part of their teams. That onus is on you. Just because you have a senior position and title does not mean that your team should immediately defer to you. Trust is earned. You play an equal role in earning the trust of the people you count on as they do in earning yours.

SAM: Even when you interview a potential candidate, that is emphasized, right?

NICK: Correct, correct. Back to how has my leadership evolved. Well, there has been a good number of iterations. When you are working at a small enough company, you can be in the trenches and still "leading the company." As the company gets bigger, and by bigger I mean making and selling more beer, we have added layers of business process that never existed before. We started a quality department. We started an IT department. We started an HR department.

SAM: Legal.

NICK: We started a legal department. We started an accounting department. It adds more complexity, more things to attend to, more processes to manage, more people to manage. You find yourself less and less in the trenches. The trick is figuring out how to be just as effective as a leader when you don't have the opportunity to work with all the members of all the teams anymore.

As time rolls on, there are fewer and fewer people who remember that you used to be in the trenches. When people first start, they don't truly understand why it is so important not to just understand "what" you do, but to also understand the "why." If people feel meaningfully connected at the how, the what, and the why, then we are doing our job as leaders. That's what distinguishes Dogfish from so many other companies.

Soon after I joined Dogfish—nearly 10 years ago, now—is when Cindy, our VP of HR, joined. We would have conversations at the end of the day before going home about where we wanted to see Dogfish get. We would discuss why we had such a hard time keeping brewers when our beer had such a great reputation in the marketplace. What is it about being a brewer working here that is not as attractive as somewhere else? Why can we not retain them?

That is what made us start asking some of those very preliminary questions that ultimately led us to assess the culture of our organization. How do things need to change internally so we do not view people as robotic non-human assets? How do we go from thinking about coworkers as a cog in a wheel to where they are actually people? This is what collectively defines our culture of internal centeredness.

SAM: It was mostly related to brewery production because we did not have much of a sales team back then.

NICK: We did not need much. You were one of our hands out in the field doing beer dinners, driving beer, and delivering beer. You were sort of kind of tending to that end of the spectrum while we were beginning to have some of those initial questions.

Cindy came from a corporate world similar to the one that I came from, and we did not want to replicate that culture. Those were the beginning sparks of asking ourselves, "Can we not be a better place?" Then in the search for the answer, you realize you need to start making small changes. Every few months, you make a small change. People do not realize the place has changed, but ultimately you get to where you want it to be.

SAM: When you say "Can we not be a better place?" that to me is tied into the whole concept of corporate douche-baggery.

NICK: Yes.

SAM: Maybe you could elaborate a little more on your term there and what it means to you in the context of Dogfish and how it applies to the bigger world.

NICK: Yes, well, eventually in any organization that gets big enough where you have to introduce layers of complexity, you have entry-level people, junior associates, associates, and senior associates. Then that leads to some new title that there is a junior, medium, and high level until you eventually get to the president levels. You get these massive layers. When you get so big that those who make decisions affecting the direction the ship is going can no longer even recognize or have any communication with the people who are in the engine room and the other areas of production and making the thing work, then there is a huge internal disconnect.

Internal disconnects usually manifest themselves as classic communication breakdowns. A huge one is "departmentalism" where you create silos—which leads to power struggles creeping in. And people jockeying and positioning for higher-level positions; whether they are capable and willing to do them is irrelevant.

The quest to climb this corporate ladder can easily lead somebody to do less of what is in the best interest of the collective and the company, and more of what is in their personal best interest.

SAM: It is usually about "How do I make the person above me in my department look better" so that they rise up the chart.

NICK: Then little things start creeping in like, "Well, if I have more people work for me than somebody else for them, I look more important. If I have a larger budget to control than somebody else does, then I look more important than that other department." Therein lies the very nonaltruistic, selfish approach to how people navigate their way through corporate careers.

All of that can turn someone into a corporate douche. That is the stuff that will tear an organization apart from the inside. That notion popped into my head, "corporate douche-baggery." In the corporate world, most people will say, "If only that department would change, then we could do a better job sitting over here in my department." You point fingers and say, "If only they changed, we could do better. We would hit our numbers. We would whatever." It is a way of sitting back and pointing fingers elsewhere to look for that change.

On the other hand, if everybody thought of themselves as a service organization, the first question you ask is, "How can we change to make everybody else's life around us easier and make every other department that relies on us upstream and downstream better?" If everybody took that approach, you are unlimited where you can go in terms of problem solving or handling difficult situations, growth, external forces, internal forces. You cannot fail if that way of thinking is embedded in the culture.

The other way is for everyone to sit back and wait for somebody else to change first. That leads to complete stagnation. That approach forces you to have a bigger voice in order to affect somebody to move faster so you can be successful. You need a bigger budget and more people. That is at the heart of being a corporate douche bag, the fundamental difference between thinking of how can I change to better my coworkers versus would somebody else change so that I can be better.

It seems so simple, but at the heart of it, this service concept is what we are building the internal culture and organization of Dogfish Head around. The ideal is to couple that with people who come in from large organizations where they have acquired amazing skill sets. When somebody comes in and tries to change us to become like where they were with department silos, it doesn't work. We need them to evolve and adapt their amazing and rich skill set to fit Dogfish.

Probably the ultimate of all corporate douche-baggeries is the one that says, "If I am the only one that knows how to do something, I am irreplaceable." Think of the contrast in our culture, where you want to be the person who is capable of training anyone to become excellent and absolutely fully proficient at something. Now we are talking about somebody who is super valuable. The guy who has the mentality of wanting to be the only one who knows how to do something in order to hold the company hostage and have job security ends up accomplishing the exact opposite in our culture.

In large companies, yes, you can hide for a very long time being the only person who knows how to do something. That is not us. That is not what we are about.

SAM: When I do my part of what we call Carniv-ale, which is the name of the onboarding program for any new coworkers, I always explain that nobody at Dogfish works for me. I do not have any employees. We all work for Dogfish. If our first instinct is to think about the other people that work for Dogfish instead of our own best interest, imagine how strong we are when everyone is looking out for everyone else.

NICK: That's why for us I think it is incredibly important to meaningfully connect every single person in this building to something that truly is meaningful for Dogfish. Not to do it in a tricky way, but a way that gives them a greater reason to show up than just to collect a paycheck.

SAM: Can a strategic plan also be a way to liberate Dogfish Head from bad tendencies and connect us more in the direction we want to go?

NICK: To me, there is no downside to a strategic plan. The timing of it could be arguable but not the act of setting a course. You are saying, "Here's where we are going. We do not care what external forces are and what everybody else does." Now along the way, it does not mean that you cannot take some detours. You need flexibility in there. But the plan tells everybody where we are going. Absent this guidance, you are asking some 200-odd people—

SAM: To guess.

NICK: To jump on a moving vehicle and say join us. If they ask where it's going, we should be able to answer. It is pretty simple. That is what a strategic plan does. Come join us. Here is what we stand for. Here is where we are going.

If that plan resonates with somebody, you attract likeminded people who are choosing to want to be part of that vision, as opposed to joining for the wrong reasons. There are some fundamental questions that should be able to be answered in a strategic plan. Who are we? What do we stand for? Where are we going? It enables everybody to use the same words from a recruiting aspect, from an onboarding standpoint, at all coworker meetings, in every communication we have.

It affects actions on a daily basis. It makes people want to strive to be better and to find better, faster, cheaper ways of whatever the definition of success is in their job. People begin transforming from just doers to thinkers while they are executing the plan. You are an incredibly powerful organization when you have that unity.

chapter 2
LAID UP IN ZERO GRAVITY

I grew up in western Massachusetts in the bucolically named town of Greenfield, at the cusp of the Berkshire mountains and the gateway to the Mohawk Trail. Our house was across from a big pond that froze in winter. Pretty much as soon as I could walk, I was playing hockey on that pond.

My dad gave me my first stick. He had gone to Canada on a business trip and brought it back, super proud of the gift. His sport as a kid had been football, which meant that he didn't know hockey sticks come in left-handed and right-handed models. He had unknowingly purchased a left-handed stick. "Don't worry," he responded when I protested that I was a righty. "You'll learn how to play with it." And he was right. Throughout my career, in middle and high school and then on the team at Muhlenberg College, I played left wing as a right-handed person with a left-handed stick. Just one of the many reasons I never turned pro and went into the brewing game instead.

When my younger sister, Christa, started skating, she inherited that first stick, which I had outgrown. I'd take her along with me to the pond, where she'd be able to play "up" against me and other guys my age. I was pretty good, but Christa became world class; she starred on her college team at Harvard and made it all the way to tryouts in Colorado Springs for the Olympics. Like me, she played left wing with a lefty stick and does everything else in life right-handed.

The thrill I get in growing a business is a lot like the one I get from hockey. You take risks; you're dependent on a team but can make strong personal contributions; you're always trying to score goals, the competition is intense, and even when you don't win, playing is still fun (just not as much fun!).

In Delaware I kept playing hockey as an adult, in a club league on a team sponsored by Dogfish Head. We'd schedule a couple dozen games each year between October and March, against a mixed crew of opponents. We got lousy ice time, meaning our games started at 9 or 10 p.m. After getting off the ice at midnight and driving almost an hour back home, dragging myself into the office the next morning was grueling.

The action on the ice could get violent, as I would painfully discover one night in 2012.

The other team was on a power play, which meant my team was one man short because of a penalty. I was skating backward on one of the opponent's offensive surges, moving fast to cut off the winger with the puck. He flipped the puck off the boards to go around me. Our big burly defenseman got there first and raised his stick back to ice the puck to the other end of the rink with a slap shot. I was still moving backward, my momentum carrying me right into our guy's massive slap-shot follow-through—his stick hitting the back of my skates. I never saw it coming. My legs were cut out from under me, and I crashed to the ice, going way up in the air before landing hard on my tailbone.

I felt the pop of my spine compressing.

Somehow I managed to crawl back to the locker room. Driving 40 minutes back home to Lewes was excruciating. I took a hot bath, dropped a few Advil, and—ever the optimist—willed myself to be okay when I woke up. Wrong! The next morning I was in terrible pain. I bent down to do a yoga stretch to loosen my back. In the midst of a downward facing dog pose I nearly blacked out. The pain was so bad that I had to be driven to the hospital, where I learned that one disc was fully ruptured (L4) and another (L5) was bulging badly.

Over the next couple of months I saw specialists at Johns Hopkins and in Philadelphia, some of the best spine specialists in the region, leading experts in sports medicine. The prognosis wasn't good. Surgery could be done, fusing my spine or inserting a plate between my vertebrae and discs, but both options would likely lead to other problems because the doctors also found early-stage arthritis up my spine. In effect, an operation could leave me in a wheelchair, it could solve my pain, or it could do nothing. The experts told me my back would continue to deteriorate and eventually

I would need an operation, but their advice was to live with the pain until it got so bad that I had to literally crawl into surgery on my hands and knees.

I began going to physical therapy three days a week and read everything I could find on the Internet and in books about relieving your own back pain with yoga and core exercise. I developed an exercise regimen that I continue to do religiously, every day for half an hour. Somewhere I heard that the comedian George Burns attributed his longevity (he lived to 100) to the flexibility he got from rocking on his spine every day while pulling his knees into his chest, so he became a bit of a role model for me. Even if my back was particularly achy on a certain day, envisioning old George Burns doing a version of elderly break-dancing put a smile on my face and gave me hope.

At Dogfish Head, as a result of my injury, I was operating at half speed. Even on good days, I had great difficulty summoning up the let's-go-get-'em energy that has always been ingrained in my personality and so essential to inspired leadership. The mental space that should have been devoted to the things that most needed my attention—participating in leadership discussions, working on new products and projects, managing my in-box—was taken up with the constant awareness of my pain. My work was affected for a year and a half. The daily physical release from exercise I always relied on to clear my head wasn't available. I couldn't ride a bike; I couldn't kayak. My routine took on a depressing sameness: I'd stand up all day at work, and then come home to put on ice packs and sit in a zero gravity chair.

Thinking back on that time, my most vivid memory is of being depressed and feeling spiritually wounded. I went back to reading the Bible and I began praying hard, particularly that my health not cause hardship to my family or the company. The worst thing of all was how the pain affected my self-confidence. By nature I am outgoing, energetic, and enthusiastic about life. But this was such a difficult time for me. In bleak moments I envisioned what life would be like if I were permanently debilitated and couldn't walk, but I never dwelled long in that dark space and I didn't share these fears with anyone.

I started reading books on Buddhism and reread the *Tao Te Ching*, trying many different ways to find peace within myself. My mother-in-law, Rachel Grier Reynolds, who lives down the street from us in Lewes, was a big inspiration during this time. Almost 10 years earlier, she had been diagnosed with an aggressive form of cancer, but she's such a positive and powerful person that she refused to accept her prognosis. "I'm going to be stronger than my disease," she told herself. "My positive energy is going to my cells." We talked a lot about not letting external prognoses determine one's fate. While I learned a lot in everything I read about spirituality and exercises, I learned the most effective medicine from Rachel, who inspired me to look within myself and listen to my own intuitions on the best way to heal my body.

While I still can't do a lot of activities I used to enjoy, like hockey and tennis, my back has gotten significantly better in the three years since that injury. Now my go-to exercises are yoga, biking, and paddle boarding, but I still live with pain. I can't drive comfortably for more than half an hour. For longer road trips, I hire a driver so I can stretch out my legs in the back (that's when I answer e-mails and take notes while on conference calls). I take Advil three or four times a week, fish oil to lubricate my joints, and cayenne pepper, which is an anti-inflammatory.

Meanwhile, as if my rehab weren't enough, I embarked on another massive commitment that required me to focus the little extra time and energy I had on the craft brewing community. This role, as important as it was to me, distracted me from the most important and necessary work I should have been doing in my own company.

Just before my injury, I had run for and been elected the chairman of the board of the Brewers Association, the trade organization that promotes and protects the vast majority of America's 4,000-plus independent small breweries. Holding this position meant a great deal to me. The personal recognition from my peers was an honor, but what really drove me was the opportunity to serve our craft brewing industry at a critical time when the mega-giants began making incursions into our territory. I had been on the board for 10 years, running different committees and then as a member of the executive committee. The work was very meaningful for me.

Throughout my life, I've been very rebellious and the outcome of my rebellious ways hasn't always been positive: I got kicked out of high school, didn't get good grades in college, and was never particularly respectful of authority. In retrospect, I know that I was something of a conscientious outsider, always standing apart from the crowd. I prided myself on doing things my own way, particularly when my way challenged the established order. Then I became a craft brewer and found a community to which I wanted to belong. Here were other creative, intelligent, subversive people. I was one of them, another misfit who envisioned creating a beer business regardless of any technical qualifications. New Belgium's Kim Jordan was a bus driver/social worker; Sierra Nevada's Ken Grossman, a bicycle repairman. At some point, against all odds, each of us in our words has said something along the lines of, "Fuck it, I'm going to start a brewery." We were beverage punk rockers, making beer instead of music but with the same ethos: two chords and a cloud of dust!

And now that I had found my tribe, I wanted to give back and keep the circuit of positive energy flowing. My parents had always talked to my sisters and me about giving back to others to make positive change. The craft community was where I got the chance. I had hit my stride professionally, and I was ready to give back and be a part of something greater than myself and my company. I wanted to add to the positive karma of our indie craft brewing community through service.

When I was starting out on the board of the Brewers Association, I got to study at the feet of some of the most talented and experienced people, like Rich Doyle of Harpoon Brewery and Nick Matt of F.X. Matt Brewing Company. I will always be grateful to have learned from them and others like Jim Koch of Samuel Adams, a great strategist who understands the competitive economics of the entire beer industry as well as anyone I have ever met. I don't consider myself a particularly brilliant business mind when it comes to operational or financial acumen, but I recognized that I had acquired a pretty unique set of skills to add to the collective mix of industry leaders on this board.

Early on I had developed a reputation for being an honest, creative, hardworking, fun-loving person who truly wanted to see the entire industry succeed. I traveled around the world talking about the craft beer business, not just Dogfish Head. We were one of the first breweries to reach out to others to create collaborative brews. Other brewers came to trust that I represented them well. I think that what I brought to the table as the association chair was the street cred of an "everyman brewer" who started out tiny (we were once the smallest commercial brewery in the United States) and worked hard to get bigger and better every year without copying the breweries that came before us. The chance to share those experiences and the things I learned along the way was why I wanted to be leader of the Brewers Association.

As chair, I was writing documents, participating on subcommittees, attending events, fielding media requests, and doing general marketing. A large component of the job was public affairs. I'd go to Washington, DC, to meet with senators and political types alongside other craft brewery leaders and Brewers Association staffers to discuss issues that were important to our industry.

After the back injury, though, I was in so much pain that I questioned whether I could carry the added responsibility of the Brewers Association chairmanship. In the last decade, I doubt that I've cried six times (when my grandparents passed on, when my dog died, a few other times), but a few days after the injury, I broke down while talking with my father on the phone. "I don't know what to do," I confessed. "Please come down to help me." Besides being my dad he is also a retired oral surgeon, so I knew he would be helpful as I assessed next steps with my injury.

Within days he and my mom arrived. We visited doctors together and he offered medical advice, but what he most provided was what I most needed—a sounding board to help me sort out my confusion. "Sam," he counseled at one point, "there's no shame in going to the leadership of the Brewers Association to say you're in too much pain for the travel and work." Still, I felt guilty about having to give up the chairmanship. I didn't want to quit.

THE GOLIATHS AND DAVID

The first session that I presided over as chairman after rupturing my back entailed several days' worth of meetings to develop a two-year strategic plan for the association (the irony was not lost on me that at the same time, I was supposed to be working with the Dogfish leadership team to develop my own company's strategic plan). It was an ordeal.

Even after my injury I continued to attend beer events to man the Dogfish booth. I'd be pouring beer, high-fiving folks, getting my photo snapped with people until my lower back went into spasms. Once every hour I'd retreat to a bathroom stall and lay flat on my back for five minutes. (I always kept a couple of yoga mats nearby). It was an ordeal, but in my mind, the end justfied the means—I was able to connect with diehard enthusiasts and introduce our latest beers to new fans as the face of the company.

The prospect of attending the Great American Beer Festival that year, however, was daunting. This festival is our industry's biggest tribute to the folks who love drinking unique, diverse craft beers. Having never missed this fest for over a decade I didn't intend to miss it that year, although I was in pretty bad shape. There was more at stake that year than my personal record. It was particularly critical that I be there because, in my role as chair, I was representing the smaller brewers at a critical moment when a controversial issue was facing our industry.

Several months earlier, under our board leadership's initiative, the association had publicly called out the big foreign-owned giant breweries for intentionally trying to confuse the public with beers that were marketed and sold as if they were made by small indie craft breweries but actually came from massive conglomerates, for example, Blue Moon (owned by SAB Miller) and Shock Top (Anheuser-Busch-Inbev). In December 2012, we issued a public position statement, "Craft vs. Crafty,"[1] that shed light on the practice and brought the issue out into the open: "The large, multinational brewers appear to be deliberately attempting to blur the lines between their crafty, craft-like beers and true craft beers from today's small and independent brewers. We call for transparency in brand ownership and for information to be clearly presented in a way that allows beer drinkers to make an informed choice about who brewed the beer they are drinking."

Needless to say, the Goliaths were not happy that David had dared to share this message with the beer-drinking populace. Many of my fellow brewers were understandably nervous about awakening the sleeping giant. I'll admit that I was a bit anxious as well, having seen the dire competitive consequences for craft brewers when the big boys unleash their wrath (and vast marketing budgets). I realized that, because of this "Craft vs. Crafty" manifesto, somebody might well decide to go after Dogfish Head or other craft breweries whose leaders served on the Brewers Association board. Even so, I considered it imperative that we, as a community, stake out our market with the message of truth. The beer-drinking public was being misled, and it was time for us to stand up and call the big brewers out on it.

I was scheduled to represent our position in a face-to-face panel with the CEOs of the big breweries we had just called out in our "Craft vs. Crafty"

---

[1] Brewers Association, "Craft vs. Crafty: A Statement from the Brewers Association," press release, Boulder, Colorado, December 13, 2012.

statement, the head honchos from Anheuser-Busch and MillerCoors. It was a speaking commitment I couldn't possibly break. This event, called the National Beer Wholesalers Association convention, began the day after the Great American Beer Festival ended.

I arrived in Las Vegas from the Great American Beer Festival in a terrible state. Greg Koch of Stone Brewing and his girlfriend, Sara, drove me in from the airport and virtually carried me into the conference center because I couldn't walk. I spent the next 36 hours in my hotel room, hurting so bad that I reached out to my Delaware doctor to call in a pain prescription to a local pharmacy.

The morning of the panel discussion arrived, and I was still in blinding pain. I brought a bottle of our Palo Santo Marron 12% ABV (alcohol by volume) beer with me, poured it into a coffee mug, and drank it to bolster myself before going on stage. Somehow, I managed to take my seat along with the corporate brewers. Everyone was professional; we agreed to disagree, but I didn't back down.

Rather than address the charge that they were actively deceiving consumers, the big companies appealed to our shared interest. Since both craft and corporate brewers use the same distributors (distributors are our direct customers, the ones to whom we sell our product who then resell it to liquor stores, restaurants, etc.), they reasoned that we were biting the hand that feeds us all by creating dissension in the industry. Even through my haze, I wasn't buying that lame argument. My response was something along the lines of "We're not trying to be negative, but you guys are just not being honest with the public; you're pretending to make these beers in small independent craft breweries, which is not the case at all, and consumers should rightfully demand to know where their beer is coming from."

I obviously wasn't at my lucid and focused best that day; I'd give myself a B-minus/C-plus, but the necessary points were made.

The moment the session ended, I drank a second bottle of Palo Santo Marron and hobbled back to my hotel room bed.

INTERNAL COLLABORATION

I kept soldiering on for the next months. I owe a lot to the leadership team at Dogfish for their efforts during this era. They saw my pain, they saw me laid out with ice packs, but they never asked me to give up the chairman-ship of the Brewers Association. I didn't deceive myself, however. A severe blow to your health forces you to pay attention to things you used to take for granted. No need to overdramatize, but I couldn't pretend anymore that I was young and could immediately bounce back from this injury. I wasn't invulnerable. Or immortal.

Nor could we keep delaying the fundamental changes we needed to make. The industry was rapidly transforming, and Dogfish needed to keep moving quickly. The company was suffering because I hadn't been fully present in my focus, and nobody else was empowered to act on major strategic decisions without my involvement. We were too big, at about $90 million a year in revenue, to operate according to one man's directives (and, I admit, at times mercurial enthusiasms). Over 200 coworkers had staked their livelihoods and families' welfare to accompany me on our journey. They deserved stability and a future in which they had confidence. I owed it to them to be the best leader I could be by surrounding myself with other great leaders and giving them the opportunity to more fully participate in leading our company.

The moment had come to stop focusing so much energy on external collaboration at Dogfish Head and start putting more internal collaboration into practice.

Mariah and I spent much of the summer of 2014 thinking about what we should do. I always felt that because I was a combination of brewer/founder/entrepreneur, I had the final say on all important high-level deci-sions within the operational chain of command. Our conversations, how-ever, finally convinced me that this was no longer the way to go.

That fall, at the annual meeting with distributors, in the presence of my coworkers, I announced that henceforth Nick Benz would be chief exec-utive officer. He first came to Dogfish Head as chief financial officer and subsequently served as chief operating officer. Until Nick's appointment, we had never had a CEO. I hadn't thought we needed one. I always had the title of president and founder. But I wanted to get our company more oper-ational leadership bandwidth beneath Nick, and I thought this promotion was a good step in that direction. It was.

As I have shared before, Mariah is more financially responsible and organized than I am, but neither of us has a great mind suited to the intri-cacies of corporate finance. And we weren't passionate or knowledgeable about driving the cost side of our business toward world-class standards. My joys and strengths are mostly around creating new beer recipes, products, projects, branding, and events. Mariah's strengths are more inbranding and community building—online, and locally as well. We knew we needed help. That's when Nick Benz first entered the picture: as our chief financial officer (and now CEO). Nick has brought a high level of financial capabilities to our company and built a solid accounting team.

Prior to the official announcement of Nick's new position, I had made it clear as our managerial design evolved that I intended to still retain considerable autonomous authority. "I want you to run all the day-to-day operations with all the vice presidents directly reporting to you," I had told Nick. "But there will be one key way in which you won't be the typical CEO." The difference was that I would still exercise a directing voice when it came to strategy. To explain how this would work, I used the image of a five-pronged star. I explained to Nick and Mariah that I wanted to shift from controlling all five prongs of the Dogfish strategy star to having each of them hold one prong and me hold three—basically my way of saying I wanted them to have more strategic input, but I wanted to keep strategic control myself.

In retrospect, I see how misguided this was. Despite my grand pronouncement at the gaslight retreat about me finally accepting that it was time for Dogfish to develop a strategic plan, we hadn't gotten anywhere on it, which was my fault. There were reasons why, but the bottom line was that I hadn't done a good job driving the process. Yet here I was still holding onto those reins, in effect instructing Nick and the team that they could create components of the plan, but it had to be a plan I agreed with and ultimately directed.

At Nick's annual review in December 2014, he didn't hide his dissatisfaction with this arrangement. The tone of the meeting was respectful but heated. He said I was suffering from "founder's syndrome"—the well-known organizational malaise that occurs when an entrepreneurial company suffers adverse effects from an overly influential, micromanaging founder. From my end, it felt like I was spending more of my energy rebelling against other internal leaders, who often didn't believe my ideas were fleshed out or developed enough to move into new products or projects, instead of us collectively rebelling against the domination of giant marketplace competitors and other external forces.

I accepted and sympathized with a lot of what Nick was criticizing me for, and I shared my frustration that he often refused to take direction or criticism from anybody else, me included. At this meeting Nick wasn't interested in listening to the constructive criticism I shared with him but we have talked about it since. I know he came in to that meeting with a lot of specific information he was focused on getting across. The conversation was, indeed, candid and honest. Most of his points were well taken. We made progress.

I spent a couple weeks thinking a lot about the leadership structure at Dogfish and what would be best for our company's future. Ultimately I agreed to surrender being the keeper of the North Star and I shared this new understanding with Mariah and Nick, but there was a proviso. "For the first time ever," I told Nick directly, "I'm giving you some specific annual goals to accomplish this year. You'll be accountable for three things: overseeing the hiring and onboarding of the two vice president positions on our leadership team (Vice President of Sales and Vice President of Happy Customers) and oversee the construction of an inclusive, holistic three- to five-year strategic plan." Nick and I do respect what the other brings to the company, and I think we found a workable middle ground by hearing each other out and moving forward in agreement on what was best for Dogfish's next steps.

INTERVIEW

Charlie Papazian, President, Brewers Association of America

Charlie Papazian founded the American Homebrewers Association in 1978 and became president of the Brewers Association of America in 2005 when the two organizations merged. He continues to serve as president of the BA. As the author of The Complete Joy of Home Brewing *(nearly 1,300,000 copies sold), he is legendary in the craft beer world.*

I've gotten to know Charlie through the years, since Dogfish Head sponsors the Great American Beer Festival. I also know him well through my time spanning a complete decade as a board member of the Brewers Association. Like me, Charlie's a hard-core beer geek first and businessperson second. We share a passion for sharing what we have learned on our journeys in beer and craft brewing. He has one of the most down-to-earth approaches to leadership of anybody I've ever met.

"People Can Do a Better Job Than Me"

SAM: Your book *The Joy of Homebrewing* and books by beer writer Michael Jackson were what really got me started as a brewer. They made me think maybe I could make a career out of my love of drinking and making beer. Can you talk a little bit about the early years, when you were teaching home brew in Boulder, Colorado? Did you have an epiphany moment when you realized you were building a community?

Sam and Charlie

Also featured in color photo insert

CHARLIE: We're talking about the period of the early 1970s. At that time, I didn't even know what the word epiphany meant. I wasn't thinking in those terms at all. And I wasn't thinking in terms of vision. In 1970 I was 21. That is when I first started home brewing. I graduated in 1972 from the University of Virginia, and moved out to Boulder, Colorado.

SAM: Right after you graduated?

Charlie: Right after. People got wind that I knew how to make beer. I thought that was cool. They asked me to teach a class at the Community Free School, kind of an adult or continuing education school.

SAM: A hippie Boulder type of thing?

CHARLIE: Yes, but most people who taught weren't hippies but rather free thinking individuals. If you had an idea about teaching something, you could do it through their network. So I did, starting in 1973. And that first class grew into this craft network and community, and the collaboration, and support group, and the passion. The seeds for all that first emerged there.

SAM: Your home brewing class?

CHARLIE: Yeah. And I didn't even have a place to live then. I was living in the back porch of a house that some students were renting in Boulder. Class was held in the living room. There were four people that took my class in 1973, three of whom I'm still friends with. One right now is a brewmaster for Sandlot Brewing Company (an extension of Coors). Another helped me found the American Homebrewers Association eight years later. By the second class I had moved out of the students' place and rented a house with some others. We're still all friends. So that gives you an indication of the type of community and bonding and shared passion that beer brewing established the framework for.

SAM: It's amazing when you talk to beer lovers in a room how quickly you connect with them. I think that sense of camaraderie is true in the beer world in general. Why do you think beer is such a great catalyst for community building?

CHARLIE: Well, for starters you're in a relaxed atmosphere. Casual. You don't feel threatened. Whether it's the alcohol or just the comfort and confidence that beer gives, you open up with people. Even people that you just met for the first time.

SAM: I definitely agree with that. My buddy Pat McGovern, the molecular archaeologist who's one of the world's foremost experts on ancient beverages, talks about how the era 10,000 years ago when humans discovered beer is right around the same moment when humans shifted from hunting and gathering nomads to settling down in villages. That's when they started creating civilization as we know it. They were growing grains; that's why they were building communities—to nurture and propagate these grains as they were growing. And as Pat says, "You know the way alcohol works is, it was probably the first thing that made humans let their guard down."

So back to your early years. As you look back at what's happened, what were the big moments for you that led to formalizing an association and the establishment of a sustainable industry?

CHARLIE: I'll answer that by going back to your original question about epiphanies. One of the core building blocks of all we're doing with the Association began at the same time that I was teaching the classes. There'd be 15 to 18 people taking the evening classes at my house and we'd sit around. We'd try a few beers. We'd have a lesson about some aspect of beer. Brew a batch of beer, drink beer, talk, learn, ask questions.

I would also invite guests—people who were interested in this phenomenon that was my beer class. There were beer distributors and importers, retail store owners, liquor store owners, and people who were just kind of curious. They had heard about this thing. And they'd come in and be blown away by some of the things going on in brewing—things we take for granted today.

SAM: Like what?

CHARLIE: Like the fact that half the people sitting around were women. For the most part, back then, beer was thought to be a man's drink. Even more, we weren't just having random conversations. We were talking seriously about the different beers we were drinking. We talked about the nuances and the different character of the beers and how they were brewed, asking each other questions and exploring the world of whatever we knew about beer in those days—which wasn't much—and really soaking up information.

SAM: And the guests who would attend were surprised by that?

CHARLIE: Absolutely. It was a game changer for them. They had never seen anything like that in their lives. And they were in the business of selling beer! Of moving beer. That made me realize that something important was starting to happen that had sustainability and that nobody could squash because it was starting with the people.

SAM: Craft beer!

CHARLIE: Right, craft beer. People wanted it; it wasn't being pushed on them by a marketing machine. The core ideas behind craft brewing emerged on those living room and dining room floors where we sat because there were not enough chairs for everybody.

We enjoyed doing things together. We had potlucks at different homes; people would invite friends, and bring food and share, and bring the beer they had brewed. There were all kinds of things to experience that no one had experienced before, and people still remember them as the best parties ever.

Then, in the mid-1970s, we hosted our first organized event—the annual beer and steer up in the Colorado foothills. We started out with 200 or 300 people. One year, there were about 600 attendees, but that was too big so we decided to limit attendance.

SAM: And, it was extremely collaborative.

CHARLIE: It was total, total collaboration. It was communal. People loved volunteering. Taking charge of the beer, taking charge of the food, taking charge of the construction of the stage. Someone was in charge of the music program, someone in charge of cleanup, someone in charge of gatekeepers and security. There were doctors in charge of first aid in case of an emergency. Everybody contributing their skills.

SAM: The passion was there even then. It's just been amplified by the brand you have built with the Brewers Association, whose mission is to promote and protect craft breweries. But I'd say a big part of the brand that you have fostered is a love of enjoying good beer and increasing your knowledge of good beer, whether it's homebrewing or commercial.

Going from those early days to today's Brewers Association, what is your role as it builds on that spirit? How do you promote collaboration within the organization? How do you evangelize about it?

CHARLIE: What does collaboration mean to you?

SAM: I'd say in the context of business, an example of external collaboration would be two brewers creating a beer together or a brewery launching a beer in conjunction with a musician. Internally, collaboration means that instead of operating within the traditional silos where you only engage with your own department and then everyone reports up to one big boss, different departments work with and for each other.

The directive has to be a priority for the biggest bosses wanting that kind of collaborative culture instead of the more traditional up-the-ladder chain of command culture.

CHARLIE: Well, my experience as a leader started out with me doing everything that's being done now in the Brewers Association. I pasted up galleys (that's the ancient method of pasting typeset copy onto a large format page sheet that eventually was sent to the printer) for the magazine. I sold advertising. I did accounting.

SAM: Ran events.

CHARLIE: Every possible thing. That meant that I understood the extent of the responsibilities people were charged with accomplishing later on when I had to let go of that stuff. I think that if you expect people to collaborate and share, the leader has to understand what their responsibilities are and what the pressures are, the stress levels that arise and the ups and downs.

SAM: What's been the toughest part of shifting from being an entrepreneur starting a business, where you wore a lot of hats and did a lot of different things, to being in a leadership role? What's been the most rewarding part of that transition for you and what's been the most challenging part?

CHARLIE: I'll start with what I've enjoyed. During the initial period, say the first five years, I worked my ass off. The Brewers Association was my life. I'd get up in the morning, and I'd go to bed late at night and there was nothing in between there but doing stuff to keep it going. I thought I had to do it all. Then we were able to get volunteers and then hired people here and there. By then, managing them and still doing stuff myself, I was ready to burn out. At that point, Priority Number One became taking care of myself. So I said screw it, I'm taking a vacation and spent three weeks overseas in Thailand.

SAM: Doing a walk-about.

CHARLIE: I didn't have an iPhone or Internet access, so I had to have confidence that my staff could run things while I was gone. When I got back, I learned a huge lesson. Not only did I have a much healthier outlook but also things at the office were actually better off than when I left. Since that experience, I don't have a problem letting go of stuff. To this day, whenever I travel, I don't feel the need to constantly communicate back to the office or try to micromanage what is going on. Instead, I see my absences as opportunities for people to develop managerial skills who haven't had that experience of being in control. I let them do stuff and make mistakes and figure out how to correct them before I'm back. And they do. I can't recall any time when I came back and said, "Oh man, I shouldn't have gone." It's never happened.

SAM: Yeah!

CHARLIE: And then to answer your question about what's the hardest thing, I think it's when you get to a point where you really have a great staff within your business and you have to take a hard look at what you're doing and how you're contributing. I'm not a good manager. With me, it's more like, "This is your job, I'm not going to be on your back all the time." I don't meet with people and try to support them every moment and every day.

At that point, you find yourself in very strange circumstances. The hardest thing to do in this new role, in this role of the experienced leader rather than the hands-on entrepreneur, is to know, what do you do to provide the best value. You end up having periods of time where you don't have anything on your plate and feel like shit. I feel like I should be contributing more because all these other people are working their asses off.

However, that downtime for you as a leader can also become the creative time when you can think about the business more strategically or come up with new solutions or ideas. It's a time to have the beer with people outside your circles and inside your circles and see the big picture and help. The ideas that you pass on or the introductions that you make to relevant people in your organization could be ideas and encounters that no one else in the organization would ever get if you didn't take a step back and look for new opportunities or solutions.

You're on this big ship, and you're not making the sharp turns this way and that way. You're just trying to maintain the direction for the whole organization.

SAM: Helping to set the course but not steer the boat.

CHARLIE: Yup. That's a way to put it. You can't be so involved and immersed in operational details because it just doesn't work when you are a leader. Particularly if you've started a company and people want access to what your thoughts are. You can't busy yourself with that kind of stuff and you've got to get used to that idea. That's the hardest thing.

SAM: The hardest thing for me to transition out of is the creative side. That's my favorite thing, thinking of something new—a new beer recipe, a new concept for an event, a new design for an ad—and it's hard to continue to do that because it brings me way back down into the small details in certain departments.

CHARLIE: I've felt that challenge. You know, I'm involved in a pilot project of chronicling the craft brewing pioneers on video and archiving photographs to make sure that they're preserved and accessible. That's pretty much busy-work, but I'm the only one who can do that because I'm the only one who can identify who these people are from the 1980s.

SAM: You're the constant in the timeline.

CHARLIE: Yeah. And I'd better do it while my brain is still functioning pretty well.

SAM: But that's an incredibly important responsibility for a founder to sustain the legacy of the organization, which is what you're doing with this project. You're codifying and documenting the brand of craft beer and the people who helped collectively, communally, collaboratively to create it.

CHARLIE: And also encouraging people to value things that many brewers now really, really regret having thrown away when they moved or expanded. Old business plans or labels from their original beers or brewing logs. Documents that were important to the founding of the organization.

SAM: Going back to the leadership thing. Recently we named our first CEO, Nick Benz, promoting him from within. You've got a CEO at the Brewers Association. What's the greatest thing that leads to the success of your relationship and your interaction professionally with the CEO? And where do you guys find the challenges?

CHARLIE: I think we're still in the process of that transition. From my perspective, this initial phase requires I start letting go and not interfere, giving space. I think the challenge down the line will be how to reconnect and establish more communication when it's necessary. We're probably not having as much communication now as we did before the transition, but that is probably a healthy thing in succession development.

Ultimately, an organization doesn't have a president and founder anymore. Things move on. But establishing how you, Sam, or I can contribute value to a CEO is different than you or I figuring out how to contribute value to the organization.

SAM: What are your thoughts about what lies on the horizon for craft beer and how do we best stay collaborative with each other instead of starting to compete with each other?

CHARLIE: Well, you can still be collaborative and still compete. That's what we're doing right now. Right? We're still doing that.

SAM: As craft brewers, every day we compete in the marketplace but we do it collaboratively to grow the category of craft beer.

CHARLIE: Well, I think there's a role for an organization like the Brewers Association to keep that spirit of passion and excitement alive and fun.

SAM: Instead of just business as usual.

CHARLIE: We need to have an association—an organization that provides a network for people to work out issues. It's really valuable. There are so many, many other places—countries, industries—that just lack that network and aren't able to trust in each other. Not because it's inherent. It's just that they never had the situation to do something with somebody else, so the mistrust results in cutthroat competition. And where does that come from? It doesn't happen instantly. It's a mentality that gets passed along like some kind of genetic code—call it the genetic code of distrust, that gets passed down from generation to generation. If we lose that fun part and being able to enjoy each other's company and recognizing the successes of others and how they contribute to our own success, if we forget that, then the association is going to start falling apart.

SAM: Right.

CHARLIE: It's nuance behavior that translates into not letting somebody, say another brewer, into your facility to see things because you think they're going to steal your ideas.

SAM: But your instinct should be to trust, not to distrust. That's what our industry was founded on: trusting and helping each other grow, even though we are technically friendly competitors.

CHARLIE: You talk about collaboration. Fostering a collaborative culture or industry has to start out by establishing trust with the people that you work with and letting them in your world so that they can contribute to the company. But that's a hard thing, trusting somebody to do something that you've always done yourself.

SAM: I understand that. It's hard.

CHARLIE: As I said, though, after that first epiphany when I traveled to Thailand, I never had a problem stepping away. Because I realized: "Wow, people can do a better job than me!" Or as good a job.

SAM: Or a different job. Everybody does it a little differently, but it's still happening in a way that's good for the organization.

CHARLIE: That's not to say you don't have to keep people on track and to correct things if people go astray. But that's what the leadership is about.

chapter 3

THE RADICALLY CHANGING BEER BUSINESS

Making money is art and working is art and good business is the best art.

—*Andy Warhol*

As Dogfish marks its 20th anniversary, the new world order of the craft beer industry couldn't be more different from when we started. The beer and spirits industries are on the cusp of a gathering storm. In the 20 years since Dogfish Head opened, this is the most competitive environment I've ever seen. Independent brands are being bought at record valuations, with multiples as high as 20 times earnings. But the bath, as brewmasters say, is always frothiest just before the bubble bursts.

Change is the ultimate constant in any business. It is inevitable. Nothing stays the same. The marketplace is fluid, dynamic, and constantly evolving. The hardest thing about confronting change is being ready for it—you're either anticipating it or reacting to it. As an entrepreneur you need to build up a tolerance to change-induced anxiety in the same way you must build up a tolerance for risk.

Our industry is in the midst of a major transition; our challenge is to determine what this will mean to Dogfish Head and get ahead of the curve. Tectonic plates are shifting as drinkers in the United States and around the world are starting to lose their taste for the industrial light lagers the megacorporate brewers have built their empires on.

A BRIEF HISTORY OF
THE AMERICAN BEER INDUSTRY

Prior to 1920, when the 18th Amendment was ratified, a robust brewing culture existed within America with well over 3,000 breweries (most focused on their local neighborhoods) making a wide selection of beer, from English ale to German lager. Nearly all would be wiped out during the next couple of decades. Those that could repurpose their operations managed to stay alive—Adolph Coors sold malted milk to the Mars Candy Company; August Busch entered the baker's yeast business. When the sale of alcohol again became legal in 1933, the survivors had a huge advantage over potential competitors who had to start up from scratch, and this advantage was compounded by the new reality of national distribution made possible by refrigerated rail cars and highways. The rest of the story is well known.

The abundant diversity of beverage choices pre-Prohibition is now returning. The alcoholic beverage category in the United States is really coming of age today. Boutique wineries are back. We're making creative cocktails with designer spirits. We are embracing pricey wood-aged brown spirits meant to be sipped. And the American craft beer movement is booming.

The year 2014 was a particularly historic one for our industry. For the first time, craft breweries captured more than 10 percent of the total market. This figure is all the more dazzling when compared to what the scene was like when Dogfish started 20 years earlier. The industry was in its infancy, craft beers were a novelty, and inventory on store shelves was scant.

The contrast from those days to today couldn't be greater. When I attended a festival or gave a talk back in the mid-1990s, the room kind of looked like a Star Trek convention in a small city—a bunch of scruffy white dudes in their 20s and 30s. Fellow beer geeks informed enough to seek out something different were willing to give the wildest concoctions a sampling, but, truth be told, there weren't many such daring drinkers. Hardly any women, hardly any ethnic diversity, hardly anybody older than 45. Now, with consumers so much more savvy and an exploding awareness and excitement for craft beer, the crowd at an event like the Great American Beer Festival spans all ages and ethnicities, and men and women are nearly equally represented.

In the late 1990s craft brewers hit a big bump in the road. In the decade leading up to that moment the craft brewing industry had been growing quickly, but unlike today, back then it was mostly perceived as a fad by the average adult citizen. Some small brewing companies in that era were slaves to their own growth; as they became bigger it became more difficult to deliver consistency and quality. Making inconsistent, mediocre beer is not hard; making good tasting beer is harder; making a great beer just once is even harder. To make a great beer consistently takes knowledge, strong technical skills, modern brewing equipment, and experience. And then to build a business around the liquid in the bottle—to ship it across state lines (and national borders), to sell and market it really well—takes skill and teamwork. There are a million details to coordinate so that each batch is properly packaged to prevent oxidation, maintains consistency and quality, and is moved quickly from brewery to distributor to retailer to consumer to ensure freshness.

The companies that made it through that earlier shakeout survived mostly by mastering the fundamentals of making consistent beers to pre-set stylistic guidelines and relied heavily on word of mouth. The commercial craft brands that have stuck around (and the newer ones that learned from the past) have figured out how to both make good beer and get good beer to customers. Consumers are much better educated and have better access to information online. Demand has grown not only in scale but also in expectations of beer quality, consistency, and distinction. Bad product gets quickly outed.

Today, craft beer is no longer an obscure little niche that appeals only to the converted. There are some 4,000 craft brewers in the United States, producing over 22 million barrels and accounting for over $20 billion in sales. Brewpubs grew 20 percent and micros 30 percent collectively in 2014.[1] And the anticipated growth curve remains steep; craft's share of the market is expected to double again in five years to 20 percent by 2020.

At the same time, industrial lager is losing a bit of its iron grip on America.

While the sales of craft breweries surge (Dogfish, for example, has had double-digit growth for 16 consecutive years), beer, as a beverage, is slipping

---

[1] Bart Watson, "Craft Brewer Capacity," Brewers Association, April 23, 2015, https://www.brewersassociation.org/insights/craft-brewer-capacity/.

within the general category of alcoholic beverages. A-B InBev, for example, the Belgian-Brazilian brewer that acquired Budweiser in 2008, continues to account for over 45 percent of the beer in the United States, but its market share of alcoholic beverages has declined. Light beer, which accounts for over half the volume at A-B InBev and SAB MillerCoors (the other mega-giant, a joint venture formed in 2007 with South African Breweries owning 58 percent), has been particularly hard hit.

It's important, though, to put these numbers in context. Ninety percent of the 4,000-plus breweries in the country put together have less than half the capacity of a single MillerCoors facility in Golden, Colorado. And while the biggest companies—A-B In-Bev, SAB MillerCoors—continue to make most of the beer brewed in the United States, their choke hold on consumers is loosening.

This is partly in response to the shift in consumer behavior away from big-box, price-driven decision making and back to unique, handmade, and custom products. For the growing craft community, which truly believes in the virtue of small and independent companies, the eroding dominance of the global corporate behemoths is good news. The forces of virtue—folks who value integrity, authenticity, and the individual daring of bootstrapping entrepreneurs—are gathering momentum. Spirits and wine overall are stealing market share from cheap domestic light lager. Craft beer is not only benefiting from light lager drinkers trading up but also attracting crossover drinkers as it steals occasions from wine and spirits. More and more people are opting for interesting, tasty, artistically brewed beers. Over the past 10 years people have been paying a premium for these beers, saying to themselves, "Hey, I'm willing to treat myself a little bit by buying a better beer." That's an incredible endorsement for craft beer in the worst economy many of us have lived through.

But there's also potential bad news in this turn of events. An exploding market also comes with its own problems. More and more start-ups are launching in every industry in response to changing consumer focus. In our industry it is microbreweries and regional brewers that are popping up. In just the Chicago area, for example, a recent count turned up more than 60 microbreweries, nanobreweries, and brewpubs.[2] Two new commercial craft

---

[2]Karl Klockars, "The 62 Best Chicago Beers," *Chicago Magazine*, www.chicagomag.com/Chicago-Magazine/September-2013/best-beer/.

breweries now open up each day in America. There's not enough shelf space
or tap handles to handle them all. Many of these brewers will make awesome
world-class, well-differentiated, high-quality beer and deserve to exist and
grow. But some of them will not make world-class beer and their inconsistent,
poor-quality beer will reflect poorly on the overall reputation of craft brewed
beer. Some of these inferior craft breweries will go out of business.

Thus, craft breweries are facing an ever-more-difficult challenge differ-
entiating themselves from each other and capturing market share. Take the
IPA dilemma, for example. As India pale ale has become the dominant craft
beer style over the past few years and pub patrons expect multiple styles on
tap, almost every new craft brewer is launching with an IPA. Of course, no
matter your business, you have got to move with the market. But I'd hate
to be starting out today trying to build a brand and feeling obliged to lead
with a basic flagship beer model that is a derivative of the biggest style trend
in the history of the craft brewing community.

Shakeouts, of course, are part of capitalism's selection process. At some
point in any boom, supply exceeds demand and companies must corre-
spondingly adjust (or go out of business). It is not clear that craft beer
has reached that point. Bart Watson, chief economist for the Brewers
Association, has gone on record saying breweries are doing a good job of
matching capacity with forecasted growth, although he makes a point of
noting that expectations can quickly grow unreasonable. "If you're a brewpub betting on 50 percent compound growth for five straight years," he
warns, "that may be a problem."[3] I hope Bart's right about the longevity of
current craft trends, but there are warning signs in the form of discounting
and challenging sell-through rates with many brands.

There is another factor today, however, that makes these even more per-
ilous times. There is a growing presence of quasi-craft brands masquerading
as true craft beers, creating confusion in the market to take market share away
from the bona fide indies who are in control of their own destinies. I call beers
quasi-craft, comparing them to the Brewers Association definition of a true
indie craft brewery. By those standards, there are brands being positioned and
marketed as craft beers that, in my opinion and in that of most small brewery owners, don't belong. Goose Island sold out 100 percent to A-B InBev

---

[3]Bart Watson, "Craft Brewer Capacity," Brewers Association, April 23, 2015, https://www
.brewersassociation.org/insights/craft-brewer-capacity/.

in 2011; Blue Moon is made by MillerCoors and has always been owned and made by this company; Shock Top is an A-B InBev product; Magic Hat bought Pyramid and then sold both operations to North American Breweries (which owns Labatt); and Leinenkugel is owned 100 percent by SAB Miller.

There's no hidden mystery about why this is happening. With industrial lager losing market share, mega-brewers are looking to craft for growth. At MillerCoors, for example, the division that oversees Leinenkugel and Blue Moon, known as Tenth and Blake Beer Company, accounts for less than 10 percent of the parent company's sales volume, but because there are higher profit margins on craft brews, these sales contribute a higher portion of operating income.[4] Anheuser-Bush abandoned its signature yellow tint when it launched a suite of amber and dark beers—Black Crown, Black Bok, Rolling Rock Black Rock—intended to mimic the taste and look of craft beers.

HOW THE BREWERS ASSOCIATION DEFINES *CRAFT*

Small

The annual production is 6 million barrels of beer or less (approximately 3 percent of U.S. annual sales). Beer production is attributed to the rules of alternating proprietorships.

Independent

Less than 25 percent of the craft brewery is owned or controlled (or equivalent economic interest) by an alcoholic beverage industry member that is not itself a craft brewer.

Traditional

A brewer that has a majority of its total beverage alcohol volume in beers whose flavor derives from traditional or innovative brewing ingredients and their fermentation. Flavored malt beverages are not considered beers.

Of course as more and more breweries that were once solidly inside the Brewers Association definition of a craft brewery make deals by

---

[4] Tom Daykin, "MillerCoors Draws Profits from Craft Beers," *Journal Sentinel*, August 14, 2012, www.jsonline.com/business/millercoors-draws-profit-from-craft-beers-v16fsoe-16619 4536.html.

selling out to bigger entities to a degree that they ultimately fall outside these guidelines, they become vocal against the very definition
many of them once supported. While the Brewers Association definition may not be perfect in the eyes of all consumers, it is at least the
most clear and definitive line in the sand that we as an industry have.

Our industry emerged from folks growing small businesses built primarily
around their passion for beer (most, like me, even starting out as home brewers). The purity of motive for true indies is as important as purity of ingredients. I've said more than once when talking about my fellow craft brewers
that it's great to be in an industry that is 99 percent asshole free. With very few
exceptions, we're collaborative by nature. But it's precisely this spirit of collaboration that's at risk as business leaders who prioritize profits over a passion for
beer take control of many craft breweries. If beer to us is an end in itself, to
them it's the means to another end measured in profits and revenue. In some
cases, instead of creating the ultimate IPA, their goal is the ultimate IPO.

I believe there is a spiritual component to the production and con-
sumption of beer. Throughout history, it has played a ceremonial role in
bonding people together. I suspect a considerable number of my fellow
craft brewers share this romantic notion of their beer as social sacrament.
Corporate conglomerates and deal makers, on the other hand, see their
breweries as capital investments to be fully monetized. They pay lip service
to product integrity (and they may well believe what they say), but their
ultimate responsibility is answering to the dominant voice of external investors who expect a big return on investment.

A big reason craft beer has grown over the past few years is that its
individual consumers consider themselves part of a much bigger community that stands in opposition to the globalization and commodification
of the stuff we eat and drink. Indeed, the craft ethos is one element in an
emerging cultural paradigm that distrusts dominant marketplace influencers and emphasizes transparency and personal autonomy. This carries
through into their consumer behavior. They want products made with
only natural ingredients produced in a socially responsible manner by real
entrepreneurs with whom they can identify. In a word, they want authenticity. Authenticity may be a buzzword but it is still the most resonant
descriptor in this instance.

A GATHERING STORM

The net impact of the changes taking place in our industry is, as I said at the beginning of this chapter, a gathering storm. With the multitude of new brands and breweries appearing, the massive international conglomerates bringing quasi-craft brew within their brick-and-mortars, and financial players treating craft breweries as deal tinder by taking over control of these once indie businesses, the collaborative commitment so strong in our earlier days is at risk of being marginalized. There's a real danger that the cohesion of the craft community, the sense of camaraderie that has been so responsible for our collective success, is becoming more brittle after decades of becoming stronger and stronger. Instead of the authentic product, the honest messaging, and a genuine love for the art of brewing that has characterized the craft brewing industry, this new stratum of mega breweries masquerading as indie craft brewers will have the resources and incentive to potentially confuse consumers with well-fabricated images, well-financed hype, and cut-rate pricing. Corporate budgets and marketing can outmaneuver integrity in some cases but we are hopeful the large pool of consumers who truly care who makes their beer will see through the shenanigans.

I get the reasons why this is happening: some craft brewery owner patriarchs and matriarchs are closing in on retirement age and are trying to figure out the future of their companies and their own financial security. But the world's largest breweries are still being disingenuous in their intentions. Their strategy is to let the original smaller brick-and-mortar craft brewing facilities they buy out continue to make esoteric, specialized beers but take the flagship brews into their giant, fully automatic mega-facilities where they can brew in huge quantities with lower cost materials and methods than indie craft breweries can do themselves. We've already seen what happens. Without naming names, a major international brewing conglomerate will buy a once-independent craft brewery, and suddenly its IPA kegs are in bars for half as much money as they were before they were bought out. While the liquid might still taste similar in some examples, often it doesn't, and either way it really shows that the conglomerates are using these former indie craft brands as pawns in a price- and distribution-power war game to knock true indies off the board. The power is in the hands, minds, and wallets of the consumer to choose to prioritize true indie even if it costs a buck or two more per pint or six-pack. Over time, making this choice in aggregate will keep the diversity and distinction of choices viable and sustainable for decades to come.

There are heavily financed ad campaigns designed to confuse and to manipulate craft beer fans. The solidarity of the community is going to be tested as marketing campaigns seek to undermine trust and the truthful portrayal of brand ownership. The worst-case scenario is that the forces of corporate greed win out, the shakeout strips the community of its vitality, and it will be too late by the time consumers catch on.

The nasty, back-biting Budweiser commercial in the 2015 Super Bowl, "Brewed the Hard Way," foreshadows the way I see things heading. In mocking fruity funky craft beer recipes ("Let them sip their pumpkin peach ale"), the company was disrespecting a craft brewer it had fully acquired, which brewed precisely such a peach pumpkin beer recipe. Rather than be intimidated by what it must have cost to produce the ad or how many people saw it, I saw it as a great wake-up call for the beer-drinking public because it showed how confused and conflicted the world's biggest brewery is about how to engage beer drinkers whose tastes are changing. The more they spite us for brewing beers beyond the bland lagers these global juggernauts mostly produce, the more we're going to stand for something very separate from what they're about. The more they make fun of craft breweries and craft beer drinkers when promoting their core light lager brands, the more they will alienate consumers on their own quasi-craft brands like Shock Top and Goose Island. It's imperative that the public know the reality about what's going on behind the tap handles. Then they can choose for themselves if they want indie craft or quasi-craft.

BUD IS PROUDLY "MACRO" AMID MICRO-BREWS IN SWAGGER-FILLED SUPER BOWL AD

New Campaign Takes Shots at Fruity Craft Beers, Brings Back Old Tagline

Budweiser stole the Super Bowl pregame with a cuddly, cute puppy. But the King of Beers came out swinging in its second Super Bowl spot with a hard-hitting approach that proudly declared the nation's third-largest beer as a "macro" brew.

The campaign's debut ad is notable for its swagger. The spot takes what appear to be shots at fruity micro brews and beer geeks. Bud is "brewed for drinking, not dissecting," the ad declares over footage of three men who are caricatures of beer snobs. Then comes this: "Let them sip their pumpkin peach ale, we'll be brewing us some golden suds."

While those lines are sure to get attention, Budweiser VP Brian Perkins said the intent was not to criticize competitors or craft beer in general. Indeed, Bud-owner A-B InBev owns several craft breweries itself—including Goose Island—and also has jumped on the fruity beer craze with its Bud Light Ritas franchise.

He said the goal of the ad, called "Brewed the Hard Way," is to "talk in a positive, affirming way about Budweiser quality." Still, Mr. Perkins added that "occasionally we do have a little bit of fun with some of the overwrought pretentiousness that exists in some small corners of the beer landscape that is around beer snobbery. That is the antithesis of what Budweiser is all about."

Although there are nods to Bud's heritage in the Super Bowl spot, Bud plans to speak with a contemporary voice that says, in a nutshell, that a brand can be big, and good.

"We can make millions of these per day," Mr. Perkins said. "But this one's for you and it's the same quality standard and the same attention to detail as everything else."

The "macro beer" phrase is an attempt to reframe the "prevailing discourse in a lot of industries, and certainly in beer, that small must be good and big must be bad," Mr. Perkins said. "I don't think anyone has really talked about macro beer before with pride." Bud, he said, wants to own that phrase.

E. J. Schultz, *Ad Age*, February 1, 2015.

That's only one of the ways these guys play hardball. They can be ruthless in trying to marginalize brewers they perceive as competition. I learned that lesson firsthand with the Discovery cable series *Brew Masters*. In it, a documentary film crew accompanied me around the world to produce six episodes about some of our more exotic beers made in collaboration with other small companies, artists, and scientists we had already established relationships with. We had a blast making the series because we liked the production company, and we were already planning on doing the projects they filmed so the footage was authentic and real and not forced or manufactured like much of what you see on reality television.

About one week before the first episode aired, the network informed me that one of the international brewery conglomerates had bought out all the program's initial ad blocks at the front end of each segment of each episode of our show for one of their quasi-craft beer brands and that they would be creating ads that would look very much like the design and branding aesthetics of our show. Just as I knew would happen, a social media firestorm broadsided us when the show was broadcast: craft beer lovers wondering why Dogfish allowed a quasi-craft beer to be the lead advertiser on a series that was presumably about the indie craft brewing community. I was outraged, but as Discovery reminded me, I had no control over the ads that air during the commercial breaks. What we *could* do, though, was respond and tell beer lovers online and in person what really happened. When beer lovers shared their disappointment in our show being co-opted by these ads, we let them know how we felt about such deception.

Representatives from the big brewery who made the ads immediately made it clear with the network that they were furious with our actions of calling bullshit on social media and prepared to pull millions of dollars of advertising from the channel unless the network deemphasized our show. Discovery was contractually obliged to air all six episodes, but they effectively killed *Brew Masters* by changing the time slot from week to week to confuse the audience—even intentionally putting us up against *Monday Night Football*, one of the highest rated programs of the season—and then blamed cancellation on bad ratings. To this day, people walk up to me at beer events to tell me how much they love the show (which is now available online at sites like iTunes).

We are currently working with one of the same producers, who was the show runner for the *Brew Masters* series, on a web series that is a joint venture between Dogfish Head and the Complex Media network called *That's Odd, Let's Drink It!* In each 12-minute episode I hook up with iconic talented folks like chef Mario Batali and Chris Bosh from the NBA's Miami Heat to make a boundary-pushing beer together. Since this new show is a joint venture, we are not at risk of having a giant brewery come in and affect the success or viewer-accessibility of our show. We learned a great lesson in how the world's biggest networks and the world's biggest advertis-

Also featured in color photo insert

Sam and Chris Bosh on set.

ers can work together in ways that are certainly legally but ethically questionable. This experience, specific to Dogfish in the case, only increased my belief in the importance of the Brewers Association definition of an indie craft brewery.

MAINTAINING THE BRAND
IN TURBULENT TIMES

I am constantly asking myself what this shifting competitive beer industry landscape means for Dogfish Head and what we can do to make sure our business style remains suited for turbulent times. The foundations of our corporate culture remain pretty much what they were when we were the smallest commercial brewery in America. We opened Dogfish Head Brewings & Eats in June 1995, debuting with our first batches of Shelter Pale Ale and Chicory Stout brewed in 12-gallon batches atop propane burners. From the get-go, our MO has always been to push ourselves outside our comfort zone. We were the first commercial brewery to focus on culinary-inspired beer recipes. These were real oddities at the time that got us a lot of visibility for being off-centered. We branched out into hoppier beers, making what we've been told was, in 1997, America's first com-

mercially brewed dark IPA—and got more publicity and recognition. Two
years later, after watching a TV chef demonstrate that the secret to complexity and flavor in soup was to add cracked pepper in equal volumes
and in incremental pinches as it simmered rather than in one big dump, I
got an inspiration. Until then, the traditional approach to adding hops to
a beer occurred at two distinct moments: one at the beginning of the boil
and one at the end—the first for bitterness and the second for aroma. We
experimented with introducing small doses of hops throughout the boil
process, created a custom machine for doing it on a large scale, protected
the name "Continuous Hopping," and voilà . . . 90 Minute IPA was born. A
couple years later we brewed a lower alcohol version called 60 Minute IPA.
From there, as they say, the rest is a big part of Dogfish Head history: over
70 percent of the beer we sell incorporates our unique continual-hopping
process.

We were able to effectively build a brand around experimental innovation. Now, with consumers much more knowledgeable and the playing
field so much more crowded with adventurous small brewers, simply being
"experimental" is no longer a differentiator. When we first made Punkin
Ale in 1994, I don't believe any other brewery was using real pumpkin meat
combined with brown sugar and fresh ground spices in a commercial beer.
Twenty years later, in one of *Beer Advocate*'s 2015 rating contests, there were
over a hundred different pumpkin brews on the list.

The challenge my coworkers and I face is to maintain the vitality and
adventurousness of the Dogfish Head brand in this new era. I don't want
to suggest that our company is at a phase of critical risk. In our early days
there were scary moments when we could have easily gone under, but that's
no longer the case. The question for us isn't whether we'll be in business 10
years from now. We're strong, we're creative, and we've got strategic plans
that we're dialing in. Our operational capabilities are solidly established; we
can package thousands of bottles an hour. We can package many hundreds
of kegs per day. We have strong distribution that we need to work harder
to make even stronger, but our brand is widely recognized and distributed
in 31 states.

I know that Dogfish Head will be here as long as we keeping making
similarly smart and creative decisions to those we've made up to now.

That's all reassuring. Our customer base has consistently grown and
been loyal, but I've been around the industry long enough to understand

that craft drinkers are always trying out new beers and receptive to changing taste. A label can suddenly become hot, all the more so now with the huge role social media plays in shaping awareness. When you hear buzz about a new brewery that is doing something cool and unique, all you need to do is pick up your smart phone to check it out online. But that sword cuts both ways, which means a popular beer can go out of fashion just as quickly.

So what's our battle plan at Dogfish Head? It's simple to state but tough to execute: maintain the relevance and distinction of our brand in an increasingly competitive and brand-blurry marketplace!

For some, the word *branding* immediately triggers negative associations. One is reminded of the slick, phony images that are the hallmark of big advertising agencies. To my coworkers and me, the Dogfish brand stands for the integrity of our company and our community and our off-centered but authentic and respectful approach to everything we do. Our brand and branding weren't invented externally by a crew of Madison Avenue hotshots. It's an organic reflection of our passion, history, our evolution, and our character. We are who we say we are. But there is still a challenge to keep a brand fresh, engaging, and top of mind with our public so that when a purchase or sampling occasion arises, they're primed to think Dogfish. The turbulence in our industry virtually guarantees that craft drinkers are going to be blasted again and again not just by authentic messages from certain brewers but also by deceptive messages from other brewers designed to confuse them. With the biggest global corporations invading our world, our audience is going to become targets for heavy-duty marketing propaganda. To defend against these barrages of inauthentic messages, it is more imperative than ever that we (and those like us determined to remain faithful to authenticity and controlling our own destiny) nurture the vitality of our brand.

Art, like beauty, is largely in the eyes of the beholder. In my eyes, Andy Warhol was spot-on when he called good business "the *best* art." There are moments when I regard Dogfish Head itself, the entire entity, as a gigantic piece of conceptual art. Like artists, we're most passionate about the opportunity to create things out of our imagination that didn't exist before—new recipes, new events, new architectural spaces—more so than we are passionate about making money.

Also featured in color photo insert

This hangs on the brewery wall, right near my cubicle.

But unlike, say, a painter or sculptor in her studio, we are also a commercial creature. Our art, in bottles and on dinner plates, gets replicated again and again (as does a Warhol silk screen) and tested in the marketplace; our organization must be capable of sustaining the quality of that art and satisfying the demand for it, always within the discipline of operating profitably.

As an industry becomes more cluttered with an abundance of new brands, it is imperative to maintain what one stands for. For Dogfish Head, that means we cannot let tumultuous moments change our priorities. While others might compromise on quality or freshness or discount to undercut competitors, we continue to resist. We understand the potential danger that retail stores and bars might opt for cheaper product. We could lose relevance. But we're holding fast. Why? Because we won't compromise our commitment to use top-of-the-line ingredients and charge a fair price for what our beers cost to make. Ingredients like chicory, saffron, raisins, and orange flesh have always distinguished our brewery. They are expensive, but quality is fundamental to our identity. A stubborn refusal to compromise is embedded in our brand.

We will always be off-centered; that's the core of our being whether you're talking music or clothes or events . . . or beer. Our brand is about continually stretching limits; about never being content with the same-old, same-old; about envisioning new possibilities. We're inspired to innovate in order to render positive karma to our beer, our company, our customers, and the entire craft community. Our marketing mission is to compellingly communicate that passion for originality. That's the essence of Dogfish Head and the cornerstone of our brand.

chapter 4

LEADERSHIP 101

love the mistakes

I feel an everlasting itch for things remote. I long to sail tumultuous seas and land on barbarous coasts.

—*Herman Melville*

It's never easy to admit mistakes. To err is human, of course, but for an entrepreneur it is probably harder than normal to confess to screwing up. Your personal reputation is tethered to your professional reputation and your business is your heart and soul (to say nothing of your life's investment, in many instances). You don't want anyone to think you'd ever do anything stupid to put your business or your own reputation at risk. Then there's the ego factor. An entrepreneur wouldn't be an entrepreneur without a high level of self-confidence. Your natural instinct is to trust yourself, particularly in the face of contrary opinion; to make the right bet. Once you're established and you have found your own sustainable niche in the marketplace, the inclination is to keep doubling down, taking new risks, and making new bets with the hope that each one will prove you right as they have before.

Being proven wrong can feel like a blow to the gut, especially when you have made decisions by your gut, your intuition, that prove to be unsustainable. This was especially true in the early days at Dogfish Head, when I could be pretty headstrong and single-minded. I'd discuss major initiatives with our leaders, we'd have lively conversations about them, but in the end it usually came down to my telling them—as the owner and vote-holder of the company—what I had decided we were going to do. I would listen to their input and sometimes I would be swayed to reconsider the direction I initially wanted to go in with a new product or project but I would make the final decision pretty much unilaterally.

I have had a pretty good batting average following my gut on new recipes and projects. If I look across our portfolio of beers, for example, I can see that over 90 percent of the beers we distribute were originally conceived by me and over 80 percent of our current volume comes from beers I came up with over a decade ago. Almost every one of them has grown in volume almost every year. Through the years the talented team of brewers, cellarmen, and QC folks have continued to dial in and perfect the recipes and beer concepts that I have come up with. Inevitably, though, you can beat the odds most of the time but you can't beat them all the time. Reality will periodically kick in with a big wake-up call. What you had fearlessly envisioned growing into a successful new product or project simply can't always turn out that way every time. The pieces won't fall into place. You failed to read the tea leaves right. As an entrepreneur, this is the moment when you can be either smart or stubborn. The mark of a truly effective leader is to choose smart, which means learning from errors so you don't repeat them. Yes, it's tough to eat humble pie, but even with all the after-the-fact "I told you so's" ringing in your ear, I believe mistakes can be hidden blessings when they teach you how to raise your game. Fail forward, meaning take new risks, but learn from your mistakes so you don't make the same mistakes twice.

The frustrations that we experienced in our efforts to establish Dogfish Head beer-centric packaged foods is a great example. It taught me a big lesson about the value of internal collaboration.

My inspiration for the food business started with a passage from *Moby Dick*. The story itself is very meaningful to me. Much of the action in this story occurs along the Atlantic coast where I grew up and where our company is based. More than that, though, I relate to the hero Ishmael's description of himself: "I feel an everlasting itch for things remote. I long to sail tumultuous seas and land on barbarous coasts." I recognize in those words the same sentiments of adventure that are central to the primal, universal entrepreneurial urge, and certainly my own.

Since I'm always trying to learn new information that can enhance the creative journey of our company, I do all my reading through the filter of how the story/book/newspaper article applies to Dogfish. I had a flash of inspiration along those lines one day a few years ago while reading *Moby*

Dick, when I came upon a passage where a character describes the ultimate clam chowder. The secret ingredient in the recipe was hardtack, the dry biscuits rationed to 19th-century sailors as a survival staple. These crackers, brittle enough to stay intact for months and not let insects in, were used to thicken the chowder. "That would probably taste real good if you mixed in some dark beer," I thought to myself. A few days later, in my kitchen at home with cans of gourmet chowder, I started experimenting with adding different Dogfish Head beers to the chowders. When I got to our Palo Santo brew, with its brown sugar and robust roasty caramel notes from months of wood aging, I knew I had found what I was looking for.

PALO SANTO MARRON

An unfiltered, unfettered, unprecedented brown ale aged in handmade wooden brewing vessels. The caramel and vanilla complexity unique to this beer comes from the exotic Paraguayan Palo Santo wood from which these tanks were crafted. Palo Santo means "holy tree," and its wood has been used in South American wine-making communities.

This highly roasty and malty brown ale was a huge hit at our Rehoboth Beach brewpub when first released in November 2006—and Palo went into full production at the end of 2007.

It is now available in 31 states.

At 10,000 gallons, our two Palo tanks are the largest wooden brewing vessels built in America since before Prohibition.

When I have a new idea, I want to act on it as quickly as possible. I am very action oriented. All "id," some would surely say. What feels so good to me is to have an idea and rally the support of my talented coworkers to bring it to life. That's my most cathartic reward. It's fine to always work this way if you're an artist or a one-man show, but you can't operate unilaterally as part of a bigger organization where you are relying on other people to do the hard work to make the vision sustainable. And, as I learned with our food business, without incorporating the input of your fellow leaders early in the process, you'll never get full buy-in.

With my idea for a Dogfish Head chowder still fresh on my mind, I showed up at a Monday Team meeting brimming with excitement for a brand-new product line that nobody saw coming. I brought the food idea to them pretty much fully baked. We debated recipe details. (Hardtack, the biscuit in the *Moby Dick* chowder recipe, is made of grain, so adding one of our hoppy best-selling IPAs made from brewers grain might be the first instinct but we learned that these beers made the chowder too bitter so we ran trials with beers that were sweeter and roastier like Palo Santo.) We tried different versions, and I would later invite them to sample my subsequent inspirations for the beer-infused bratwursts and pickles that would fill out the line of beer-infused foods. But I hadn't considered there might be feedback about the much more important, fundamental question: Should we even be in the packaged food business in the first place? And if so, are we ready to allocate the right resources with the right professional background to be successful?

In effect, this is how that presentation went in terms of my message to the rest of the leadership team: "You can make suggestions or subtle tweaks but we're doing this no matter what; now you guys have to help me make it happen." At Dogfish we've adopted a not-so-affectionate term for ideas that are brought to the team already fully developed by one member of the team without consensus and without all of the right work input considered to make it as successful as possible. We would call that a "shit sandwich," as in "Sam gave us a shit sandwich that we had to eat." To be painfully honest, there were a few instances where they felt this way. Since I have been the one bringing the majority of the creative ideas at Dogfish forward up to the present, I was the shit sandwich delivery guy in most of the cases. Thankfully, it was only a handful of times. Sometimes the ideas would still be successful. Sometimes not so much.

I did a very half-assed job of involving the Monday Team in the process of launching this entirely new packaged food business that, despite my determined optimism, turned out to be an incredibly big resource suck for the company for a very low return on investment, at least as defined by profits and revenue. The brand value of playing in spaces no other breweries were playing in was certainly positive but subjective and difficult to quantify. We didn't put the right attention and resources behind the project to ensure success, but we had limited resources and some things had to give.

I forced this initiative forward, still convinced of its merits, without earning support from our leadership team and coworkers. How could they feel invested, since nobody but me had ownership of the idea? Yet more demands and pressure were being heaped on them and their departments to participate in the launch of the beer-centric foods, even though none of them had been consulted in advance. By default, I became the idea's sole champion, and since I'm not particularly good at operations, beer-centric foods would face continuous operational challenges and resistance.

At the same time, we were also in the throes of another major initiative. Having successfully changed the Delaware law to allow the sale of pints of beer on-site, we were now building a tasting room at the brewery. Why not offer food, too? True to form, I forged ahead, personally naming our food truck Bunyan's Lunchbox, determining its design, hand drawing what I wanted the truck to look like and even drawing the logo.

Just to keep things interesting, I announced a firm date of June 15, six months hence, to both launch our line of foods and open the tasting room and food truck. I did this without first analyzing the impact this opening schedule would have on the rest of the business.

The packaged food business was driven by my personal passion, but there was also a legitimate, plausible business model. Yes, I enjoyed researching different kinds of clams and vetting chowder manufacturers, but I also was intent on getting our beer into unexpected positions on supermarket and grocery store retail floor spaces that other breweries couldn't access. I envisioned cans of Dogfish Head chowder racked next to cases of Dogfish Head beer in a unique, attention-grabbing promotion that would get us new customers and more brand recognition. Same with other foods that fit our profile. Brats were a natural: sausage and beer is a classic pairing. Hop-infused pickles were a little departure from the obvious, but they were still in the wheelhouse. On paper, the whole scheme sounded good.

In the real world, things were different!

Myriad details that I hadn't even considered began gumming up the works. The management team had reason to be distrustful when I brought them whatever packaged food concept I dreamed up next, which, invariably, would unleash a tsunami of internal stress and strain. We screwed up the way we came to market with the chowder, imposing an unwieldy distribution model in the process. We'd buy the truckloads of soup at the local production facility 10 miles from our brewery, house it in our own brewery, and then distribute it ourselves. Instead of being solely focused on selling more beer, our sales department was suddenly being asked to manage chowder inventory and do the accounting.

I personally chose our food partners, making it clear that anything bearing the Dogfish brand had to be of the same meticulous all-natural quality as our beer. We're a company that's obsessed with consistency. After a while, a sample of chowder showed up that our sensory panel tasters didn't like. When pressed, the company who canned our chowder admitted they had mistakenly doubled the salt during the packaging process. With us it's a no-brainer what to do when a batch of beer isn't perfect: nobody's happy, but you dump it down the drain and write off the loss. The chowder manufacturer's reaction was different. Their position was basically, "Okay, it tastes saltier than it's supposed to, but we're still within the legal limits so let's sell it anyway." I had clearly picked a partner that was not a good fit for us.

Despite this rocky start, Dogfish Head beer-centric foods made their way to market and some of the items are a modest success. The business now is frankly a question mark. We've killed chowder. If we continue doing brats we may bring production in house and just for our own food truck or we may take our food truck men in a totally new direction. Pickles are doing the best of the three. People love the taste, and we sell a lot at the brewery. The producers take care of all the distribution and sales. The big question is how good a distribution job can they do getting it next to the beer?

The most significant return from this foray into packaged food, though, is something that will never show up on a profit and loss statement. It has proved invaluable to my evolution as a leader. I've had to learn to absorb some difficult criticism. My dedicated and proud coworkers have helped me understand, once and for all, that my "little ideas" can quickly turn into massive resource sucks. The lesson learned is applicable to any entrepreneur with a growing team of leaders: big decisions that involve the time and resources of multiple people need buy-in; they need team support. There are still creative decisions and projects that I want to take the lead on fleshing out at Dogfish Head. I need to be ready to invite coworkers into the creative process earlier, and I need to be ready to take the support role on more creative projects and not always need to lead.

A SHOW OF THUMBS

I began using this process when I was on the Board of the Brewers Association and we now make use of this process on the Dogfish leadership team as well. A show of thumbs is a good way to do a temperature check on where people stand on critical issues when all opinions should be heard. It allows you to get the status on issues collectively in real time before delving into each person's position. The process is similar to the way a vote is put forward in a board of directors environment, but is less formal than a Robert's Rules of Order voting approach. Basically, with a show of thumbs one stakeholder is tasked with distilling a concept we have been discussing into a single statement. Then we ask for a show of thumbs in regard to our individual positions on this statement.

Thumb up = I agree and commit to actively support it.

Thumb sideways = I am neutral, but I can live with it and commit to actively support it.

Thumb down = I do not agree, and therefore I cannot commit to it.

If all thumbs are up there is nothing more to discuss. We note and record the vote and move on to the next piece of business. If we have mostly thumbs up and some thumbs sideways, we ask to hear from our members who are thumbs sideways as to why they don't love the idea to see if we can get them to move to thumbs up. If we can't get them to move to thumbs up but they will stay thumbs sideways and still support the idea, the idea moves forward and we leave the room fully committed to supporting the idea. If there are thumbs down from some, we listen to their concerns as to why they can't support the idea. We have a respectful debate with the goal of trying to get the thumbs down members to at least move to thumbs sideways. If we can't get them to thumbs sideways—so there are leadership stakeholders who are stuck at thumbs down—we almost always do not move forward on the idea.

We did not have our consensus-building show-of-thumbs process in place when we were moving the packaged food concept from idea to launch. If we had, I am sure this project would have been handled very differently. Matters reached the low point when the Monday Team started looking at some of the packaged food product ideas as complete distractions for the company. I was excited about an off-centered partnership with a small private soup company. What could be cooler? What I never considered was all the things required to make that relationship work that didn't affect me: staffing the different production and selling components, establishing policies and contracts between the different companies involved, overseeing special preparations of the beer to be added into the chowder. . . .

During this era of the packaged food line launch, I'd often be on the road, selling beer, meeting with distributors, and hosting events—removed from the falling morale. But at meetings of the other leaders, particularly the Thursday Group of Nick's direct reports, they would share their frustration with each other. Instead of the weekly discussions of operations and departmental priorities and activities, which these meetings were supposed to address, they occasionally turned into high-level critiques of some of the projects we had embarked on at my insistence. Rather than discuss "How do we do this?" the conversations ended up being "Why are we doing this?" or, worse, "Here's why I resent us doing this." I was the person responsible for the why and the only person who could respond. But I wasn't in the room.

In the context of this specific business initiative, Dogfish Head was in the midst of a trust crisis in all directions of leadership. I was not trusting the other leaders enough to involve them early in the creative/strategic decisions, and I felt they didn't always have my back to put the right people and resources into place and hold them accountable when we launched new projects and products that I was passionate about.

Back in this era, as the company's often unilateral big decision maker, I was ultimately willing to trust my own judgment. The whole premise of Dogfish Head and off-centeredness is about proving the status quo wrong. My entire career had been about challenging what others took to be true. My reflex was to presume that I knew what was right in every situation that pertained to Dogfish Head, and the more people doubted me, the more sure I was that I was right. That kind of logic loop makes it hard to hear dissent.

At the same time, my colleagues had lost some confidence in me on certain projects. And, as the execution of our beer-centric food business was proving, in some regards, I had earned their distrust.

We had reached an impasse. I knew I had to be open to a change in direction and a leap of faith into a more collaborative approach to consensus building.

INTERVIEW

Pearse Lyons, President and Founder, Alltech, Inc.

Pearse Lyons is an Irish businessman, with a master's in brewing science and a PhD in biochemistry. His journey took him to Kentucky, where he started Alltech, Inc., in his garage with an initial investment of $10,000. Alltech is now a multibillion-dollar global animal health and nutrition company. He also established the Lexington Brewing and Distilling Company, known for Kentucky Ale.

In the alcohol business, there aren't many companies that produce both beers and distilled spirits. Both Dogfish Head and Alltech are exceptions to that rule. I had heard great things about Alltech's leader. When Dogfish Head bought a world-class copper-clad distilling system from an equipment manufacturer in Kentucky based a few miles away from Alltech, I used that opportunity to meet Pearse. Since then, we've become fast friends and confidants.

"Chairman's Choice"

SAM: It's perfect that we're starting where we are. When I came in, you mentioned that you just gave your entire sales force a talk about selling where your point was not to talk about the competition.

Also featured in color photo insert

Sam and Pearse

PEARSE: Why mention them? You're only doing them a favor because you're either bringing attention to them or you're making yourself look small by considering yourself in the context of another company.

SAM: Exactly. I think anyone like you and I who began as start-up entrepreneurs . . .

PEARSE: With nothing, yeah.

SAM: With nothing. We're obviously going to be a David in an industry dominated by Goliaths. And one of the major premises of this book is that there's ultimately more business value that comes with embracing the good karma of prioritizing collaboration instead of focusing on the negative energy that surrounds competition. Even among potentially "friendly" competitors.

As a leader, how do you bring the spirit of collaboration into your company's world so you don't have people on the org chart in different business units and silos competing with each other?

I know you have been successful in a number of highly competitive industries.

PEARSE: All of them.

SAM: You've been successful without getting distracted by competition. I'm curious about your journey in that context.

PEARSE: First of all, you have to be aware of your competition. I don't really see it as a competition, though. I see this more as market information. Alltech is in the beer business, for example, and I'm fascinated by beer.

But if we're talking competition, you have to know your competition. The famous sprinter . . . he won four medals in an Olympics . . .

SAM: Carl Lewis?

PEARSE: Right, Carl Lewis. I'm a distance runner and I've got a good story from the New York Marathon to illustrate this point about how you handle competition. Lewis was the honorary starter the year I ran. By sheer chance, I encountered him later that evening in a bar. We chatted away and the subject of competition came up. He told me, "In my business and in my chosen profession, I'm aware of my competitors, but if I looked over my shoulder at them, the competition passes me and the race is over." And within the essence of 10 seconds, you can see that.

SAM: But competition is real, isn't it? You can't just ignore it.

PEARSE: Of course not, but his point was so valid. Be aware of the competition. Know their strengths and their weaknesses, by all means. But don't get hung up about it. Run your own race.

Take beer. Let's say you, Sam, bring out a new beer, for example. I've got a sales force for my beer of 400 maybe. What are they supposed to do? Drop everything because Sam has brought out a new beer so they forget about selling our beers on their merits? Of course not! Yes, the competition is there and the competition has an idea. But I don't want my team distracted. What I need is passion, integrity, speed. And I need urgency. You can't get bogged down worrying about what others might or might not be doing.

SAM: That sounds to me like you're describing an entrepreneur staying true to his vision.

PEARSE: Right. As I mentioned, speed is usually critical and nobody has the same sense of urgency as an entrepreneur. It's absolutely critical. You don't have any choice, especially when you start out. You're operating with little money and no safety net. It's your beer, your bottles, and ultimately your passion.

SAM: Have you got a good illustration of passion?

PEARSE: Sure, here's a recent one from this year. For basketball March Madness, we brought out a limited edition set of beers called Platoon, in honor of how Kentucky's Coach Calipari substitutes players in five-man platoons. In the same six-pack, with blue and white labels, which are Kentucky's colors, we put three bottles of a Belgian white wheat ale and the Belgian white accented with blueberries and honey. It was a natural—stock up on Platoon and cheer for the Wildcats.

We put them out with beautiful outer packaging. So I go around to a retail outlet, the Liquor Barn, to find it. I couldn't. I asked the guy, where is it? He points over there. And that outer beautiful packaging is now brown because we couldn't get the box done in time.

SAM: The consumer can't see it.

PEARSE: I opened the box and I started putting them out. And here I am, the boss!

So then I asked our guys, "Well, how many cases did you do?" They say a thousand. I said, "Guys, you're nuts. If Kentucky gets to the Final Four, that thousand cases is going to go in a minute and you only have one chance to do it." "Well, yes, but the case is out the door and we couldn't get the honey . . . ," do da do . . .

I called my distributor and they weren't going to deliver to the stores until Monday. This is Thursday. Monday! There are games all weekend. "Get it in tonight! Or tomorrow morning." How are we supposed to do that? "In your car, whatever you have to do, just get it over there!"

SAM: A sense of urgency!

PEARSE: Anyway, they did just that. Out into the store the following day, just before the big game. Da, da, da, da, da. All gone.

SAM: So it sold right out.

PEARSE: All gone. And now we have 4,000 more cases that we're doing. "Well, we're short of this and da da." Get it done!

This sense of urgency, it's absolutely crucial. And entrepreneurs have it. You clearly had it when you started your business. You didn't have any choice. You had your beer and your passion. And little money.

SAM: Very little money.

PEARSE: So you had to do it! The challenge for craft brewers and all entrepreneurs, I think, is to not lose that bite when they get a little bigger. They start knocking other brands and selling cheap. They lose the passion of their own identity. And selling cheap.

SAM: It's bad karma, bad energy.

PEARSE: And our friend Anheuser-Busch, to put out what they put out knocking us.

SAM: I was asking about these silos within your own company. If you get to a certain scale, you don't want them to compete. You want them to collaborate. But there's a room full of MBAs at Anheuser-Busch InBev who are charged with reviving the Budweiser brand. And they don't care about the room full of MBAs on the other side of the giant building who are charged with growing Goose Island and Kona—the brands marketed as indie craft brands, which they 100 percent own and control. So they'll step on their brethren across the C-suite hallway for the short-term benefit of their flagship over here.

PEARSE: Right. It's incredible.

SAM: Yeah. Shortsighted.

But keeping an entrepreneur mind-set can be hard when the company gets bigger and starts to scale. You wear a lot of hats in the beginning and you make most of the decisions. Clearly, you've got to move quickly or you're going to get stepped on by a bigger competitor. It's up to you to make the calls. But now our company, Dogfish Head, is just too big for that.

I've been charged by some of my coworkers as suffering from founder's syndrome, where you still love going deep into the detail parts of the company. I see their point and I intend to get better about being more inclusive. Taking the lead on some creative projects but playing a supporting role on others. We need leaders throughout the organization. But as you get bigger, departments separate into silos whose specific interests can be in conflict with each other. Scale can breed internal competition. You want everyone to work for the good of the whole.

We're on a scale now that we have to start thinking about a holistic strategic plan in order to get agreement about the goals and objectives. We want everybody on the same page. But I've fought that for two decades because I felt if we built a strategic plan, we'd be building it in the context of what others are doing. We'd lose the inspiration to go on our own journey. How do you navigate that?

PEARSE: First of all, you're not an MBA, I don't think.

SAM: English major.

PEARSE: Okay. In my case, I've a technical background. Reluctantly, I should add. I didn't want to go college. But my mum had never gone to high school, much less college. And so she said you're going to school.

I'm 26 now, finished with school, and thought I'd go to Guinness. I'd already worked in Guinness every year for maybe five years.

SAM: In the summers?

PEARSE: In the summers. And I was being groomed. And now I'm doing my master's and PhD. And then I come to get an offer from Jameson's to design the brewing process for the first whiskey distillery in Ireland in some 20 years. I see all these marketing guys and they all have nice suits and expense accounts and fancy cars, which I didn't have. And so on and so forth. I saw clearly, marketing and business is where it was at.

So I applied to do an MBA. And this is relevant, I think, to your question.

I applied to do an MBA and got rejected. No problem. You're rejected. And why should they pick me? And here I was a new PhD but I didn't have business experience and so on. So I decided to do a commerce degree at night to get myself ready for the MBA, which I did. After the end of the third year, I got accepted.

So here's my question, how long did I last on the MBA?

SAM: After you enrolled and started the MBA program?

PEARSE: Yes.

SAM: Were you also doing that in your own time in addition to a job or were you doing it full-time?

PEARSE: On my own time, but the company freed me up at twelve o'clock to focus on that.

SAM: I'm guessing you lasted two semesters. Three semesters?

PEARSE: Three weeks!

SAM: Three weeks! Not even one semester. Why?

PEARSE: Because entrepreneurs are not structured. By definition, they cannot be structured in advance. I say this from personal hindsight. The stock-in-trade of entrepreneurs is creative, inspired, daring, game-changing moves that can't be programmed in advance. Can't be taught. It evolves organically.

To make my point, look at the British Empire. I studied industrial history as an undergraduate, learning about why Britain went into India and so forth. It was commerce that drove it. Businessmen like you and me went there largely on their own for the opportunity to grow businesses and trade. And her Majesty—the imperial government—only came in when the job was done to protect what those entrepreneurs had built.

So when I hear people saying, "Well now, we have to have a strategic plan," I say nonsense. I say nonsense.

SAM: Can you explain what you mean by that? Why you say that?

PEARSE: Here's a great example! In Dublin a few years back we had the Alltech Craft Brewing and Distilling event.

SAM: Right. You graciously invited me to that.

PEARSE: Millennials over there called it "the Alltech."

SAM: Which you were happy with.

PEARSE: Delighted. They never called it by this long string of misery as it were, blah blah blah blah blah. They'd just say, "See you at the Alltech. Have a beer at the Alltech." Fantastic event. "The Alltech, the Alltech, the Alltech."

So here's my point. Whose decision was it to do the thing the first time? Mine. Call it a chairman's choice, the boss's choice, the entrepreneur's choice. Whatever you like. But after that, once the organization takes over and it gets put into several silos, it's no longer solely up to you anymore. If Sam the entrepreneur goes back to Dogfish Head this afternoon and says we have decided with Alltech to do A, B, and C, it'll happen. If you put yourself into a silo, it's not your call. Now it has to be part of a plan.

Second time around, we decide to do the event in Normandy, France. And it was a mistake, in my opinion, because we had our brand already there. Why would we double brand? But we had a plan in place by then, with all the effort and strategy that goes into that. To use your phrase, various silos were invested. So I decided we'd stay with it. We had half our marketing team over there for the best part of six months. I became more and more frustrated with it because I knew it was wrong. And what did we get out of it? Scarce little. If I had put all the money we spent in Normandy into promoting beer, we'd be bigger than Sam Adams; we could have built ourselves a million-barrel brewery.

But here's my point. You do something once, chairman's choice. You do it the second time, it is now by virtue of a general choice. Not my choice. Strategy people tend to force you to toe the strategy line. You're an entrepreneur. That's all you've got going for you, which is a hell of a lot. The silo people are managers.

SAM: I agree with that as long as you're inspiring your coworkers and there's a level of faith that's always going to be part of your work as chairman and majority owner. But what about the value that comes with your leadership team having input and buying into an idea so that they have some ownership and then champion it to the same degree that you do?

PEARSE: They never champion it to the same degree that you will. If you pull your team, as you're calling it, into buying into the game, that's fine if you're a public company. But you've just given up all the flexibility that you have as a private company with one majority owner.

SAM: Leadership by democracy can be painful, right?

PEARSE: Business isn't a democracy. Entrepreneurship is not a democracy. It's the opposite to a democracy. You make the decision and you are responsible for the consequences.

SAM: And yet you've inspired a lot of talented people that I admire to join you at your company on this journey.

PEARSE: Yeah, because I look after them and we're flat, a flat organization. And I talk with them. I run with them. I kid with them. A guy called me this morning and he's in tears. He gets me the tickets for the Kentucky basketball games. I've never asked the price. Never. Because if I have to ask the price, then he's the wrong guy. And he goes out and buys them. But he's all broken, cut up because the prices are now so high. He literally was crying on the phone.

SAM: Because basketball is a religion of sorts here in Kentucky.

PEARSE: Right, and he felt terrible. He felt that he was betraying me in the sense that he wasn't doing his job, which is to get the tickets. But here he was, he couldn't do it at what he thought was an exorbitant cost. I told him to get me the tickets; it will cost me a lot but I won't ask the price. If you look after people . . . no, if you're *nice* to people, if you're *normal*, if you're whatever, then people look after you.

The people who work for you for money, they're not the people you want. Now you're paying me well, okay. And maybe I get a bonus or whatever. But if I'm in it for the money, as opposed to in it for the thrill of competition or the satisfaction of accomplishment, I'm never going to be fully successful for you.

SAM: A rallying cry of mine at Dogfish is "We never let the tail of money wag the dog of inspiration," you know.

PEARSE: Inspiration is key. You are an inspirer. That's the other thing about an entrepreneur. An entrepreneur, that's to say good ones, never say "I." It's "We." Entrepreneurs say "Thank you."

I don't know what your salary is and I don't care what your salary is. But the fact is you own the company. I suspect if you didn't own the company, you'd work just as hard. It would certainly be true in my case. I did it for the last company where I was an employee. I did it for Irish Distillers.

SAM: It's how you're programmed.

PEARSE: How you're programmed. To build a team, be a good guy. Last week was a huge, huge week for us. You know what the highlight was?

SAM: A big sports game? Your pending M&A acquisition?

PEARSE: We went running, me and a guy named Declan, who wrote a book called *The Green Platform*. A great guy. He was a priest for 18 years. My son calls him the world's most positive man. We run along and we see this guy, he's just sitting there, looking scruffy. Declan says I'm attracted to hobos. I went over and asked, "How are you doing?" And the hobo says, "Well, not so good today." So we stopped.

SAM: Just went over there and talked to him?

PEARSE: And I said, "Well, we can change that, can't we, Deco?"

"Yeah, sure, we can change that."

"Deco," I say, "what you got in your pocket?" I always have money with me, so I see what I've got in my pocket. Together we gave him maybe $80. You should have seen the guy's face.

SAM: He was hoping for a quarter.

PEARSE: Yeah, and he got this. Those moments are the essence of life.

SAM: That exploration of goodness, there's a karmic component to it where you're not expecting a quid pro quo.

PEARSE: Never.

SAM: But if you put it out there, inevitably, the goodness comes back to you.

PEARSE: You have the "win philosophy" and your job, whether as entrepreneur or leader, is to instill it in your people. That can go really deep. You make them *want* to go further than they think they can. A good way to motivate your team is to keep asking them, in subtle ways, "Why should I have a bigger dream for you than you have for yourself?"

Athletic teams and brewing and business, they're all about the same principle. The people who are saying, "What's in it for me?" inevitably fail. Those who say, "How can I serve the team?" succeed. In Alltech, we see the connection between that attitude and peak performance.

And one of our rallying cries, an article of faith, is this quote from a Buddhist monk that says, "The master in the art of living makes little distinction between his work and his play." In fact, he hardly knows which is which. He simply pursues his vision of excellence in whatever he does, leaving others to decide whether he's working or playing. To him, it's always both.

SAM: There's a Robert Frost poem where he says the greatest anyone can wish from life is to make their vocation their avocation.

PEARSE: Well, that's what the Buddhist guy is saying. Then there's this. I spoke a while ago to a group in Dublin that operates chains of pubs. I said to them, "You know what you're selling? Not pubs. You're selling dreams. People come to pubs for three reasons: to be entertained, to be engaged, and to hear and tell stories. And you need to be different, you need to offer people something else, something more, that they didn't know they wanted." You know what Henry Ford said, if he gave people what they wanted, they'd . . .

SAM: Still be on horses?

PEARSE: They'd ask for a faster horse.

chapter 5
PREPARING FOR SUCCESS

Coming together is a beginning, staying together is progress, and working together is success.

—*Henry Ford*

The Monday Team was understandably skeptical when I agreed with them that the company needed a more collaborative approach to leadership. For almost two years I had been telling them I wanted to be more inclusive with our leadership team but it hadn't really happened consistently. To some degree, they regarded me as the boy who cried wolf once too often when it came to my capabilities at sharing strategic direction. When it came to choosing how Dogfish Head would deploy its resources, the decision-making process remained decidedly Sam-centric.

Those earlier promises had been sincerely made. I hadn't been acting in bad faith. I have always believed collaboration is important in theory, but I had failed at the execution. When it came time to go all in, I found it more challenging than I expected. I have since learned through my travels, interviews, and casual discussions over pints that many other entrepreneurs at growing companies have faced similar challenges. There is a muscle memory factor to a founder's tendency to make decisions based on gut instinct. My personality, my capacity for trust, my reflexive compulsion to cast Dogfish Head according to my vision for our brand, all kept me from pulling the trigger. Now, though, I was truly ready to commit. My journey over these past several years had given me a new perspective. It was more a gradual realization than a transcendent conversion experience, but, at this moment, I fully understood the company could never achieve maximum potential as long as I, alone, had the final word on all important decisions. I had become a true believer. Collaboration wasn't just good karma; it was also good business.

It's one thing to see the light; it's a whole other thing to sustain the glow. I knew that it would take more than good will and conversations about team spirit to make this work. We had to radically change our company culture. I was confident that this was the right move, and so were the other great leaders around me. Our Monday Team believed in this evolution for our company as much as I did, and we were all equally responsible for moving the evolution forward. The gathering turbulence in our industry has made it imperative that Dogfish become more flexible and agile than before. Previously, our leadership model had been a solar system with me as the sun around which the others spun in fixed orbit. Now we envisioned a multidimensional matrix. The Monday Team would own the Dogfish Head strategy together, but we wanted as much experience and as many smart voices—internally and externally—helping to articulate the goal tactics that would inform our internal strategy. To pull this off, we would need help.

My scorn for many components of traditional business management makes me a less-than-ideal prospect for consultants. That's not to say that I don't respect people who go through the rigorous academic training to get MBAs. My sister has one, as does Nick. The problem I see is that, in many ways, formal business education essentially prepares you for something that already exists—an industry, a specialization, a set approach. It teaches how to succeed in the present context rather than prioritize how to change an industry. You might say, "How would you know, Sam? You don't have a business degree." That's true, but in 20 years I have worked with many people who do. At Dogfish, I've had to learn as I go. To be sure, I wish I was better at finances and reading balance sheets and profit-and-loss statements, things I could have learned in business courses.

When we were small, I tried to look at Dogfish Head more as an artist collective than a proper corporation. In those early days, I embraced a broader definition of off-centeredness with my coworkers than was probably healthy for any company. We accepted eccentric personalities in the name of creativity. We'd tolerate a hothead, for example, because he was a great chef or she was a talented brewer. But as we scaled up, I recognized that Dogfish was very much a business. I had always trusted people to follow my example and emulate my work ethic—to try their hardest because I always tried my hardest, and treat customers with consideration because I did. But as the work force grew, *trusting* them to try their hardest was no longer the best way to lead the company; instead, *motivating* them to do their best became a big part of my responsibility. And motivation entails great communication so that everyone understands the what, the why, and the how of where we collectively are going—and the role of each individual in getting us there. This meant setting goals, holding people accountable, and conducting regular performance reviews—none of which, in my romantic anti-authoritarian punk-rock mode, came naturally to me. But if the internal collaboration was going to succeed, I had to become a better leader, and I had to give the leaders at Dogfish with more traditional people-management skills than I more room to inform our leadership process.

BRINGING IN THE EXPERTS

Dogfish Head chose to integrate an external work–life coach as a resource for our internal leaders about a decade ago. The earliest professional coaching sessions at Dogfish were geared toward addressing individuals' deficiencies or discomfort in managing people. This was in an era when folks were placed in management roles largely because of their technical prowess rather than a demonstrated ability to be effective communicators or leaders. At the time, our culture had yet to emerge as something to be nurtured let alone something to frame our hiring choices, and some of our hiring decisions clearly reflected this. For Nick, Mariah, Cindy, and me, many of our early conversations around assigning individuals to work with a professional coach were held in the context of: *Some of these great people we have promoted into management positions are having challenges; let's get them help to "fix them."* To the credit of our earliest coach it was made clear that IF people are in agreement, open, willing, and truly believe in where we are going and how they contribute to this journey, THEN positive change can occur; the "if" was the big unknown. For some of our leaders, we tried this approach and did not get the desired outcome. But in the vast majority of cases our investment in training and coaching has paid off. Many talented and passionate coworkers have grown into great leaders as they have helped us grow this company.

As we developed as leaders within the growing organization, we began to realize that "fixing people" wasn't the right mind-set. We abandoned this idea of being in the business of people repair, instead entering into the business of individual self-enhancement. We expanded our program to include all the managers at Dogfish and framed the coaching around strengths. The program that emerged leveraged those self-identified strengths to improve performance and increase opportunity. Nick was steadfast in his belief that proactive communication should be on everyone's improvement list to move this from an organizational need to an organizational reality. As our program has grown, we have folded into the coaching program supervisors at all Dogfish companies. We don't script the sessions, preferring to let our managers and their coach take conversations where they need to go.

Our coach, Tammy Ditzel, president of Inesse Consulting, has been working with the leadership team at Dogfish Head for about four years. Tammy works with our leaders both individually and in teams and has helped us not only grow but mature on our leadership journey. Her work with our team has been instrumental in helping us identify our goals and objectives as well as more effectively work together as we develop our strategic plan. Tammy and her work have been integral to the evolution of our company and our capabilities as leaders and internal collaborators.

In addition to her coaching work at Dogfish Head, the leadership team has also worked with Tammy to facilitate the development of our three-year strategic plan and to help us articulate and finalize the foundation statements upon which we are constructing the plan. I will not share the strategically sensitive language of our foundation statements but I will describe and define these statements because I think every leadership team and every company, no matter the size, would benefit by creating their own foundation statements to define their present and map their future.

THE DOGFISH HEAD APPROACH TO FOUNDATION STATEMENTS

Vision/Purpose

Our raison d'être serves as our vision at Dogfish Head. It translates to "reason for being" and it keeps us focused on the *why* and the *where*: why we are here, and where we aspire to be in the future.

Mission Statement

Our *compass* serves as our mission at Dogfish Head. It keeps us focused on what we do, who we do it for, and how we do it.

Strategies

Our strategies are simply our top priorities for the next three years. They unite all of our coworkers in a common language designed to keep us aligned to our compass, and keep us moving closer to achieving our raison d'être.

Goals

Each goal we set is aligned with one of our specific strategies, run through our filters, and while they are specific, measurable, actionable, realistic, and time-bound—we make sure they are focused on the big picture and flexible enough that our coworkers can design their own tactics to achieve them.

Tactics

Our coworkers at Dogfish own their tactics 100 percent. Tactics are action items identified by our coworkers to achieve the goals.

SWOT Analysis

Our TOWS serves as our SWOT Analysis—we like to end with a positive! We not only analyze our own threats, opportunities, weaknesses, and strengths—but we also brainstorm during our planning process those of our competitors—both our friendly competitors (other craft breweries we respect) and our less friendly competitors. We also separate out our responses by internal and external.

Business Plans to Drive Each Strategy

We make sure that everyone at Dogfish feels connected to our strategic plan. This means that Sales, Marketing, Operations, Human Resources, and Hospitality all have their own stake in how they contribute tactically to each of the three strategies.

Filters

Our leadership team works together to "filter" ideas at Dogfish. As a group of creative souls, we can sometimes (unintentionally) create chaos! To diminish chaos, without sacrificing creativity, we run every idea through nine filters to make sure that each of our decisions is in the best interest of Dogfish and our coworkers.

Consensus Process

Our *One Voice* serves as our consensus process at Dogfish. We are passionate people—passionate about beer, yes. But also passionate about the art of goodness and sharing it with people in our backyard and around the globe. In order to keep us operating as One Voice, our consensus process gives each a voice in our decision-making process and prepares us to actively support the decisions we make. Our consensus process includes our "show of thumbs" voting exercise, which I described in Chapter 4.

Tammy's firm is Inesse, from the Latin meaning "to be from within," which is how she coaches. Her intellectual mentor is Alan Fine, the author of *You Already Know How to Be Great*. His big idea is that the key to improved performance is eliminating the psychological interference that keeps us from implementing knowledge we already possess—which is to say that we are constantly forming beliefs about ourselves and other people that impose arbitrary, unnecessary limits on what we think can be accomplished. Tammy's methodology builds on this premise that the thing that holds most people back is themselves. Become clearer about who you and your coworkers *really are*, accept that these different ways of seeing the world are equally legitimate, and then adjust your behavior accordingly to minimize misunderstanding and maximize results. The foundations of effective collaboration come from interactions that are grounded in this mutually shared awareness.

Nick and the Monday Team, with some of their direct report managers, had been meeting with Tammy for several years. Then Mariah joined in for one-on-one coaching sessions as well. If they all thought Tammy's work was a good investment for Dogfish, giving coworkers a forum for self-expression and both professional and personal growth, I supported it. But I resisted their recommendations to get involved and participate myself. I was still in a place where I didn't want to change.

During my 2014 annual review for Nick, when he somewhat accurately diagnosed me as having a case of founder's syndrome, he urged me to work with Tammy. "She has helped me grow as a leader; she can help you, too." Reluctantly, I agreed. If I were truly committed to acting collabora-

Dominance
Person places emphasis on accomplishing
results, the bottom line, confidence

Behaviors
- Sees the big picture
- Can be blunt
- Accepts challenges
- Gets straight to the
  point

Influence
Person places emphasis on influencing or
persuading others, openness, relationships

Behaviors
- Shows enthusiasm
- Is optimistic
- Likes to collaborate
- Dislikes being ignored

The "D" and "I" in DiSC

tively, which I was, there could be no excuse for not making use of every available asset that could help me facilitate the transition.

My work with Tammy began with an appraisal of my behavioral style in the workplace, using an analytic questionnaire. Using the DiSC personality assessment, I was analyzed on the four different DiSC dimensions: dominance, influence, steadiness, and conscientiousness. The key quality of exceptional leadership, I learned from Tammy, is being able to adapt one's communications, directions, and actions to the different personality types of the people you work with. By recognizing my own strengths and weaknesses, I would be better equipped to align myself with the equally valid but varied styles of the other members of the Monday Team.

Steadiness
Person places emphasis on cooperation,
sincerity, dependability

Behaviors
- Doesn't like to be rushed
- Calm manner
- Calm approach
- Supportive actions
- Humility

Conscientiousness
Person places emphasis on quality and accuracy,
expertise, competency

Behaviors
- Enjoys independence
- Objective reasoning
- Wants the details
- Fears being wrong

The "S" and "C" in DiSC

My personality fell right on the dividing line between dominance and influence, iD in DiSC parlance. The description of this DiSC positioning was unnervingly spot-on for me: "a goal-oriented person who seeks exciting breakthroughs . . . you want to have the freedom to set your own course . . . strong ambitions, probably attracted to high-profile assignments that will allow you to maximize your talents . . . extremely passionate and expressive, your enthusiasm is often contagious . . . a strong ability to persuade others to adopt your vision . . . persuasive powers allow you to work toward your goals by gaining the buy-in of others." There was also a stark cautionary note: "People who are more analytical may challenge some aspects of your plans that you have left unaddressed."

It spelled out the priorities in the workplace for people with my specific personality type. No surprises there. I like to act fast and keep moving, stay optimistic and upbeat to maintain momentum, focus on innovation rather than minor victories, and put a premium on results. The report, however, found one trait in my results that was unexpected according to the standard formula: "You often turn your focus to cooperation and group effort, which is not typical of the iD style." In other words, I valued collaboration.

As Tammy shares in her coaching, the primary reason to identify workplace personality styles is to improve communication. The problem she often sees among teams is that members, in trying to do the right thing, will treat each other the way they, themselves, want to be treated—a noble proposition superficially but it contains a logical fallacy. What happens if the way you want to be treated isn't necessarily the way the other wants to be treated? Say I'm working with a style S, who is steady and doesn't share my sense of urgency to move from conception to action? Or a C, whose chief wants are precision, stability, and reliable outcomes? Obviously, there are going to be disconnects if we're looking at each other as reflections of ourselves.

Each style also comes with its own respective set of stressors, aspects of work that provoke anxiety. In my case, things that make me uptight include having to sustain interest in routine projects, following strict rules, setting realistic limits, and—again unlike the typical iD—working in isolated environments that don't allow ongoing social exchange.

The solution to navigating these sinkholes? Model behavior that keeps you from pissing somebody off unknowingly because your style rubs his or her style the wrong way.

From the get-go, I have enjoyed my time with Tammy and recognize its value. And the DiSC process has helped develop trust and communication among the members of our leadership group. It's easy to administer and understand, it doesn't take a lot of time or resources, and it gets the discussion going about what kinds of leaders with what kinds of personalities are at the leadership table together. It can even be used as a new leadership candidate vetting tool. Strong applicants can take it during the interview stage, and you can see if their DiSC results are complementary to the existing team's results. The goal is to find great balance and diversity of DiSC orientation in individual members to create a diverse, complementary whole.

As the first to take the DiSC assessment at Dogfish Head (her earlier engagements had addressed actual situations, not specific personalities), I suggested that the whole Monday Team do likewise. But, to my surprise, that took some convincing. There was discomfort and insecurity about sharing intimate information for certain members of our team. Since we were now consciously trying to work more collaboratively and democratically as a group, I didn't feel comfortable simply telling them they had to do so. Again, a certain level of distrust and group insecurity had surfaced. But, I felt that was precisely the reason to take the DiSC assessment. In discussing my hope that we could do this DiSC work together and in addressing their concerns, I acknowledged that sharing the more personal, psychologically oriented stuff isn't easy. But if we all went into it with the best intentions and trusted each other to be respectful, we'd learn a lot about and from each other, and grow as leaders collectively. In the end everybody agreed and embraced the project, and we all contributed positively to making it effective for our group. We still keep sheets handy that remind us where each other is on the DiSC spectrum along with notes about the best way to engage with each other.

Once everyone completed the DiSC assessment, we devoted a Monday Team meeting to reviewing the results. Tammy's take was that we are pretty diverse, which has both disadvantages and advantages. "There's more conflict in a diverse group," she explained, "but higher probability of better results." She described our types. As she went around the table describing characteristics, there were lots of aha's and knowing smiles as we recognized the description of each other's traits. I was surprised to see that Cindy and I sat so closely on the DiSC circle. Mariah and Nick were pretty similar. Tim was in a different position from everyone else. As was Neal. Sorting out my role within the internal collaboration paradigm is tricky because while at an operational and strategic level I now consider myself one among equals, as owner of the company I'm still the one with the ultimate control stake in the company (Mariah and I own 86 percent of Dogfish Head). Tammy is coaching me to have confidence in the leadership team so that I can let go of more operation direction. I'm all in on that. But there's still another big uncertainty in the equation: how this new approach will impact our long-term goal—mine and Mariah's.

I need to surrender more operational control for lots of reasons, personal and professional. But the act of relinquishing many aspects of control would be different, and easier, if the endgame were to sell Dogfish, or do an ESOP (Employee Stock Ownership Plan), or combine with a strategic partner. Instead, my intention has always been to maximize our independence and keep Dogfish a Calagione family-controlled company so that we have the ability to become a multigenerational family company if the time and circumstances align for this to happen. My plan is to have a model similar to that of Sierra Nevada Brewery, which has made it over that hurdle. Its founder, Ken Grossman, has long been a mentor and friend; we talk at least once a quarter, with one of our ongoing conversation topics being family succession. At this time, two of his children, Brian and Sierra, have leadership roles in the company.

What makes the situation at our company more challenging and what makes my stepping back so delicate is that our kids are nowhere near the ages of Ken's kids, so it is way too early to know as a family if either or both of our children are interested and capable (they would have to be both) in keeping Dogfish a family-controlled company. Also, I am disproportionately personally identified with the brand as the analog face and voice of Dogfish and the person who spends a big fraction of my work time focused on creating and participating in consumer-facing events and content (books, magazine articles, media interaction, web series, etc.). From a business perspective, this is an important competitive asset.

In the past, I have had my own hierarchy of priorities in terms of the most important and value-driving activities for Dogfish Head. Other members of the Monday Team have their own perceptions of major priorities. Only recently did we begin our work to align those strategic priorities and agree to recognize them as shared and unified.

The constant at Dogfish has always been Calagione family control. We have had different minority-share investors come in and out of the company and on and off our board of directors for the last 20 years. My orthodontist and family friend was an original investor and adviser. My dad, Mariah's dad, and Mariah's uncle, a Wall Street veteran, each has invested in Dogfish Head, sat on our board at overlapping times, and helped us consider strategic opportunities, acting as sounding boards and mentors.

While I know there have been different advantages to bringing in different external minority investors with strong business resources to complement our internal strengths, I also know that every time we do this it comes with a degree of risk. I began considering bringing in a new external resource in 2014 as we saw our industry becoming more complicated and competitive and less of a jovial, familial club of like-minded entrepreneurs. Don't get me wrong, most of the 4,000 indie craft breweries in the country still recognize each other as compatriots. But the landscape where the larger breweries operate has changed more rapidly in the last two years than it had in the previous 18 years our company has been in business. More and more of the breweries that were once controlled by craft brewer founders are now controlled by publicly traded international brewing conglomerates or financial enterprises—yet compete with craft breweries because they have acquired craft breweries. To ensure we remain competitive and continue to reach a bigger market, we needed to invest in the business. Before we could consider bringing in outside investors, who would have their own opinions about what Dogfish should be focused on, however, I wanted to make sure our internal leadership team was ready to work with a greater harmony of priorities.

It is a goal at Dogfish to have our portfolio of beers be recognized as a great value at higher price points than the average craft breweries' pricing. How do we do this? For us the answer starts with making unique, consistently great beers, but it goes further. We strive to be recognized for our exploration of goodness—always working outward from the foundation of world-class liquid in the bottle and not just world-class branding and story-telling. We have a multimillion-dollar quality assurance laboratory and a team of talented coworkers dedicated to QC on everything that we make. We intentionally keep circling back on the message that our beer is still a great value at its price, all the while reinforcing that premium position through the brand-building ideal of what it means to be off-centered. To keep the brand high profile and exciting, we need to continue doing things that make Dogfish distinctive and memorable—not just in beer but with our spirits, our inn, our merchandising, and our restaurants as well. Others have added to the list, things like our Beer & Benevolence nonprofit work, our green initiative (recycling thousands of tons of grain as cattle feed and millions of gallons of water), and our pride in sowing good karma through generosity.

However we end up defining our forward-looking vision, I know it is imperative that it be built around a foundation of well-communicated and well-differentiated strategies, goals, and tactics. Conceding the need for such a plan was, as I've said before, a new threshold for me. Accepting that I'll be only one of many with meaningful input to our first-ever strategic plan is to some degree a great leap of faith and trust for me.

Consolidation and the growth of the craft beer segment are happening quickly in our industry. But in some ways the beer business is slow moving; a new beer, from concept to coast-to-coast distribution, when done thoroughly and correctly, takes about 10 months. Fleshing out our departments with talented, well-trained coworkers and major capital expense projects can take one or two years. For most components of our business, results don't happen overnight. With our industry's product life cycles, our leadership team decided that three years is the right chunk of time for us to collectively plan our goals. I'm comfortable having Nick, our CEO, be the "Driver of the Strategic Plan" and giving him and his team of VPs as much help and latitude as I can in the three-year run room for this plan. The plan itself will be a living document updated frequently by us as the leadership team with the input of our coworkers. As the chairman of the board of directors and with my ownership control, I can exert more formal direction to our long-term plan if necessary, but I am hopeful we can build the strongest company through our strategic work together as an internal leadership team.

The creation and ongoing implementation of that long-delayed strategic plan is the most important work we are doing as a leadership team at Dogfish Head. I wanted to maximize the prospects for success with this plan, to weigh the odds in our favor. Aside from our work around the DiSC assessment, I also knew that we could do a better job at being more well-rounded leaders by understanding what is important in the leadership team members' personal lives, outside of the work we are doing at the company together. Then one day, while browsing through a Harvard Business School article, I stumbled upon a writing excerpt by Stewart Friedman and found it insightful and relevant to our leadership journey at our company. A long-time professor at Wharton, Stew is the author of the *Wall Street Journal* best-seller *Leading the Life You Want: Skills for Integrating Work and Life*, and *Total Leadership*, among other notable claims to fame.

I reached out to Stew about consulting with the Monday Team. Several conversations confirmed my hunch that he could really help Dogfish Head at this moment of cultural transition. The fact that his office was in Philadelphia just two hours from the brewery, making for an easy commute, clinched the deal.

His work shows how companies that encourage coworkers to maintain balance in their own lives become much more powerful organizations than those that always prioritize the work above the people doing the work. That message, restoring personal control through self-intervention, resonated with concerns I was having about my own future and those of the other members of our leadership team who all work very hard. But I was drawn by more than self-help evangelism. As a consultant at Ford, Stew had launched a corporate-wide portfolio of initiatives involving some 2,500 managers that is now recognized as a global benchmark for leadership development programs. In our own way and at much smaller scale this also jibed with my ambition and hopes for Dogfish Head. Could we work together toward nurturing a company culture where leadership would be embedded throughout the organization and good ideas could bubble up from below instead of always being driven down from above? Sustainable internal collaboration on steroids!

Stew asserts that sustainable change—both personal and organizational—comes when you optimize your commitments to work, family, community, and self (meaning mind, body, and spirit). The key word here is *optimize*, not *maximize*. You make conscious choices about priorities in each of these categories and allocate your time accordingly. Doing this changes the game from a zero-sum trade-off (when work wins, life loses) to a more dynamic equation. The irony that Stew has found is that by doing less, one accomplishes more. With four-way wins, all parties benefit. People feel part of something bigger than just themselves and that positive attitude carries over to the job. The function of leadership is to facilitate these four-way wins and, by so doing, empower the organization to thrive.

I figured his more personal approach would perfectly complement Tammy's professional coaching for our leadership team. She was teaching us tactical skill sets to become more effective, mutually supportive teammates. That was all good. Stew's strategic emphasis on how to determine long-term choices would make us better leaders.

INTERVIEW

Stewart D. Friedman, Founding Director of the Wharton Leadership Program

Stew Friedman has been on the faculty of the Wharton School of Business at the University of Pennsylvania since 1984, becoming the first Practice Professor of Management for his work on applying theory and research to the real challenges facing organizations. In 1991, he founded both the Wharton Leadership Program and the Wharton Work/Life Integration Project.

Stew's most recent book is Leading the Life You Want: Skills for Integrating Work and Life *(Harvard Business, 2014), a* Wall Street Journal *best-seller.*

Harmony in All Aspects throughout Life

SAM: To give some background: I was on a plane and I was reading a collection of articles from *Harvard Business Review*, when I came across an article that focused around your book *Total Leadership*, and it really spoke to me.

The content certainly can help anyone in any realm of their life but is particularly relevant to folks in mid-sized and growing companies. As a startup entrepreneur at a mom and pop organization, you're forced to wear a lot of hats, and that balance between the different quadrants of your life—work, home, community, and self—is something that you don't have the luxury to consider in that start-up phase of "fight or flight, and am I even gonna make it?"

When we were starting out, there were many times when I thought, what got us through that moment of *are we gonna be able to make payroll?* Are we a business that can sustain ourselves for more than this year? There were times when I thought, okay, I don't have to worry about going bankrupt next week. We have a sustainable business now. Are we growing in the direction that is best for our brand and are we growing in the direction that's best for us as leaders and as coworkers at this company, in terms of our personal health? And so the article you wrote in the *Harvard Business Review* really resonated with me.

STEW: That makes sense to me. I would just add that when I think about harmony among the different parts of life, I like to think of it in terms of the whole course of one's life. At different phases, you emphasize different aspects of what matters to you in terms of your work, your family, your community, and yourself: your mind, body, and spirit.

Certainly when your business is in start-up mode, it's hard to focus on anything but the survival of your business, but it doesn't mean that you can't attend in some small way to the other parts of life that are important. I would say that, had we connected back when you were in that struggle and just launching. But now that you are launched and growing, and you have the confidence and the resources to be able to breathe a little, it's easier to take account of the other things that matter in life.

SAM: I see what you're saying too because that sense of being overwhelmed or sort of out of sync with all the positive components of a healthy life are the same whether you're in start-up mode or you're now at a different point in your career. It's only that we finally have the luxury . . . created the luxury of time to make it a priority, right?

STEW: Much better put, yes. I'm glad you made that adjustment in that sentence because it's a choice to make an investment in trying to find a sense of harmony or integration. And it's always difficult. It's never easy no matter what life stage.

SAM: The context of my book is more focused on the work quadrant of my life, but I note numerous times that the only way you can be as healthy as possible at work is to make sure that the leadership, and eventually all of the coworkers, are conscious of all aspects of their life. When you talk about these choices, I think you do a really good job of describing them by saying the stereotypical approach is a zero-sum game of the choice between focusing on your life or your home versus your work. Can you talk about why it is a futile exercise to have that perspective?

STEW: I think most people use the word "balance" to describe the relationship between work and the rest of life. And I think the notion that there is a scale that needs to get into perfect equilibrium is a misguided metaphor. In my experience, it's impossible to do that. But more importantly, when you think in terms of balance, you always think in terms of trade-offs—what do I have to give up to be successful in my business—instead of asking a different question, like how can I find the strength and support and resources that I need to be successful in my business by tending to the other parts of life that matter to me?

When you ask that question—which I sometimes refer to as thinking in terms of four-way wins where there's positive impact that you can make, not only on your family and your personal life and your community, but of course in your business too—when you ask yourself that question rather than assuming you must make a trade-off—assuming balance, assuming zero-sum—then you're much more likely to open your mind to the possibility of taking action that's going to benefit all of the different parts of your life—rather than just assuming it's not possible.

It's really a kind of mental exercise and a very action-oriented exercise in exploring where there are such possibilities. So that's why I prefer thinking in terms of harmony or integration over the course of life because, when you think in those terms, you're much more likely to see possibilities for change, for innovation that then enable you to have that greater sense of harmony.

SAM: Yep. In terms of being self-reflective, for the readers of my book and the readers of your book, what's the best way to diagnose yourself—to identify which quadrants of your life need the most enhancement or attention first?

STEW: Well, in my book, *Total Leadership*, there are a series of exercises that help bring to life three principles, which we've found to be practiced and followed by people who are good at this naturally. The first is to be real—to clarify what matters most to you—so that's where it all starts, and really ends. The second principle is to be whole, and that means identifying the key people in your life who matter to you and to explore what they really need from you. The third principle is to be innovative, and continually experiment with how you get things done.

To answer your question about the best way to diagnose yourself: it begins with identifying your values and your vision and your assessment. And we've got some free simple tools for people to use to explore what really does matter to them.

It doesn't take long, but it does take some time to think through: What are my core values? What are the critical episodes in my life's history that have shaped those values? Why are they important to me? What's my vision of the world I'm trying to create in the future, and where do I allocate my time and attention *now* relative to what I think is important within the four different facets of life? It starts with a series of activities that are best done with others whom you trust, whom you can talk to about your answers to these questions and get some reactions.

SAM: And the best results are achieved when this is done with the people around you who may be going through a similar journey or people whom you trust very relevant to at least one of the quadrants in your life, correct?

STEW: Exactly.

SAM: You have both a really robust online course and you also have the book. And you've got the website. What do you think are the best ways for people who want to go on this journey to learn more about this? What do you recommend as the first steps to exploring?

STEW: It starts with you, but it's important to then take the next step, which is to think through who are the people who matter most, now and in the future, and you actually name them and identify what you think they expect of you, what they need from you, and vice versa. Then do an analysis of where there's conflict and where there is harmony or compatibility among those different people. How does what your parents expect relate to what your customers and your coworkers and your friends and your family expect, and how does all of that fit together?

Where is there conflict? Where is it not? And what do you learn from looking at those questions in light of the first set of questions that identified what you care most about? And then you talk to those people, and you develop skills. And in Chapter 5 in my book there are instructions for people to actually have these conversations to clarify what matters most to the people around them. What you often find out is that what others expect of you is usually a little different from what you thought, and actually it's usually less. Most people don't believe it when I tell them that, until they actually do the inquiry and find out that it's true.

It's all a big piece of the diagnosis. Before you can come up with smart ideas for innovating and experimenting, there is also a component of learning and correcting assumptions.

SAM: We're a mid-sized company now. We're not so small and I'm personally working hard to evolve from the quintessential founder's syndrome, from directing every creative and strategic major decision to building a team of thinkers, not just doers, with the other leaders at Dogfish: using the total leadership process as a tool to better understand how we can support each other and what our expectations are of each other. The total leadership process becomes this great template for an even bigger world of our work with each other and our work for each other, and I think a big part of that is understanding and caring about the three quadrants that aren't the work quadrant for the other leaders at our company.

STEW: Absolutely, and it doesn't cost a lot to do that. It doesn't cost a lot to care about the whole person in the people around you. It doesn't take a lot of extra effort or cost for you to—in a nonintrusive but truly caring way— find out what it is that matters to those around you outside of their work. As leaders we need to understand what has an impact on what we do together and know how we can support the interests of others in life beyond work. For some people it's kids. For other people it's writing the Great American Novel or going to school. It can be anything, but the key, as you pointed out, is that when you invest attention into the lives of people beyond their work, they return loyalty and commitment tenfold compared to what it costs to understand and really try to support those wider interests.

My book guides you through simple exercises that help you identify and define what you care about, and who matters to you, and then talking to them so you can come up with ideas for experiments. The simplest way is to have people do these exercises and then share in small groups—groups of three are best—share with them what your responses to the questions are. This is done better in writing if possible.

Part of what I've done in my book's Appendix is to provide guidelines for being a good coach. What I found is that the social experience of exploring what matters most to you, who matters most to you, and then trying experiments designed to pursue four-way wins—doing that in a social context with two other people who are doing the same thing—except, of course, entirely differently because it's their lives and not yours, but you're trying to help them and they're trying to help you: it is very powerful because you learn a lot about yourself from trying to help other people.

SAM: We're doing that here. I know you work with quite a list of other companies. Are we an anomaly at Dogfish in that with our leadership team almost all of us had more focus on a quadrant other than the work quadrant, even though that's where we know each other the most?

STEW: Not at all. The locus of activity for these experiments can be any-where in your life. The key is to be thinking about the impact that you have either directly or indirectly on all of the different parts of your life. It's doing that kind of action, pursuing that kind of goal that you then discover how the pieces are connected in ways that you didn't see before. So you're kind of like a scientist in the laboratory of your life, and you're experimenting, and you're seeing if I make this change in my family life and I'm looking for how that's going to have a positive impact on my work relationships, I'm going to see those because I'm looking for them. So the key here is, no mat-ter what part of your life you're focusing on in terms of where the change occurs that's an innovation for you, the key is to be looking for impact on all of the different parts, and that's how you really shift your mind-set to see opportunity for harmony rather than trade-off. It's not at all unusual for people to make changes in their family lives first—that's the most com-mon—or for themselves personally. Many people feel stressed, burned out, unhealthy physically, psychologically, spiritually, and so they do something that's going to in some way nourish them.

They're looking for not just a greater sense of health and stability, but how that's going to have an impact on their work. One of the reasons that's such an important thing is that when you look for ways to try things differ-ently, it's going to affect other people at work, and they may need to support you. So let's say that you wanted to change your work schedule, so that you could have more time to work out or to be with your kids because that was critically important to you, well, you may have to negotiate that with people around you at work, and the key in making that successful is to help the people at work see that you're doing this for them. You're not just doing it for yourself and for your kids. You're doing it for the people at work, and you want to measure the effect.

You want to give demonstrable evidence that shows that that's actually working. So you build that in, and you help the people around you at work see that what you're doing in your family is intended to benefit the people at work as well. That's because you'll have more energy if you exercise, for example, and you'll be more focused at work and less worried about family issues if you can attend to them better. You'll be more committed to work and less resentful if you're able to focus on what's most important to you, your family, and your community. That's what makes this kind of change sustainable because you're acting as a leader in all parts of your life. That's why I call it *Total Leadership*. You're acting as a leader, taking action that's intended to benefit the people around you, the people that you care about in all of the different parts so they want to see the changes you're making even more than you do.

SAM: It's like that old adage, don't just work hard, work smart. I think a lot of times at small, private companies that are growing or even at big companies where there are pressures—by doing this exercise where you're asking people to be more forthcoming and honest about all four quadrants at the same time, you're giving them permission to work smarter and not just to work harder.

STEW: Exactly. Smarter means it's better aligned with what you really care about and better aligned with what the people around you truly need from you, and that's why all of that diagnostic work is so important. But you're absolutely right. Being more mindful of how you choose to invest your energy and attention is really the key. And I think what you and your company are doing is part of a shift that we're going to start seeing more of, in terms of people wanting to organize their lives this way, and that the old model that you just referred to will be gone.

SAM: What are the healthy, first steps that you see companies taking toward getting out of the rat-race mentality? What are the examples that have come up in your work—something common to the companies that are on track, whether it's consciously through the total leadership principles or just that the company is on a track toward something that's sustainable and more in keeping with sort of the millennial or new generation's expectations of a happy life?

STEW: Yeah. It's exactly what you're doing. Usually there's some kind of event or episode that causes people to step back and think, we've got to do something differently. For example, we're losing our best talent to the competition and why is that happening? Or, we're seeing our healthcare costs skyrocket, or people are reporting in our human resource surveys that they're not engaged, they're not fulfilled. What's the problem, and what's that going to cost us in terms of not just turnover, but productivity and the ability to attract great people? So it's some kind of event or data that shocks people into thinking, we've got to do something a little differently. Identify your vision; tell the story of where you've come from and how that has shaped your values; do what I call taking the four-way view, look at your work, home, community, and self, and ask how important is each.

Take 100 points and divide those up into the four domains. Which ones are most important? Now, where are you focusing your attention, and how satisfied are you in each domain, and how well are you performing? Where are there gaps between what you care about and what you do? And how's that affecting your satisfaction and performance? What does it imply about what you might try differently? It's asking these diagnostic questions that gives rise to ideas for innovation, and that's really where it begins.

SAM: That's part of why the exercises in the book are so great. If you're doing this with a group, you're all doing the exercises together so that even as a sounding board, being there to support each other on individual exercises means each of us will be getting better at being a supportive leader for others.

STEW: Now you're getting at one of the great byproducts of this process of the social learning of leadership, and that is that you build your skill as a coach. What you want is a company of teachers, a company of coaches, a company of people who are there to support the growth of other people. What you become is a culture that really emphasizes the growth of capacity for leadership. And it's not just a renewable resource; it's a limitless one.

One of the things that I find useful about the total leadership approach is that it's very flexible and it's built to be adapted to different contexts in which people pick it up. So yes, investing the time and attention and resources in the growth of future leadership is something that most smart organizations have figured out they need to do, but that was not always the case.

The concept of small wins is also critical. It's like learning to do scales—and then you can play a song, on a guitar or another instrument. You've got to take small incremental steps.

We're just going to try this little thing, so nobody has to freak out that the whole world's going to change. It's a small thing, so let's just see how this is going to work, and if doesn't, we'll adjust. That can lower the anxiety and resistance associated with the process. It gets people to support you, and of course you have a greater sense of confidence and competence in trying something new if it's smaller in scale.

You don't climb a mountain in one step. You take a lot of steps. So you take that small step and then you realize: I can actually see a little different view here. Let me take another step. Great. The view is getting better, and I can still do this, so let me take another step. It builds confidence and it has all kinds of benefits, and I find that's essential. You need to have a big idea, which is why we start with your vision, a big concept like what's the point of my life? And from there you work back to now what's the next step?

What we're ultimately trying to help people to learn with *Total Leadership* is how to initiate innovation in a smart way. Based on a clear-eyed view of what matters most, who matters most, and where you want to go. To be smarter about how you get support for ideas that you care about, and that builds your strength, your capacity, your confidence at being able to innovate intelligently. That's really the core of it. When I first created this program back at Ford Motor Company in 1999, when I was head of leadership development there, that was the primary task that I had. The CEO hired me to create a change in the culture of the company to get people to be less afraid of taking risk, and this was a response to that.

Thank you, Sam. I'm excited to see you guys again and see what's been learned and where we take it from here.

chapter 6

INTERNAL COLLABORATION
marrying off-centeredness
to a world-class organization

I have been hosting beer serving and speaking events for over 20 years now. I love doing these events and spending time with the people who love our beers. At this point in my career, I know how to work a room but I am not so great at working an org chart. When our whole company could literally fit in one big room, back when everything we made—beer and food and distilled spirits—was done under one roof in Rehoboth, my creative fervor was enough to allow me to be a good leader and get the right messages to the right people efficiently: customers and coworkers alike. But as we've grown this company—with multiple locations; multiple product lines, including beer, food, and clothing; an inn; coast-to-coast distribution; and some 230-plus coworkers and counting—when it comes to addressing my need to amplify my communication skills proportionate to the growth of our company, I've come to learn what my strengths and weaknesses are.

An important contributing factor to our success as a company is that we have consistently been able to "fail forward." Over the past two decades there have been some errors that led to wasted time, energy, and money. Rather than break us, though, these mistakes have made us stronger and more resilient. Why? Because almost all of them have been due to Dogfish Head's willingness to take risks. Rather than become immobilized by the possibility of failure, we've always been emboldened. Additionally, as a leadership team we have done a pretty good job of confronting our failures, pulling no punches as we address the challenges and mistakes we make in order to correct our path as quickly and smoothly as possible. In fact, we are so quick to analyze what we are doing wrong we have to remind ourselves to celebrate our successes occasionally instead of always going deep on the things we need to improve upon. Generally, I believe this happens because we know we have more to gain by addressing the areas where our company needs improvement as compared to sitting around slapping each other on the back over the things we are doing well. While you shouldn't dwell on and bask in your successes, you should note them for the record: say a quick "good job on this one, team!" then confirm together what was successful in this instance and how it was achieved, and move on to address the next challenge.

As we move into our new model of a shared leadership approach, however, I am sensitive to our need to still remain a risk-taking company to the degree that is important to our innovative off-centered brand. As we begin our third decade, we're running a fiscally super-tight ship. We're creative in the places we need to be and conservative where we need to be. In our consumer-facing activities, we continue to aggressively innovate with new recipes, events, products, and projects. But internally we're pretty buttoned-up and conservative about things like our financial debt-equity ratio or our human resources practices.

Letting go can be very difficult for me. Tammy, our leadership coach, has helped me to see that this is natural; that an entrepreneur sacrifices so much to build his company that he's fearful to entrust its destiny to others. Hence, the founder's syndrome. That clarity has been invaluable for me. Nick, our CEO, pointed this out to me as well. The way out of this dilemma is for me to have enough trust in the leadership team so that I can confidently relinquish a great degree of personal control on most components of our business.

The biggest, most important step we've taken to implement internal collaboration has been to assess and discuss our leadership culture as a leadership team. For us to all live with our collective decisions and for me to not be tempted in a moment of frustration to play my trump card and say, "I have ownership control of the company and this is what I want to do," it's imperative that the Monday Team be fully conscious of how our separate personalities contribute to actions. Internal collaboration done as comprehensively as possible now involves flowcharts and set management practices and HR guidance. There's organizational structure to it, even though I hate even using the words "organizational structure." But moving to the next level is not just a matter of techniques and directives. In order for it to work, we have to continue to respect the things that made us strong in the first place—our recognition that we are coworkers, not employees, that we are doing this together. Our culture needs to be well articulated and permeate all levels of the company. Our values, particularly the willingness to take calculated risks at opportune moments, must be fully embedded in the workplace or we could fall into the trap of becoming excessively cautious and failing downward instead of failing forward.

As I mentioned earlier, Tammy Ditzel's coaching work is helping us better operate as a group. Culture, in her view, is not simply the average of different people but rather the sum total of such factors as individual style, dominant styles within the group as a whole, cohesion or tension, and consensus (or lack thereof) about collective mission.

Tammy calls Dogfish Head "the most unique culture [she's] ever encountered." From the meetings she's attended throughout the organization, she's impressed with how deeply off-centeredness runs in our organization. Nonconvention is not the exception but the rule. Tammy reports, "I'll hear people give all the standard ways that things are done and then they'll ask, 'What's the opposite?' That's what they want to do." This is an awesome foundation to build on.

The challenge in our new collaborative mode will be to consolidate and guide that iconoclastic energy so we don't devolve into anarchy. We have a strategy to do this, first at the leadership level and then throughout the company. Basically, our plan is to grow our appreciation and understanding for each other's unique abilities and perspectives and capitalize on the various individual strengths each of us has. Sounds simplistic, perhaps, and our success will ultimately be measured by outcomes, not just group harmony. But this is our leadership plan.

To execute this plan, we began by identifying the dominant personality styles of the team using DiSC analysis, as I described in Chapter 5. The majority of our leadership team, four out of six, fall into two categories within the four DiSC quadrants. Two of us are Dominants (D), which is higher than the usual percentage in an average group. Ds make quick decisions, like direct answers, and enjoy a competitive atmosphere. Interpersonal communication within the group can suffer at the hands of Ds, who are highly results oriented. Two of us are Influencers (I), again higher than typical, whose traits are optimism, enthusiasm, and socializing. They offer a warm environment that fosters creativity but tend to hold too many meetings. Both D and I are active styles that combine to foster an energetic, outgoing atmosphere conducive to charismatic types. Two of us, however, have more passive styles. One is a Steady (S), whose hallmarks are stability, predictability, and consideration for others. Such folks put a premium on teamwork that leads to reliable results, but they also tend to avoid tough decisions in order to spare feelings. This sensitivity can inhibit change and stifle innovation. The other is Conscientious (C), a type that prizes accuracy, analysis, and perfect results. Cs contribute greatly to the culture by clarifying expectations and delivering exceptional quality control, but their drawback is that they can be super-critical in the face of what they consider to be exaggerated enthusiasm.

Personally, I am something of a hybrid. I fall a shade on the D side of the intersection with I. No surprise, this is a personality combination that enjoys exercising passion to lead a group toward major accomplishments as quickly as possible. His ideal is a culture that is adventurous and colorful. When corporate priorities force an iD to rein in ambitious plans, he stresses. He also stresses when forced to moderate his pace, partner with overly cautious people, and succumb to a slow, systematic approach. My personal DiSC analysis follows.

YOUR DISC STYLE IS: iD

Because you have an iD style, Sam Calagione, you're probably a goal-oriented person who seeks exciting breakthroughs. Most likely, you want to have the freedom to set your own course. You may have strong ambitions, and you're probably attracted to high-profile assignments that will allow you to maximize your talents.

Most likely, you're extremely passionate and expressive, and your enthusiasm is often contagious. You probably have a self-assured attitude that many people are drawn to. You often use gestures and anecdotes to emphasize your points, and you tend to speak freely with little concern about filtering your thoughts.

You probably have a strong ability to persuade others to adopt your vision. More often than not, your persuasive powers allow you to work toward your goals by gaining the buy-in of others. However, people who are more analytical may challenge some aspects of your plans that you have left unaddressed. While you're often able to create forward momentum in a group, you may need to delegate more in-depth responsibilities to others.

Like others with the iD style, you're very active and energetic. You have a strong need for variety, so you like to have multiple projects on your plate, and you probably dislike sitting still for long periods or being forced into monotonous routines. You enjoy the gratification of kicking off a new project, but after the excitement wears off, you may lose interest and fail to follow through on your plans.

Because you enjoy having influence, you may strive to be among the inner circle in an organization. Most likely, you feel a strong need to be heard, and you do your best to make a favorable impression. You appreciate being recognized for your contributions, and you may thrive on public recognition. And, because you value such compliments, you're often generous with your praise of others.

Most likely, you enjoy meeting new people and building on your large network of friends and associates. You may be particularly drawn to other people who share your charisma. You're probably not afraid to share personal information, even with people you've just met. Because you enjoy making connections, you're happy to introduce people who may have common interests. Furthermore, you may embrace opportunities for friendly banter or brainstorming.

When conflict arises, you probably try to focus on the positive. In fact, you may try to brush unpleasant issues under the rug for as long as possible. However, you also have a tendency to jump to conclusions, and if you become very upset, you're more likely to express your anger than to shut down. In such cases, you may lash out at other people without trying to control your emotions. While unleashing your feelings may seem cathartic, you may underestimate the impact that this intensity can have on others.

You're not afraid of the unexpected, and you probably enjoy the excitement of being spontaneous. Because you're so adventurous, you're eager to seize new opportunities, even if it means changing directions quickly. You're open to taking risks and making decisions based on your gut instinct. Because you can be overly optimistic, you may dismiss potential obstacles too quickly.

Sam Calagione, like others with the iD style, your most valuable contributions to the workplace may include your ability to initiate change, your passion, and your drive to succeed. In fact, these are probably some of the qualities that others admire most about you.

These results were prepared by Tammy Ditzel with the Everything DiSC© tool, courtesy of Inesse Consulting, LLC, the certified partner, distributor, and administrator of Everything DiSC©.

So how does an entrepreneur integrate himself or herself into a collaborative leadership culture? Much as I hate conventional wisdom, three tried-and-true strategies apply.

First, you need to be patient and give others time to put ideas together and come to conclusions, lest they feel like they're operating amid chaos.

Similarly, you've got to encourage and support the process and analysis required to ensure you have the best chance at getting things right the first time and won't have to redo work later. Equally important, you must give credit to the members of the team.

The third imperative is to acknowledge problems rather than gloss over them. It is important to keep a positive attitude, but also to temper excessive confidence or haste in the early stages of a project so you can be more likely to avoid unpleasant consequences later on.

Diverse personalities and skill sets are critical for collaboration to work. With a diverse group, you might have a little more conflict than with a homogenous group, but you also get better results. Different perspectives and even priority values need to come into the conversation in order to produce the best choices. Teams where all the members are alike tend to struggle. They are most fragile because all the members want the same things and, as a consequence, unknowingly wear blinders that make it difficult to see contrary factors.

Collaborative diversity, however, doesn't come easy. Everybody sitting around the table has to be allowed to act in a way that is true to him- or herself, even when that slows down the process or bruises feelings. They need to express their personal priorities, needs, and even fears.

Internal collaboration depends on fully utilizing the different strengths of every member of the group. Thus, understanding the varying personalities within a team can help ensure effective teamwork and ultimately success of a project. Someone who, for example, is more reserved or pensive could easily be shouted over in a conversation, and his or her unique contributions, the special powers that others lack—such as attention to detail or methodical planning or insistence on accuracy—would be lost in the commotion.

In a business setting, people who don't feel free to be themselves—who suppress their natural behavioral tendencies to try to conform to what they perceive to be the group's values—will often end up unhappy and resentful. The tagline for Tammy's coaching is "Helping people and organizations create joy on the job." You can't be joyful unless you're true to who you are, and you can only feel free to do that and be that person in an environment where there's trust. The bottom line: internal collaboration is all about building strong-assed teams that value, respect, and trust each other.

The development of our calendar of new beer releases is an example of one way Dogfish Head collaborates internally on projects. In previous years, the calendar was a project I created with the input of only one of my coworkers, our VP of sales. I'd say, "I think we'll sell this many cases of this particular beer," based on what Dogfish had done previously and my gut instinct about what sales for that specific beer would look like in the future. I would go through our entire lineup of roughly 30 beers this way: "I want to release this beer and then this beer and then that beer at these volume forecasts." Our VP of sales would chime in with his own gut check and away we would go. Consumers, particularly craft beer consumers, want diverse choices; they have come to expect a certain level of innovation and evolution with each annual beer calendar we execute. We keep favorites and rotate out underperformers, many of which we bring back a few years later to keep anticipation high and demand for specific beers in front of supply. This year, for the first time ever, I'm not involved in the initial draft of next year's calendar. For the first time, we asked all our coworkers what ideas they had for new beers. We asked beer geeks around the country. We worked with a couple of industry analysts to collect data about where they think the industry is going. Then we let our sales, marketing, and production leads take the first whack at the next year beer calendar based on all of these inputs—before the Monday leadership team, including me, gets to weigh in with opinions. To be sure, we can't let ourselves get tied down to relying only on external inputs. By definition the Dogfish brand makes unique, creative choices about where to place our bets. But in the spirit of collaboration, we can be better informed by all these other voices.

The team at Dogfish will be leaving some blanks in the beer calendar schedule intended to keep us innovating and trying new things. That's very much part of our culture. In the same way that I want to ensure everyone at our company has a voice and is contributing to our success, the team is also ensuring there are opportunities for collaboration for me as well. That's how I envision our collaborative culture evolving. I'm still very much a leader, just no longer *the* leader. With a great team of leaders growing around me, I am focusing a little less on interacting with our distributors and less on directing the VP of sales and VP of marketing than I used to. I am focusing more time on doing the two things I have always loved doing since I opened Dogfish Head: (1) making off-centered ales with off-centered people and (2) sharing off-centered ales with off-centered people. So I'm coming up with new innovative beer recipes and making them with my own coworkers or work-ing with external collaborators on these brews. The beers I spend my time on are not always beers that are heading toward coast-to-coast distribution. They can be one-off creative projects like the port wine and local grape-infused small batch beer I recently brewed with four of my female coworkers called Mother Nature vs. Father Time. Or the one-off collaborative brews I did this year for our web series *That's Odd, Let's Drink It!* These brews were done with external creative collaborators like chef Mario Batali, basketball all-star (and fellow home brewer) Chris Bosh, and rapper Mac Miller. Brew days like these, when I get to touch the ingredients and add them to the boiling beer with my own hands, are always my favorite days at work. I also love the days when I get to do cool events where I am talking about and sharing our beers with off-centered passionate customers or our best retailers and distributors. For example, I am typing this part of the book right now in a hotel room in Providence, Rhode Island, where I will pour beer at our booth and give a tutored tasting for hundreds of people at the Beervana beer festival. Events like these are a great opportunity for me to high-five and thank so many beer lovers who support our company and also to hear what they would like to see from Dogfish in the future. I get this feedback from them indirectly by just keeping track of which of the half dozen Dogfish beers I am pouring are most poplar at this fest and sell out the fastest—and directly, when I ask the people in line specific questions like which beers that we used to bring to festivals would they like to see come back or which of our beers they would like to see in a can when we move forward on our canning line project. I participate in an average of two consumer-facing events per week, and as I chat with beer lovers, distributors, and retailers at these events, I begin to absorb patterns in the feedback I take in. This informs my gut, which is now only one data point for our decision-making process, but it is a relevant one that comes with 20 years of experience and a pretty good track record.

On any team or in an organization, when coworkers are motivated to act like leaders and to contribute awesome ideas, we have to make sure they are empowered to make decisions on their own. We want a company where people are managing upward and constantly asking themselves, "What can I do to make sure my work has the most positive and helpful impact for my direct leader at this company?" The critical factor for success in this regard is a strong culture of open and robust communication. There has to be a shared framework for individual autonomy. It's kind of like our version of a famous John F. Kennedy quote, "Ask not what your leader can do for you, but ask what you can do for your leader."

Cindy Dunson had an eccentric off-centered resume when she first applied to be the director of HR at Dogfish. She came from the regimented, hierarchical world of banking, where she had successfully risen up the corporate ladder. While that background might not have seemed like the right fit for a funky little antiestablishment-oriented brewing company, she spent most of the time in her interview sharing her passion for her hobby of being a magician's assistant. She has grown the HR and cultural bandwidth of our company from a department of one to a robust team of many.

Cindy has been the champion for a company culture of shared responsibility and recognition and utilization of the special gifts that each coworker embodies, transforming Human Resources from a generic department name into a key strand of the Dogfish DNA.

INTERVIEW

Cindy Dunson, Director of Human Resources at Dogfish Head

One of Cindy's key responsibilities is building the structure for screening potential coworkers to make sure they "get" Dogfish Head. She believes that ours is a company of participation rather than spectatorship, and thus, when we consider a new hire, we look not only for technical excellence but also for people excellence and cultural fit—like a well-balanced three-legged stool. To build a culture of internal collaboration, it's important that folks from different departments develop relationships with each other. "The people who do best here," Cindy says, "are those with an appreciation for what we can be, not just what we are."

Off-Centeredness Is about Our Culture

SAM: As the VP of HR here at Dogfish Head, would you say there is a specific type of person we look for when you think of the folks you've interviewed and hired during your nearly 10 years with us? Is there a type of person that thrives in the Dogfish Head culture?

CINDY: Yes. First, you can't be change averse. Dogfish Head is continuously changing and evolving as an organization, and we need folks who thrive in that sort of environment. I think we also look for people who have real skills and strengths across all three of our hiring criteria—cultural fit, people excellence, technical excellence. We require that of our leaders, but quite frankly we also require that of everyone. When we are interviewing candidates for a position as brewer, for example, they might not have experience managing a team, but they still need to be excellent from the standpoint of collaborating with fellow coworkers and working with maintenance folks. Basically, they still need to have a good balance of those three components.

I also think we're more of a culture of participation rather than spectatorship. So folks who do really well here are people who want to get involved holistically rather than merely collect a paycheck—which can be done anywhere. Many of the people we hire are picking up their lives and moving to Delaware to join the Dogfish Head team. As a general rule these people not only want to get the job, but learn more about beer, and become a part of the Dogfish Head family. They want to hang out at Beer:Thirty (our weekly intercompany celebration of our great work and one another) to get to know people from other Dogfish walks of life. Those people who will take time to develop these relationships and have an appreciation "for we rather than me" will likely do best here long term.

SAM: Right now, we're all trying to shift. Nick Benz often talks about how we need to cultivate more thinkers and fewer doers in order to grow

The steering wheel of Sam's Dodge Challenger Super Bee, painted with a reminder to "Go Slowly" and "Go Thoughtfully."

Sam in his used muscle car, his 46th birthday present, wearing a road-mullet wig.

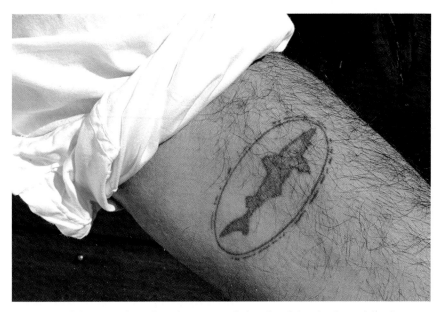

Sam's Dogfish tattoo, based on his original sketch of the shark-and-broken-shield logo, created 22 years ago.

A Dogfish Head fan's tattoo, one of the many shared with Sam throughout the years.

Sam (right) and Nick Benz, Dogfish Head's chief executive officer as of 2014, outside the Dogfish headquarters.

A piece of art that hangs in the Dogfish Head brewery, near Sam's cubicle.

The Dogfish Rules of Thumb are 16 rules for being successful at Dogfish Head. They offer hands-on tips to help coworkers interact with each other authentically and productively.

Sam (left) with Pearse Lyons, founder of the Lexington Brewing and Distilling Company, creator of Kentucky Ale, and Alltech, a multiglobal animal health and nutrition company.

Sam (right) with Charlie Papazian, founder of the American Homebrewers Association, at the Craft Brewers Conference.

Dogfish collaborates with the City Lights Bookstore in San Francisco, to create a curated library for the Dogfish Inn, the harbor-front hotel in Lewes, Delaware.

Sam (right) recording the *That's Odd, Let's Drink It!* web series with Chris Bosh, NBA All-Star and fellow homebrewer.

Dogfish Head launched a partnership with Woolrich, a family-owned outdoor clothing company that began by providing blankets to Union soldiers in the Civil War, to create the Pennsylvania Tuxedo capsule collection.

The Pennsylvania Tuxedo includes both dry goods, like a soft wool blanket, a button down shirt, and a wool coozie, and a "wet" element, a collaborative brew incorporating fresh-picked spruce tips from the forest in Woolrich, Pennsylvania.

Sam (right) and Josh Rich, an eighth generation descendant of Woolrich founder John Rich, and current vice president, International, at Woolrich.

Dogfish collaborated with two Italian breweries, Baladin and Birra del Borgo, to open a new rooftop brewpub, Birreria, at famed Italian marketplace Eataly's New York City location.

the company. I look at that in the context of our more unique, org-chart interactions: when you think of a manager interacting with a supervisor or interacting with other coworkers on their team within a department—where we're trying to say, instead of every decision coming from the top of the org chart to moving throughout the org chart. What we ask of our people is to look for ways to improve what they do for the betterment of Dogfish. Can we talk about that transition in thinking—the path we are now navigating?

CINDY: I just interviewed a job candidate from New Jersey who asked me, "What do you like about Dogfish Head?" I am often asked this question in these settings. The one thing I always bring up, referencing my own move to join Dogfish Head nine years ago, is this: I wasn't sure about working for a family-owned company where you don't know if you will be micro-managed or feel like an outsider. Taking a risk by joining Dogfish and experiencing this inclusive work environment for myself and helping newer coworkers acclimate by sharing my own experience helps build the belief that we all have the ability to do more and to contribute in many ways.

Even the doers here need to be thinkers. We all have the ability to influence the process: in each of our respective jobs, we are the experts. And so what I said to the candidate is, if you are selected to come join us at Dogfish Head as the regional sales manager of New Jersey, we're hiring you because we can't do that job. We either physically can't, or we think you are going to do it better than anyone currently working at our company would. And it's like that for each and everyone here.

And because this is true of our coworkers, that means you are also charged with doing it more safely, more efficiently, and more joyfully. For me having that line in everyone's job description about constructively challenging the status quo is a really important one. No matter what your role is at Dogfish Head, you have an obligation to make that role the best role you can make it. And that's what I think Dogfish culture represents. However, making that ideal resonate with all of our leaders and managers so that they can bring it to life is something that constantly needs to be worked on.

SAM: Yeah. That's well said. When I refer to the "exploration of goodness" at the heart of our purpose being central to our brand, it also holds true that having a focus on the exploration of goodness is central to being a successful coworker at Dogfish. We expect you to be the best person at your job, and that's why we hired you. Keep exploring what it means to get better at your job. Don't be complacent and just keep doing the same thing.

CINDY: Right. And there is room for a breadth of different kinds of people at Dogfish because no matter what your role is, if everyone takes that approach that "I am the best person for this job and I am always capable of growing," then each of us will continually strive to be better: individually, and as a community of coworkers.

SAM: How much of our hiring process now is intuition versus more objective, measured standards?

CINDY: What matters most to us is that cultural fit—the people stuff, the soft skills—and it's also the more hard-skilled technical stuff. On the technical side we'll set up paneled interactions with people who have a strong technical understanding, so that we have a bit of a bullshit barometer during that part of the interview process.

SAM: One of the things I love best about our candidate vetting process is the time that we require each candidate to spend with a variety of coworkers, intentionally people within the department they are applying for as well as from other departments. It's great because the candidate gets to see these different perspectives and what different departments care about. But I think it's even more effective because existing coworkers get to hear more about what makes coworkers in other departments tick.

CINDY: That's a deliberate process. We make sure we include coworkers who have a good pulse on culture, because we want that cultural evaluation component to continue through the day through the various conversations with the different teams and into the dinner process where folks are a little bit more laid back and a little bit more disarmed.

SAM: That evening portion is what we call the liquid, truth serum component of our interview process. Since we are a brewery and distillery and food company, we want make sure that we get to know the candidates in those environments.

CINDY: At the heart of the process is this: if ultimately we are collectively responsible for our company culture, we need to make smart hires to preserve the integrity of our culture.

SAM: Every year more and more people are in a position to join those dinners because there's more and more people who really get it and are ready to be evangelists for our culture. In an ideal world any coworker could be at that dinner five years from now, and you should be confident that their feedback is going to be through the lens of understanding our culture.

CINDY: If the culture test is there, the leadership test definitely needs to be there—especially for the management positions. These candidates do need to spend time with indirect reports, direct reports, fellow management peers, and those who will be holding them accountable. It's about putting them with enough different coworkers that we get a really well-rounded view. For the most part, we tend to come together at the end where there's a pretty consistent recommendation that's being made. I call this team our selection squad.

Being involved in those selection squads is part of each member's role in the company. It's a privilege to be included, and those folks need to respond with feedback that is in the best interest of Dogfish.

SAM: Is the Dogfish Head culture difficult for new hires to fully get? How do you integrate corporate discipline, order, and accounting into what's an off-centered culture? How have we made that easier over the years? And maybe end by coming to the evolution of the rules of thumb that are in our guidebook.

CINDY: I don't think the Dogfish culture is out of reach for new people because they are coming here to be part of something they already know a bit about externally.

Off-centeredness is about our amazing culture, and off-centeredness is about the differentiation of our beers. Developing the rules of thumb wasn't about taking judgment away from management or taking freedom away from coworkers; it was more a way to define the rules of engagement a bit. It's not just the what but it's the how and the why—it's providing that greater context, to help us interact with each other.

SAM: What recommendations do you have for growing businesses that need to start paying more attention to their culture?

CINDY: Through the years we've had some great talented people here who just weren't right for us culturally. We embrace that our culture is specific to us and different from that of other companies. What makes one successful in a different environment doesn't equate to their success with us. What makes us who and what we are is unique.

We care that what we talk about must also practically matter. We talk about exploration of goodness. Goodness therefore needs to matter to us. In our boardroom there are pictures of coworkers on the wall, and those images are there to add that necessary weight to decisions, so that we—like you often say—don't fuck it up, and that's important to us.

If those pictures are going to be on the wall, we legitimately need to care about them. Those are some of the factors that influence how we interact with each other, how we interact with our coworkers. There are other companies that, like us, have their own brand identity, their own following, and they deliver a great product or service, but that's not to say what works for us will work for them. The key is finding your own authenticity. And then, once you've found it and discovered what makes your company tick, do the meaningful work to make that thing resonate with your people.

SAM: The wall in our biggest conference room, where the Monday Team usually meets, is covered with photographs of our coworkers kept as up to date as possible: current photos so that we can continue getting to know by face and by department all of our coworkers as the company grows, but also as a reminder that they're in there as we're making those decisions, and the decisions we're making are affecting them. Watching that wall grow for the last 20 years. . . .

It was fun when it was just me, but now look at how many people are on this bus or on this wall with me. I really think we are finally making steps, and it's gonna be an iterative process, and the first phase of this strategic plan that we'll embark on will only be that: a first phase of something that's evergreen and continues to be added to.

What excites you most about moving in that direction at Dogfish?

CINDY: A couple of things excite me.

I don't think having a strategic plan means having an absence of creativity the same way that the rules of thumb aren't the absence of creativity. They provide guideposts or markers on a map although the journeys are still individual. Ultimately it is our coworkers who are breathing life into those rules of thumbs in different ways. Each coworker receives a review at Dogfish that is in three components: cultural fit; technical ability, that is, how you do your job; and goal setting. The goal-setting piece is aligned with us culturally on those rules of thumb that speak more to growth with an emphasis on how our coworkers are helping to pull the company forward versus people needing to be pushed.

SAM: Instead of them using their energy to help . . .

CINDY: Instead of them using their energy to be like, this shit is a moving process. Let me give it a heave. The cultural component is so important that we spend much time on it during the hiring process. It has to live—otherwise, it's not dynamic.

So coworkers are given feedback about those things that we have determined to be critically important to us. All of us are aligned with that through the performance management program, so how awesome would it be to do the same thing with our strategy, which in essence is where Dogfish Head is moving.

SAM: How awesome would it be to do what with our strategy?

CINDY: To take that, where is Dogfish moving, where it is that we want to go, and make it live with coworkers. To say to our people, this is where the company is headed, and this is your role in it. And that strategy can cascade out to every coworker in our organization in a way that they move with it, and that can be done via goal setting. This is so powerful. Having people be meaningfully connected, not only to their role at Dogfish, but understanding how that connects to the greater good of the company. How awesome is that?

SAM: Good stuff. Thanks, Cindy.

When vetting potential candidates, each candidate meets with an array of coworkers from different departments. Some are people with whom they will regularly interact if they get the job, but some are people from more tangentially related parts of our business compared to the candidate's intended departmental home. This process is as rewarding as it is time-consuming because the candidate gets to see these different perspectives. But it's also great for existing coworkers because they get to hear more about what makes fellow coworkers in different parts of the company, who are in the room asking questions alongside them, tick. By understanding each other more fully—what we each think Dogfish Head stands for, what we individually consider our greatest collective successes and most critical challenges—we can help each other put Dogfish Head on the best path forward.

We love the diversity of our deep talent pool of fellow workers. One evergreen attribute we hope to identify and encourage in each new hire is that they will not just be *doers* but they will also be *thinkers.* "We're hiring you for a job because either physically or technically we can't do it ourselves," Cindy says, "and so we want you to do it better than we would do it ourselves if we had that position at the company." No matter what someone's job is at Dogfish, that person has an obligation to make that role be the best he or she can. Making that ideal resonate with all of our leaders and managers, so that they can bring it to life, is something we constantly work on.

As a business grows, the leaders need to pay more attention to their culture. If you're directing people to figure out their own authentic way within the context of your company, it is beneficial if they understand the whys and hows that make a business run. Like an ensemble of jazz musicians, they need to understand established structure and general principles before they can start improvising. To that end, we've put together the Dogfish Rules of Thumb—16 rules for being successful at Dogfish Head to offer hands-on tips to help coworkers interact with each other. These *rules of thumb* should not be confused with our *show of thumbs* consensus-building technique that I describe in Chapter 4. (I guess we are all thumbs around here.)

Rule of thumb number one sets the tone for all that follow: *You must embrace that it's not just what you do but how you do it. If you think it's cool enough to simply knock out items on a to-do list without paying attention to the relationships that might be damaged, your coworkers who might be compromised, or the bodies in your wake, then you won't last here.*

A big obstacle to effective collaboration is miscommunication. It actually might be more precise to say the most common challenge to collaboration is the lack of communication. Miscommunication implies a faulty attempt occurred. That's often the case in business. But I think it's safe to say, at least at our company, we fail forward more constructively when we at least try to communicate salient details to stakeholders and fail backward when we don't communicate at all in certain situations where execution suffers. We are committed to developing static-free feedback loops between coworkers and their supervisors. Unlike traditional evaluation methods where the boss rates the employee, we have established channels where

Also featured in color photo insert

Dogfish Rules of Thumb

both sides share objective feedback with each other. Leaders meet once a month with each of their direct reports. The purpose of these meetings isn't to point out faults but rather to stimulate a conversation about what is going well and how a process, action, or decision could be improved. HR has crafted some great coaching questions for supervisors to use when meeting with their coworkers—questions like "Are you getting what you need from me?" and "What resources and tools are we missing that you need in order to accomplish your goals this year?" Leaders are committed to this type of process and are doing it faithfully, and we are getting really good results.

We do exit interviews when coworkers choose to leave our company. We ask them for candid feedback on what they feel works well at Dogfish Head and what they think we need to work harder on. But we also do occasional in-depth interview projects with a diverse selection of current coworkers. We call these our Pulse Interviews because we are taking the pulse of the people who are currently part of our family of coworkers. While both processes are beneficial, we have come to realize there is often more fruitful feedback from people who are happy at the company and plan to stay and grow with the company than from coworkers who have already made up their mind to leave us. Of course, the latter group might be more brutally honest with their feedback since they aren't staying with our company, but we encourage total honesty from current coworkers who participate in the Pulse Interview and we are building on this process from a basis of 360-degree trust and respect as we navigate it together.

EXPERIMENTAL BREWING

For any company, retaining your best coworkers needs to be a top priority. These are the folks you're relying on to perpetuate the values of your culture. They are the ones at every level of the org chart who are pulling the culture forward side by side with the leadership team, not pushing against it. One of the most fun and on-culture ways we identify talent is with our experimental small-batch brewing program.

To bring more breadth and depth to the creative pool from which we draw innovation, we developed a program that allows anybody in the company, from dishwasher to accountant, to come up with an idea for a beer. If the person is able to involve three or four other coworkers, one of whom has home brewing experience so they're not working entirely in the dark, Dogfish Head will provide all the ingredients they need to brew a 10-gallon batch that they share with their coworkers at our all-staff happy hour in the tasting room on Fridays at 4:30, which we refer to as Beer:Thirty. We have created a form for all the coworkers to fill out as they judge a sampling of the beer. This feedback gives us each a richer experience of beer appreciation and provides a sensory analysis of the beer. Afterward, the head of the small-batch brewing program tallies up the scores and analyzes the comments. Every quarter we pick a winning recipe and then that team gets to go to the pub in Rehoboth and brew a 120-gallon batch. They get the pride of selling a beer they thought of and produced. The best of those four quarterly winners gets an expense-paid weekend trip to go sight-seeing and visit Birreria, the Mario Batali and Joe Bastianich brewpub project Dogfish Head is involved with in New York City.

The small batch program and process are examples of how we are already successfully instituting collaborative practices into our business. However, for me and for the rest of the leadership team, the ultimate opportunity to make a giant leap toward company-wide internal collaboration will be the creation and evolution of our strategic plan. We have begun this process. The leadership team has generated a concise and company-wide list of three universal company strategies that will sit atop our three-year strategic plan. We are now hard at work with our coworkers fleshing out the goals that ladder up to the three strategies and the tactics developed to support each goal. I've spoken a lot in the book about this strategic plan; it marks a major inflection point in the history of Dogfish Head. One of our driving intentions is to stay at the highest end of the brewing industry. This means we must continue to stay relevant as delivering what is perceived as a great value at a higher price than what is the norm in the beer industry. But there are important nonfinancial aspects of Dogfish Head that are equally important to us in terms of our long-term strategy. I believe, and others have agreed, that our company's generosity of spirit, our authentic and respectful interaction with customers and coworkers alike, distinguishes our brand as much as the things we lovingly produce and sell. It's not just advertising hype when we say that Dogfish Head is, at its core, about the exploration of goodness. Goodness in beer, yes, but also goodness to the earth, goodness to our environment, goodness to our communities, goodness in the arts, and finally goodness to each other.

It's going to be up to Mariah, Nick, and me to orchestrate a harmonic coming together of the separate voices of the leadership team into a unified, strong, singular voice to articulate the strategic vision of Dogfish Head as we move into the coming competitive moment our industry now faces. Nick has already taken the lead to draft a list of decision-making filters that the whole leadership team fleshed out and finalized the language for so that any new concept or creative idea has a clear path toward being considered and being implemented. Two of these filters are "Is it fun?" and "Will it enhance our brand strength and/or financial strength?"

No business can be successful without prioritizing financial strength. Without profits a company is unsustainable. And financial strength is usually very objectively defined within a company. The enhancement of brand strength as described in the filters is a bit more nebulous but it is worth defining, building a strategy around, and continually enhancing. Brand differentiation and brand strength are what allow a small niche company to charge more for products and services than the massive (usually) commodity-driven market leaders who rely more often on lower pricing and wider distribution to sustain their businesses. Two key components to our brand strength at Dogfish Head are centered around community building: specifically, our social media community and the local community we engage with in our philanthropic efforts.

INTERVIEW

Mariah Calagione, Vice President, Dogfish Head

Mariah Calagione is my coworker, my fellow Dogfish Head executive, my bride, and my high school sweetheart. As vice president, she sits at the leadership table of our company and is a voting member of our board of directors. She also oversees our social media efforts and manages Beer & Benevolence—our nonprofit program, which donates hundreds of cases of beer and hundreds of thousands of dollars each year to the causes that are dear to our company's heart.

I barely know where to start in describing how important Mariah is to my life story. We've been together since high school and have basically grown up together, with very different but very complementary brains and personalities.

There's a great F. Scott Fitzgerald story, "Head and Shoulders," that I identify with. It describes the skills, the thrills, and the challenges that come with relying on your life partner to also be your work partner.

"This Is the Road We're All Going Down Together"

SAM: We are going to be talking a little bit today about how a business can authentically intertwine your community into your company and your culture. Before I ask specific questions, though, please tell us a little bit about your role at Dogfish.

MARIAH: My role at Dogfish has morphed over time. When I came on board full time back in 1997, it was in the job of being the marketing and advertising kind of person. And I also ended up doing the jobs of HR and insurance and payroll and—

SAM: Bill paying.

MARIAH: Bill paying, which is a lot of fun . . . not. Eventually I got back to marketing, once we hired people who actually knew how to do those things rather than me just making up ad hoc solutions along the way.

SAM: In addition to all that, you've also always played a leadership role with an executive seat starting back when it was just you and me as a mom and pop running our mom and pop company. We were a leadership team of two.

MARIAH: I was the pop.

SAM: You were the pop and I was the mom! Together we would make the big strategic decisions for the company, or at least first consider them and then share them with other leaders in the company. Now that team has increased, where it's really myself, you, and Nick Benz who kind of sit in that executive triumvirate. Right?

MARIAH: Yes.

SAM: Today, you are the digital voice for our company and the person who oversees all of our social media. What were the key early steps to building a meaningful online community for our brand?

MARIAH: Actually two unrelated fans of Dogfish started our first Twitter and our first Facebook accounts. I began engaging with them, enjoying that, and starting to see how that engagement worked with communities of people who appreciated what we were doing online. The more I enjoyed communicating with customers and retailers and eventually wholesalers, the more I got involved in that world. I think a lot of times a business leader wouldn't have the time or interest in becoming so involved in the minutia of social media engagement, but I was able to because we had grown to a point where other people were able to tend to other stuff I used to have to do. So I had that flexibility, which I think helped make our presence on social media more authentic. The voice resonated because it was the same voice we were using on a lot of our other marketing efforts and materials.

SAM: And part of the voice is humor. We show that while we take beer very seriously, we don't take ourselves very seriously. You and I pretty much grew up together, started dating in high school, so I think our senses of humor overlap almost completely and that has informed our brand voice. There's humor and also humility. Everyone's palate is different, so there's no such thing as the best beer. We're just proud that we make world-class beer, but we believe there are other breweries making world-class beer alongside of us. How do you make sure that our voice is pervasive and impactful when sometimes the anonymity of social media allows people to be more cruel or harsh or direct than they might be face-to-face?

MARIAH: You mean in response to negativity online? Luckily, we don't find a lot of it. There's a lot of negativity and terrible things out there but generally if people have chosen to follow you on a social media platform, they're supportive of your company and what you're putting out there and talking about. For us, moments when we have to navigate the mean, nasty side of our social media dialogue are fewer and farther between. When it does show up and mean people say mean things, I'll write a lot of mean, nasty things back to those people in my head.

SAM: But not send them.

MARIAH: But not send them. I only do that if they're really just mean. You can be negative about something that you don't like about a beer or about something we're doing. That's fine; we're all big boys and girls with different preferences. We brew 30-plus styles of beer a year; if you include the brewpub exclusives, it's maybe 60 styles a year. Of course we don't expect people to love them all or love every initiative. Constructive criticism is very helpful.

We only have problems with the people who are just nasty and mean in unreasonable ways. I don't respond to them unless they attack people personally, say, like our brewers. If there is something negative posted, our other fans will often come to our defense before I even have to, which is nice to see. And sometimes they'll say things more harshly than I may have—but probably not more harshly than I would have wanted to. So it's kind of refreshing to not have to play defender against the bully.

SAM: When you think of where these groups of fans reside, it seems like there's always a new hot social media platform. You've found that it is less critical to focus on going all-in on one platform than to always be dabbling in different platforms that seem to be getting more energy around them. If you were advising an entrepreneur or small businessman, how would you recommend they find the new platforms people are moving toward?

MARIAH: That goes back to my initial point of how we got into social media because we were interested in it and why we were initially successful. When I hear about a new platform that people are spending time on or see a new platform, or read about it in a blog or in newspaper articles, my ears are open to that kind of stuff because I personally find it interesting. I'll check something out and play around with it and if it seems to have sticking power, great. If it doesn't, then it's not a big deal. We have accounts that we've activated on different social media sites that we haven't really kept active because either the medium wasn't a great fit for us, or we felt there were better places to put our time and energy. We gravitated to Instagram and that has been successful. Vine was not so successful. Once Instagram allowed video and we had a larger audience there, we put more resources into that.

SAM: Sizable for-profit social media platforms figure out how to monetize the traffic in their community, often with advertising. We're a brewery that doesn't spend a lot on advertising. There starts to be dollar signs associated with some of these activities. What do you recommend to entrepreneurs? Are there ways to vet media when it does make sense to spend money to grow an audience online? Or do you recommend they just figure out ways to do it grass roots, meaning not spending dollars, just the time of doing it?

MARIAH: I don't know enough about spending the dollars to say whether it is or isn't effective. We've dabbled in it for niche areas of our business, particularly as the Dogfish Inn opened and came online.

SAM: Our hotel, the Dogfish Inn in Lewes.

MARIAH: That was an opportunity to do some targeted demographic advertising on Facebook to people in certain geographic markets who we knew visited the Delaware coast. And to see whether there would be an immediate impact. It was a very narrow spend and a narrow focus. We're sponsored persons in Facebook ads, but we haven't really done a lot beyond that. Something works or doesn't work as part of a holistic approach. But if you want to see if something works, do a small buy of something targeted and then you can see if it has an impact. We could tell if we targeted people in northern Virginia who like craft beer, for example, whether our Dogfish Inn posts picked up with northern Virginia reservations. It's not a direct correlation because someone might read something and then not book until six months later, but you would get a feeling if you had a flurry of calls or a spike in reservations immediately following some kind of ad campaign or sponsored post.

SAM: More and more of these platforms are getting more aggressive trying to figure out ways to monetize their traffic. There's always the possibility that after you spend your time and resources to build a community, the platform starts setting the rules of how you engage with the community that you helped build. You don't have that risk with your company's website,

or your company's YouTube presence. How do our wholly owned proper-
ties online compare to the Facebooks, the Instagrams, the platform du jour
that's external from Dogfish?

MARIAH: We use our own website as sort of a holding ground for all of our
content. If we post an article to our website, we have 100 percent control
over the content, obviously, but it's not going to see a huge audience unless
we share it socially. So we use our website as a repository of information for
subjects people ask about, like aging beer, which is a common question we
get: Which Dogfish beers could age as well as fine wines and which ones
should be drunk fresh. We can write a comprehensive article about a subject
like that and then when someone posts a question to Twitter about aging
beer, we can simply give them a link to that page, which has a lot more
information than I could ever write in 140 characters.

You're right, though. Those platforms can always change the rules of the
game and they always do. If you stay on top of that world to some degree,
then you'll see how Facebook, for example, starts giving less priority to still
photos and more priority to video. And then you can post in a way that
uses more video than still photography and get more activity on those posts.

SAM: Are there ways that we've been able to take the feedback from the
online community and use it to make our guts more objective and less
subjective when we're making event, beer, or other brand-centric decisions
at Dogfish? Are there ways, for example, that we threw an idea out to the
community, and based on how they felt about it or a trend in feedback, we
adjusted our action?

MARIAH: You definitely get feedback on everything you put out if it's engaging content, whether they like it or not. Sometimes you can tease out themes
or trends. But we don't do that very scientifically at Dogfish; it's still gut. If
you want to get feedback for something, you can easily post very specific
questions and people will give you answers. Or do a SurveyMonkey if you
want to go down that route. You can also spend a lot of time on the pages
and posts of your so-called competitors and see what they're doing and
asking. And there are many companies that will gladly take your money to
help you get through the clutter of what can be seen out there on the social
spheres. We just haven't spent a lot of time and resources on those kinds of
things, but the tools are out there.

SAM: When a small company is growing to the place where it needs at least one person devoted to its online world, is it critical that they do it internally themselves or do you see examples of small companies who successfully farm that out? If the goal is being authentic, is it better to just find your own way, to sort of limp toward success but at least do it with your own voice, or to outsource to efficient and seasoned pros?

MARIAH: I'm sure companies out there successfully farm it out or get an agency to handle their social media. With a smaller company, though, I think that authenticity does not come through if the content is not coming from within the company. If you have a small company that's doing a lot of creative and interesting things, it's hard for someone who's not in your building every day, living and breathing what makes your company and products exciting, to know everything that's going on. But at the same time, they could be a fresh set of eyes that sees something that you take for granted as super interesting that consumers would like to know.

SAM: Shifting from the virtual world to the physical world, you also oversee our Beer & Benevolence Program, which is our nonprofit arm of Dogfish. As the only member of our leadership team who's born and bred in rural coastal Delaware, you have a special place in your heart for our home base. You often act as the arbiter of how we're prioritizing our company's engagement with physical community. Can you talk a little bit about the evolution of Beer & Benevolence, and how Dogfish identifies and works with nonprofits?

MARIAH: Since we opened 20 years ago as a brewpub in Rehoboth, different community organizations have been coming to the door saying "Can you support this?" or "Can we get a gift certificate for that?" Early on, when we were a smaller company, our decisions were a bit more haphazard, but we've always been able to choose causes that were relevant to us or our customers or our coworkers. The whole philanthropy side of the company grew as the company grew. We started doing a 5K road race as a benefit called the Dogfish Dash. In the second year, we partnered with the Nature Conservancy of Delaware because we wanted an organization that had local ties and still had recognition beyond just Delaware, seeing that we had both local regular customers and customers from many different states. We wanted a beneficiary that would resonate with them. That was the first time we began to think of our donations and philanthropy as a bigger program.

We began referring to it as our Beer & Benevolence program. We tied the annual budget for that program to our barrelage sales each year. We shoot to budget $1 toward this program for every barrel we brew. So if we sell 250,000 barrels of beer this year, which we should, we budget to spend $250,000 from the Beer & Benevolence budget to support community organizations. That's been our modus operandi. Then we added a grant program where coworkers on a committee vet applications from local organizations. We also defined goals for the kinds of organizations that made sense for us as thematic and demographic fits, and we landed on three types: those that support environmental causes, those that support artistic causes, and those that support community-building initiatives. Because we are a producer of alcohol, we try to stay away from events that support children and children's needs or motor sports.

In addition, over the past couple of years, we started a program where all the tour guides and bartenders in our tasting room pool their tips every month, and we donate the total to an identified local organization. Last year that amounted to about $40,000. We encourage our coworkers, if they're involved in a community organization that could use support, to let us know, because we would love to support those programs that our coworkers are already supporting.

SAM: We're a company that relies on natural ingredients from the ground, so the Nature Conservancies makes perfect sense as a nonprofit partner for our brand fit. They protect the lands on which some of our ingredients grow. Establishing a budget, whether it's tied to a unit of sales or revenue, is something that helps any small business plan for their giving.

Shifting from our engagement with nonprofits to general community engagement, how do we as a company navigate community relations? What kind of priority is it?

MARIAH: As you become an integral part of your community, you get to know the other people who are also integral parts of the community, and you want to do what you can to support them. So even though we don't necessarily conduct fundraisers for kids, we have a number of coworkers who do. We have coworkers who serve on school boards, who serve on committees for their kids' school PTOs. As a family-owned company, it's important to us to support the families that work with us. I've served on a number of different school boards and educational entities, as has our CEO, Nick. We know that you have to support the communities that support you. If we have the resources to help our community, it makes sense for us to do so. Where we can help and where help is asked for, we're definitely willing to do our part to make things easier or better than they might have been without our involvement.

SAM: On the school or education side, it's not pure altruistic activities for us. If your company's growing, you want to recruit and reach out to very ambitious and motivated coworkers. Having good schools and a vibrant community are components in their decision whether to join our company and move here. And probably for any small company, that's a reality too, right?

MARIAH: If you're hiring or relocating people, the cultural opportunities and schools in an area, the quality of life, are all very important. So giving back to our community on those fronts makes sense. If we can support the choral society that puts on free classical music concerts five times a year, who knows when we'll have an employee who loves to go to them? When you live in an area where there's a lot of organizations that do a lot of great stuff, we want to support as many of them as we can because they make our community a richer place to be.

SAM: Do you have recommendations on how a business can best communicate with its literal neighbors around its physical facilities? How do we approach just being good neighbors in the towns where our facilities are?

MARIAH: Most people who neighbor our locations are proud to have us there. There's always going to be certain people out there who think the worst of any kind of business. And I don't know that a business, especially a small business, can ever do 100 percent of the right proactive communication with all the potential stakeholders, many of whom we might not even know are stakeholders. Do your best but don't beat yourself up if you can't, you know, get in front of everything.

One example: we recently went through a hearing for a variance in the town of Rehoboth Beach, where our original brewpub is located. At first the variance was denied. On appeal, we got approval, in large part because of rallying community support. The overwhelming response online, in the media, and in person at the town meetings shared by local pro-Dogfish citizens wasn't that Dogfish should be given the variance because they make great beer or they make great food but, rather, because Dogfish does so much for the community. That was very gratifying to hear. All the organizations we had helped and things we had done came back in spades later in ways that you might never imagine would help. At some point, you're going to want your community to support you beyond being a customer. You want to be thought highly of as a member of the community.

SAM: Let's shift to one last subject. We're talking a lot in the book about evolving from a more mercurial, quick-reacting, or spontaneous acting . . .

MARIAH: Anarchy!!!

SAM: . . . entrepreneurial company, to one that is more strategic and does more planning. I know you are certainly not afraid to voice your frustrations with how quick we are to go in new directions. Are there things you're looking forward to as Dogfish moves toward a more planned, strategic approach? What are you most excited for as we become more methodical?

MARIAH: I think I'm most pleased with the idea of everyone feeling like they're on the same page and they know the end goal. It's exciting to rally around things that everyone can envision, contribute toward, and believe in. And if you haven't spent the time and effort to really clearly define, not just in your own mind but in the minds of your coworkers and your customers, what that destination is, I think it's harder for people to rally around it. If you are a dynamic company with lots of facets, and people are only focused on one of those facets, it's hard to get excited. When the destination isn't clearly defined, coworkers can't pick their head up and look down the road and see where the company is going, and how their efforts are contributing in the right direction.

In having one direction, I don't mean it's, you know, "My way or the highway." But more like "Hey, this is the road we're all going down together."

SAM: On the other side, any concerns that you have as Dogfish becomes more methodical and creates a strategic plan and grows?

MARIAH: We always have the fear that a strategic plan means you can't change your mind or backpedal or take a different tack when your gut tells you something about the industry is changing. You know, when it's right there in your face. The question is whether we'll still be nimble enough to react to things when they're outside of our quote-unquote stated strategic plan. But we have more to risk with no strategic plan than we have to risk by forging forward with the first iteration of a plan, so I am excited we have embarked together on this process.

chapter 7
EXTERNAL COLLABORATION

Believe that what is true for you in your private heart is true for all men. Speak your latent conviction and it shall be the universal sense.

—*Ralph Waldo Emerson*

The golden rule for successful collaborations is this: the more proportionate and focused the involvement from each participating entity is, the more mutually beneficial the results will be. "Of course," you say, "that's obvious." Maybe. But not until we had a few seemingly promising collaborative projects go off course did we come to understand what it takes to sustain good ones. Everybody wants win-win in theory, but despite the best intentions, in practice, things can often get sticky. When it comes to external collaboration—with other companies, artists, or organizations—I've learned that there have to be shared intentions, a single written definition of success all parties contribute to and agree upon, and a shared level of engagement. Enthusiasm isn't enough. As our VP of marketing says, collaborations are hard.

Most collaborations begin with mutual respect between two organizations or entities. In order for Dogfish Head to initiate a collaboration, both parties must respect each other and have shared values. This might not be an approach they teach in business schools, but I'm convinced that the best strategy is to focus on the positive energy that comes from collaboration rather than the negative energy that can come from focusing on competition. The impact on your brand and your corporate culture and ultimately your long-term bottom line will usually be greater.

Karma counts. I've always looked at Dogfish Head as a catalyst for good. It's embedded in the same philosophy that I teach my two children: we are each of us born with unique superpowers. With every choice we face as individuals, we can either use our powers for good or evil. It's easy to argue for shades of gray, and there are frequently scenarios where the choices are murkier. But if you can make that good-versus-evil filter instinctual, you will at least be sensitive to every decision point you come to. Of course, none of us makes the perfectly correct choice every chance we get. But we can each always strive to make the right choices more frequently in the future than we have in the past. In my own life I did this good-versus-evil experiment for a week and took notes on my smartphone. I recorded the choices I made in those seven days, decisions as big as my contributions toward our company's strategic plan and as small as my choices to eat healthier. In the places where I remembered to consider my choices through that good-versus-evil filter, I estimated that I made good choices just over 80 percent of the time. So I guess my letter grade would be somewhere between a C-plus and a B-minus. I have lots of room to improve. And, of course, one person's definitions of goodness and evil are going to be slightly different than another person's. If you tested yourself, using your own definitions, for a week, or even just one day, where would you come out in terms of a percentage score?

This principle applies when assessing the strategic fit of a potential collaboration. Those that work best are the ones where both companies are equally engaged and are not just thinking of their own brand and their own profits when they engage in such a project. You should fight for good, not evil, for your company and you should fight for good over evil on behalf of your collaborative partner as well. Returns on investment need to be equitable, whether that return is financially or brand equity oriented. It's actually usually both. You want to structure all the aspects of the collaboration through the lens of making sure the relationship is synergistic and not parasitic. To do this, and protect both sides from future mix-ups, you have to start by assuming the worst instead of the best and by walking through best-case and worst-case outcomes together. Then put expectations, commitments, and the shared vision for success down on paper, so there is a master document both collaborative parties constructed together and can refer back to if necessary.

We put serious resources into our collaborations. In the early days, we'd arrange deals on the basis of vaguely defined understandings and e-mails. I believe there was even one instance where a semi-drunk high-five constituted a verbal contract between me and a collaborating brewer. Now Dogfish Head has a full-time lawyer and a legal assistant on staff. They work on trademark matters and supplier contracts, but I'd estimate about 20 percent of their time is devoted to contracts defining and tending to our collaborations. For example, if we're making a brew with a band, we always pay a mutually agreed-upon licensing fee.

From the get-go, the mission at Dogfish was to brew daringly and creatively but always in the service of something grander than simply shock value. I've often described how I was inspired by the celebration of cuisine in the United States that began in the 1970s with folks such as Julia Child, James Beard, and Alice Waters. The food revolution was all about fresh, seasonal ingredients of the highest standard. My ambition was to brew beers the same way, beers that could complement great food. Very few people looked at beer that way when we started Dogfish Head. Wine was for fine dining; beer was for a hot dog at the ballpark. Maybe I was simply blinded by my passion, but I never doubted that we could change this misperception. It would take some doing, of course. We needed to concoct recipes that drew from a broad spectrum of spices, herbs, and even fruit that embodied the bounty of the land. We had to consistently apply the same impeccable standards to our beer recipes that restaurants like Chez Panisse devote to their menus. And, most importantly, we had to persuade the public that there was much, much more to beer than the bland, light, homogenous drink that they had become acclimated to (dare I say conditioned to) from giant corporate brewers.

We might have been the smallest commercial brewer in the country when we began, but our ambition was grand right from the start. We set out to lay claim to unexplored territory; our intention was to participate in the creation of quintessential *American* beer. We would do this by using native ingredients and by invoking our national spirit of freedom. American beer wouldn't be a particular style so much as a full-on declaration of independence. It would be an act of liberation, freeing us from five centuries of restrictive German brewing laws that had directly or indirectly limited commercial brewing in many countries to one dominant beer style: light lager. The only limits on us were going to be our creativity and brewing skill.

By *we*, I don't mean Dogfish Head alone. In some regards we were following the lead of others such as Ken Grossman at Sierra Nevada and Jim

Koch at Samuel Adams who had already begun blazing their own trails. This was a collective enterprise. Reinventing American beer was an epic quest. First-generation craft beer lovers resisted stepping outside the seemingly sacred formulas of modern beer styles like pale ale, lager, and stout. It would only be through bold and adventurous efforts that the beer landscape would slowly change.

Growing craft beer into a significant presence (today it accounts for just over 11 percent of the domestic beer market) has entailed industry-wide cooperation. I'm proud that we have always placed a priority on finding ways to contribute to the well-being of the whole sector. The key to competing with giants is to find a way around the spaces they occupy. Of course, Dogfish competes with other craft brewers, but collectively we all have an interest in increasing the public's awareness that there is alternative space with a whole lot of tastier brews than just industrial lager. A rising tide lifts all boats.

It is a small step from this commitment to the well-being of the industry as a whole to helping a fellow brewer in need.

At Dogfish Head we have been helped by the craft beers that came before us. Wild Goose Brewery in Maryland sold us some brewing tanks they outgrew, as did Bells Brewery from Michigan. About 15 years ago we began an informal practice of reaching out to brewers we respect who are smaller than we are. As we outgrew a piece of equipment we thought they could use, we would offer it to them at slightly less than used market prices. This way we knew our equipment had found a good home with breweries as passionate about brewing unique quality beers as we are. We figured we were offering them a karma discount. For a long time all the beer brewed at Russian River Brewery came off the brewhouse we sold them and all of the beer from Allagash was kegged for a time on our old kegging line.

Recently we sold an old brewhouse we had in storage to our friend John Harris, who was opening his own brewery called Ecliptic in Portland, Oregon. Because he was a friend striking out on his own, and a first-generation craft brewery who brewed at many great Northwest breweries, I wanted to see him succeed. I knew he didn't have a ton of start-up capital. So I sold him the three-vessel brewhouse for $100. He was very thankful but called me back a week later to say his accountant wanted him to pay more for it for depreciation value. I told him tough crap. One hundred dollars and not a dollar more.

Michael Jackson, the legendary British journalist whose classic *World Guide to Beer* has sold millions of copies in 18 different languages, sprinkled lots of his magic on us and helped propel Dogfish to a new level. Until Michael's passing in 2007 at age 65, his was the most influential voice in the beer business. My generation learned about beer from him. The first time a major beer publication took Dogfish seriously rather than as a rebellious weird or eccentric brewer was in an article by Michael that was published in *All About Beer Magazine*. . . . The personal stuff he begins with is super embarrassing but the rest makes me proud.

IN THE BEGINNING THERE WAS MICHAEL JACKSON

The young woman with whom I had dinner was envious. "You are spending the whole day with Sam Calagione. Tomorrow!? He's the Robert De Niro of brewers!" She told me that he had not only the good looks of a movie star but also the sensitivity of a poet. He even took Walt Whitman to bed with him. I think she meant a book by the laureate, though I am certain she had no firsthand knowledge of this.

The Calagiones seem to be practical people. The grandparents on both sides were from Calabria, Italy. They came to Milford, Massachusetts, to quarry pink granite. Among the next generation was . . . a gentleman farmer who made his own wine and cultivated maple syrup. Son Sam found good use for the syrup.

This was not his original plan. Sam was an English major and took courses in fiction and poetry. Perhaps he was just too romantic. He was thrown out of one school for playing ice hockey in the nude in the middle of the night. Somehow he finished up bussing tables in a nightclub in Australia, developing a more than passing interest in beer and home-brewed pumpkin ale.

Dogfish Head and the Poetry of Brewing

"I did start writing, but it was a business plan," observed Sam. "I do creative work, too—I formulate beers." In 1995, Sam opened a brewpub. He named his brewpub after a promontory in New England: Dogfish Head, site of a lighthouse in Booth Bay, Maine, where his family has a weekend place.

The first brew-kettle was a converted keg. The present brewhouse was assembled from vessels acquired at an auction when a local cannery closed. Supportive local farmers refrained from bidding.

In this Mid-Atlantic region, Dogfish has begun to win a reputation for its extraordinarily adventurous beers.

The energy he puts into sales has impressed me greatly. His first shipment to New Jersey—a six-pack—was transported by small boat across Delaware Bay, requiring seven hours for the 20-mile journey.

He rowed the boat himself. He also built it.

No wonder the women are impressed.

Excerpted from Michael Jackson, *All About Beer Magazine* 20, no. 4 (September 1, 1999).

The mutually respective mojo sparked up the first time we met at a presentation Michael gave at the Smithsonian in DC. In chatting afterward we discovered a shared passion for jazz (that list of shared interests would expand over the years to include various subjects ranging from boxing and Ernest Hemingway to Charlie Parker and Raymond Carver). The next night he was cohosting an event in Philadelphia; I was going there, too, for a beer festival. "I've got a piece-of-shit pick-up truck," I told him, "but do you want to ride from DC to Philly together?" He already had a train ticket but didn't hesitate to accept my offer. It was there that he introduced me to Dr. Pat McGovern of the University of Pennsylvania Museum, whose contributions to Dogfish have been important (more on that in a moment).

Michael was the guy who got me to do our first international collaborative beer. He had seen Dogfish Head starting to get respect in America for its experimental brewing and wondered whether we wanted to help Herold Brewery, a little brewery in the Czech Republic in danger of going out of business. "You've changed the definition of IPA from what was traditional in England to something much bigger and bolder with your 90 Minute Imperial IPA," he said. "Would you want to brew the first imperial Czech pilsner with them?" My answer? "Of course!" I went over there with special citrus-forward American hops and a yeast strain that was very alcohol tolerant so we could brew a strong pilsner (I had to bring a couple off-centered

American ingredients to the recipe). Talk about cross-breeding. We got to combine our innovation DNA with the DNA of a historic brewery that dated back to the 16th century. This experience, thanks to Michael, hooked me on collaborative brewing.

HEROLD BREWERY

Herold is one of the oldest functioning breweries in the Czech Republic, in nearly constant use since 1506, and has been housed since its beginning in what was originally a Gothic castle.

Under Communist rule, the brewery was seized by the state, with very little capital invested into it (or any of the nation's breweries during the period). However, on the upside, beer was very cheap and legal, which helped establish beer drinking as perhaps the single most popular hobby among Czech men. The protagonist of Jaroslav Hasek's novel *The Good Soldier Svejk* proclaimed that the government that raises the price of beer is destined to fall within one year. In 1984 the Communists almost doubled the price of beer, and though off by four years, his prognostication was fulfilled.

Interestingly, there was a paradoxically positive consequence of Communist ownership: the lack of investment in the facility. Without major modernization over the years, the Herold Brewery still makes beer the old-fashioned way, using only traditional methods, equipment and ingredients.

From "The Microbrewed Beer of the Month Club," www.beermonthclub.com/herold-brewery-bohemian-black-lager.htm.

Patrick McGovern, the bushy-bearded fellow I met that night in Philadelphia with Michael, is by title the scientific director of the Biomolecular Archaeology Project for Cuisine, Fermented Beverages, and Health at the University of Pennsylvania Museum. Think of him as the Indiana Jones of ancient ales, wines, and spirits. Dr. Pat roves the world's oldest anthropological sites collecting evidence of what human beings first ate and drank. Using techniques like infrared spectrometry and tandem liquid chromatography and ion cyclotron resonance (don't ask!), he identifies residue traces left in the shards of jugs and drinking vessels. The opportunity to work in tandem with Dr. Pat inspired us to launch our ancient ales lineup, which now numbers seven. He comes up with the ingredients, while the Dogfish brewing team and I create a modern recipe around Dr. Pat's list of ingredients.

Our first brew together—based on fragments from a 2,700-year-old tomb in Turkey that had been gathering dust in the Pennsylvania Museum archives for 40 years until Pat analyzed them (beeswax, tantaric acid from grapes, compounds that pointed to barley)—was Midas Touch. Its appearance in 1999 came at a particularly opportune moment for Dogfish Head. Our company's well-differentiated approach of using exotic culinary ingredients from around the world in our beers was being criticized by so-called beer purists as a violation of the *Reinheitsgebot*, the Bavarian purity law of 1516. This law restricted beer-making ingredients to water, barley, and hops (yeast hadn't yet been discovered by Louis Pasteur). This was the unyielding definition of German beer for the next five centuries and became the reigning standard in other countries as well. I don't care about traditional rules, but as the craft movement began developing momentum, there were lots of drinkers who did. Bad publicity was the last thing we needed at that stage in our company's history, with our financial foundation still unsteady.

Dr. Pat's discovery pushed back the boundaries of beer history thousands of years before the *Reinheitsgebot*. Not only did this give credibility to what we were doing, but it effectively blew open doors that had long been nailed shut for the entire craft community. Midas Touch remains a favorite to this day and we've done six other ancient brews with Pat inspired by archaeological findings in Turkey, China, Honduras, Peru, Egypt, Italy, and Scandinavia.

THE MIDAS TOUCH

It all started with a tomb, the Midas Tumulus, in central Turkey at the ancient site of Gordion, which was excavated by this Penn Museum in 1957, over 50 years ago. The actual tomb, a hermetically sealed log chamber, was buried deep down in the center of this tumulus or mound, which was artificially constructed of an enormous accumulation of soil and stones to a height of some 150'. It's the most prominent feature at the site. There was indeed a real King Midas, who ruled the kingdom of Phrygia, and either he or his father, Gordius, was buried around 740–700 B.C. in this tomb. There's still some uncertainty, since there's no sign announcing "Here Lies Midas or Gordius!"

When the Penn Museum excavators cut through the wall, they were brought face-to-face with an amazing sight, like Howard Carter's first glimpse into Tutankamun's tomb. The excavators first saw the body of a 60- to 65-year-old male, who had died normally. He lay on a thick pile of blue and purple-dyed textiles, the colors of royalty in the ancient Near East. You will see what really got us excited: the largest Iron Age drinking-set ever found—some 160 bronze vessels, including large vats, jugs, and drinking-bowls that were used in the final farewell dinner outside the tomb.

Like an Irish wake, the king's popularity and successful reign were celebrated by feasting and drinking. The body was then lowered into the tomb, along with the remains of the food and drink, to sustain him for eternity or at least the last 2700 years.

None of the 160 drinking vessels, however, was of gold. Where then was the gold if this was the burial of Midas with the legendary golden touch? In fact, the bronze vessels, which included spectacular lion-headed and ram-headed buckets for serving the beverage, gleamed just like the precious metal, once the bronze corrosion was removed. So, a wandering Greek traveler might have caught a glimpse of this when he or she concocted the legend.

The real gold, as far as I was concerned, was what these vessels contained. And many of them still contained the remains of an ancient beverage, which was intensely yellow, just like gold. It was the easiest excavation I was ever on. Elizabeth Simpson, who has studied the marvelous wooden furniture in the tomb, asked me whether I'd be doing the analysis. I just had to walk up two flights of stairs, and there were the residues in their original paper bags from when they were collected in 1957 and sent back to the museum. We could get going with our analysis right away.

What then did these vessels contain? Chemical analyses of the residues–teasing out the ancient molecules–provided the answer. I won't go into all the details of our analyses, in the interests of the chemically challenged. Briefly, by using a whole array of microchemical techniques, including infrared spectrometry, gas and liquid chromatography, and mass spectrometry, we were able to identify the fingerprint or marker compounds for specific natural products.

These included tartaric acid, the fingerprint compound for grapes in the Middle East, which because of yeast on the skins of some grapes will naturally ferment to wine, especially in a warm climate. The marker compounds of beeswax told us that one of the constituents was high-sugar honey, since beeswax is well-preserved and almost impossible to completely filter out during processing; honey also contains yeast that will cause it to ferment to mead. Finally, calcium oxalate or beerstone pointed to the presence of barley beer. In short, our chemical investigation of the intense yellowish residues inside the vessels showed that the beverage was a highly unusual mixture of grape wine, barley beer, and honey mead.

You may cringe at the thought of mixing together wine, beer, and mead, as I did originally. I was really taken aback. That's when I got the idea to do some experimental archaeology. In essence, this means trying to replicate the ancient method by taking the clues we have and trying out various scenarios in the present. In the process, you hope to learn more about just how the ancient beverage was made. To speed things up, I also decided to have a competition among microbrewers who were attending a "Roasting and Toasting" dinner in honor of beer authority Michael Jackson (not the entertainer, but the beer and scotch maven, now sadly no longer with us) in March of 2000 at the Penn Museum.

I simply got up at the dinner and announced to the assembled crowd that we had come up with a very intriguing beverage that we needed some enterprising brewers to try to reverse-engineer and see if it was even possible to make something drinkable from such a weird concoction of ingredients. Soon, experimental brews started arriving on my doorstep for me to taste—not a bad job, if you can get it, but not all the entries were that tasty.

Sam Calagione of Dogfish Head Brewery ultimately triumphed. He also came up with an innovative label of our re-created beverage, showing the Midas golden thumb print.

Just one footnote: the bittering agent used in Midas Touch was not hops (which was only introduced into Europe around 700 A.D.), but the most expensive spice in the world, saffron. Turkey was renowned for this spice in antiquity, and although we've never proven it, the intense yellowish color of the ancient residues may be due to saffron.

From Dr. Pat McGovern's blog: www.penn.museum/sites/biomoleculararchaeology/?page_id=143.

When two adventurous creative entities come together with pure intentions and a sound vision for how to work together on a project, the opportunity to create something unique and exciting can be exponentially greater than doing projects in a vacuum by yourself. This has certainly been true for Dogfish. It's easy to get trapped by zero-sum thinking in business. The standard default assumption is to regard the size of the marketplace as fixed with every player out to grab the biggest slice of the fixed pie for him- or herself. Collaboration, on the other hand, can expand the size of the pie itself to make bigger slices available to everybody. Even better, by combining resources and consumers assembled from different sectors and sometimes even different industries, collaboration can even create brand-new market opportunities in spaces where they previously didn't exist.

Brewers United for Freedom of Flavor, the BUFF Alliance, is a perfect example. Three of us—Bill Covaleski from Victory Brewing Company in Pennsylvania, Greg Koch from Stone Brewery in California, and I—conceived a noble endeavor: to collectively create a beer that would highlight the camaraderie of the craft brewing movement. We first worked together on a tasting event in 2003, back when there was not a huge demand for any of our beers. For the next half-dozen years, we had many discussions about coming together to do a bigger project with each other. Then, in 2010, we gathered together to create Saison du BUFF, a herbaceous recipe based on the Belgium style called saison. After many creative recipe-direction meetings over many beers together, we decided to brew our recipe with parsley, sage, rosemary, and thyme (all three of us are raging music geeks, so the herbs in the recipe were combined as a shout-out to Simon and Garfunkel). "The brew is very flowery and fresh," said one reviewer. "At first sip, you're truly struck with how herbaceous this is." Each of our three breweries distributed our own nuanced version under separate labels, but collectively

Saison du BUFF makes a strong statement celebrating craft beer's American spirit and collective mission.

I'm a huge music guy. I have listened to at least a couple hours of music a day for as long as I can remember. My music collection includes thousands of CDs and a few hundred vinyl albums. I have been obsessed with music since I was a little kid. My parents supported my decision to take saxophone lessons and then guitar lessons when I was growing up, but between my sports commitments (football and hockey) and my crap attention span, I didn't go far with either instrument before giving up. But I did put in a lot of practice and got really good at playing the stereo. In the same way my parents always encouraged my artistic pursuits, buying me books and painting materials to feed those habits, they also allowed me to buy albums every couple months until I got a summer job in my early teens and could buy them myself. This love of music only escalated when I became a DJ at my high school radio station and then at my college radio station as well. As an adult my love of music has been woven into the evolution of Dogfish Head since day one. I have always programmed the music selection at our brewpub, originally on a six-CD changer and more recently on iPod and Spotify custom mixes. We committed to a live music program at our pub centered on national and regional acts who only play original music—not cover bands, which are the moneymakers at most seaside resort venues.

We have had some amazing bands grace our stages, ranging from the Strokes to Guided by Voices, from Built To Spill to Bonnie "Prince" Billy. We found a great way to fuse music and beer by working together with adventurous musicians to create collaborative beers. Getting to know and work together with musicians I admire is a labor of love. But it's also great grassroots marketing for Dogfish Head (and good publicity for the band, too). There's a natural synergy here. Beers and bands are both artful passions for connoisseurs. Each band or musician stands for something the fans and audience believe in. Even if some of the band's loyalists have never heard of Dogfish Head, by aligning with the band we get to share the positive energy that's so critical to our brand. When the excitement is authentic and the story and liquid turn out great, word spreads fast in our community and the music community. That kind of sincere cross-loyalty bonding can't be bought or manufactured by slick ad campaigns (try as they do); it can only be earned through mutual respect, an inspired creative direction, and shared follow-through.

Bitches Brew, our homage to Miles Davis's landmark jazz album, launched us along this musical highway in terms of being our first official music series beer. I worked with my friend Adam Block, who runs Miles's label, Legacy Records, and is as big a beer geek as I am a music geek— which is why we get along so well. I've told the tale of how this came to be in one of the episodes of our Discovery Channel series, *Brew Masters*, but it's well worth briefly repeating. The record was hugely important to me. I listened to it so often while writing the original Dogfish Head business plan in my New York City apartment that it was sort of the soundtrack for that endeavor. With Bitches Brew, Miles invented a new paradigm, jazz-rock fusion, with rhythms and improvisations unlike any heard before. Not everybody dug the sound but few could doubt its importance as a creative breakthrough (Duke Ellington described Davis as "the Picasso of jazz"). It inspired me as I wrote the business plan. I wanted Dogfish Head to be a maniacally inventive and creative brewery, to look backward and forward for inspiration: analog beer for the digital age. You could say that my dream was to have Dogfish Head, in some small way, stand for the same thing in the beer world that Miles Davis stands for in the jazz world.

We released our first batch of Bitches Brew Stout in 2010 to commemorate the 40th anniversary of Davis's album. Every year it sells out and, like the music, every year the liquid improves with age.

American Beauty, the Imperial Pale Ale we brewed with the Grateful Dead in 2013, raised the bar as a more intricate music collaboration compared to the ones we worked on before it. I think of the Dead as the quintessential collaborative band. They embrace improvisation at the core of their music, which by definition is all about the collective whole being greater than its separate parts. They bring to their songs the same open-ended "We shall see what we shall see" philosophy of Black Mountain College, the experimental community of the 1940s and 1950s, which so stirred me. When it comes to interacting with an audience, there's no better example of grassroots human-scale collaboration than the way the Grateful Dead interfaced with their Deadheads. For the Dead, in many ways, sharing their music was what counted, not selling it. They encouraged fans to tape their live shows, even setting up recording areas in venues where the acoustics were perfect. They understood that passionate Deadheads would turn on others in a cascading effect, which was an important example for me as a young guy trying to grow a business. Get your beer into the hands of the right evangelistic customer base—arm them with unique stories for each unique beer—and if the beer actually tastes as good on the tongue as the story sounds, they will help you spread the word.

A member of the Dead entourage first reached out to us to do a collective brew: their audiovisual archivist David Lemieux is a fellow beer geek who loves Dogfish Head and he turned members of the band on to us. The prospect was exciting, but in order to go forward we needed real input from the band. Without their artistic involvement in the project, we'd just be parasites exploiting their name. After some back and forth, the band members came back with their first choice for a base beer style: a strong American pale ale with 100 percent American-grown ingredients. And then a stroke of inspiration struck. We devised an authentic way in which our two fan bases could participate in the project. Collaboration on steroids!

At the stroke of midnight on New Year's Eve, we went live with a website inviting Deadheads and Dogfish Heads to propose an off-centered ingredient for the forthcoming beer, with one big requirement: they had to explain why their relationship with the band inspired their choice. More than 1,500 entries arrived suggesting such things as red grenadine from "Brown-Eyed Women," rose hips reminiscent of the motif painted on the Rosemont water tower, and jalapeños like the ones burning in one Deadhead's mouth after he first heard "Mexicali Blues." There were hundreds of nominations for weed or LSD or magic mushrooms (none of which we could do without getting shut down by the authorities).

The winner was Thomas Butler, proposing we mix in granola with the mash and hot barley. The choice was great from a recipe standpoint; the notes of almond and honey balanced out the bitterness of the big hop kick to round out the flavor profile. But it was his story that sold us. Phil Lesh, a founder of the Dead and their bass guitarist for 30 years, contributed his North Bay music venue in San Rafael, Terrapin Crossroads, for the launch, which, in keeping with the spirit of the gig, happened on July 4th.

THE FINAL INGREDIENT

Thomas Butler remembers two things from his first Dead show.

When his dad tossed him over the fence at Oklahoma City's Zoo Amphitheatre (his old man didn't want to buy a ticket for a nine-year-old), little Thomas ran into a woman wearing only a soaking-wet white sheet. It left little to his school-age imagination.

"Hey, it was a Dead show in the middle of summer and I was young," says Thomas, now 39 and living in California. "I'll never forget that."

The other thing he remembers is all the "cigarettes." He couldn't figure out why everyone was passing them around. "People here are pretty poor," his dad told him, "so they have to share."

That was life in the early 1980s for Thomas and his dad, also named Thomas. When the weekend came, they went to concerts, especially if the Dead were within driving distance. When there was no show to catch, they'd brew a batch of beer in the garage of their Tulsa home.

Thirty years later, Thomas saw that Dogfish and the Dead were seeking ingredient suggestions and stories to help shape their upcoming collaboration. He e-mailed his dad their story from that first show—the fence hopping, the woman in the white sheet, the shared smokes—and said he was going to suggest granola as the final ingredient. Granola was the main course in millions of parking-lot meals, and they both agreed it would be a sweet and toasty complement to the pale ale's all-American hops and barley.

Woven through many of our collaborations is a shared pride in American heritage. Dogfish DNA is all about the celebration of freedom (culinary and cultural, alike), and there's nothing more American than that! So one of the things I look for in a partner is somebody as fiercely independent as we are and equally committed to staying that way, which is a big reason why our relationship with Woolrich, the family-owned outdoor clothing company that began by providing blankets to Union soldiers in the Civil War, has been so successful.

Paul Bunyan brought us together. Yes, *that* Paul Bunyan, 10 feet tall and traveling the countryside with his companion, Babe the Blue Ox. Sometimes I think of him as the unofficial Dogfish icon. The legend of the superhuman lumberjack who came out of the Maine woods to cut a swath across the country has always been dear to me. Fifteen years ago, I painted a picture of him holding the Dogfish logo that we sold on T-shirts. His tale reminds me of the story of Dogfish Head, a Delaware-based brand named after the place where I spent my early summers on the coast of Maine. Maine is considered the birthplace of the mythical folk hero Paul Bunyan.

The theme of the tasting room we built a few years ago in Milton is Paul Bunyan. Unlike many of the first generation of craft brewers who had genuflected at the feet of Europe, Dogfish Head went all-in with our American stylistically irreverent approach, so it seemed only right to evoke an atmosphere that celebrated an American-born legendary hero in our décor. We even designed and built a food truck that is shaped to be a massive interpretation of Paul Bunyan's Lunchbox. For the décor we wanted the same iconic buffalo-check plaid flannel made famous by lumbermen. That led us to Woolrich, the signature manufacturers of the fabric. Based in the middle of Pennsylvania (Woolrich, to be exact, in unincorporated Pine Creek Township, population 1,560), the company has been there since the 1830s, the United States' oldest continuously operating woolen mill. Founder John Rich would travel to lumber camps with woolen fabric in a mule cart to sell; the wives of the lumberjacks finished it into clothing for their husbands.

Our clothing and merchandise business accounts for less than 2 percent of our company-wide revenue, but it represents a much bigger share of our brand identity. The clothes a person wears are part of his or her personal identity, much like the label on a bottle tells you something about its contents. Wearable branded clothing has been a big part of the beer industry since before Dogfish Head existed. If a person chooses to display the logo of the beer he or she loves, it can be very aspirational for other people. Personally, I choose to wear the clothes of brands I believe complement Dogfish, so even if I'm just dressed in old surf shorts and a stained T-shirt, the shorts are from Patagonia, an independent American-owned company, and the T-shirt is a shout-out to Grizzly Bear, a great indie rock band.

We offer an array of Dogfish-logoed items for sale, ranging from glassware (classic shapes and the unique IPA glass Dogfish and Sierra Nevada custom designed together with a high-end glass company), to a barbeque grill set, to an old-time vinyl record player. These offerings are mostly meant for fun; fleshing out the inventory is very much a labor of love: figuring out what Dogfish beer lovers will love to wear to show their allegiance to our brand. Our partnership with Woolrich, on the other hand, has evolved into a more serious and expansive brand play.

We launched the partnership in 2014 with a nautical-inspired capsule clothing collection that includes a soft wool blanket proudly woven in Woolrich's 180-year-old mill, a beach cover-up dress with a screen-printed Dogfish logo on the pocket, and even a woolen beer koozie. A "wet" element was included with the dry goods—a collaborative brew true to both companies' cultures. The story behind it illustrates how the best partnerships are hatched by a creative spark (and not as the glimmer in the eye of a financial deal maker).

The Woolrich annals recount how founder John Rich, helping with a barn raising, took a terrible fall that almost killed him. What happened? Seems he was overindulging in his own homebrewed spruce beer. That kindled my enthusiasm to bring the old patriarch's drink back to life in the form of a pale ale complemented by the resinous conifer qualities of fresh green spruce tips that we picked ourselves plus wheat and rye like he grew on his farm. What to call it was a no-brainer. We named it in honor of the company's big-selling red-and-black-patterned jacket and matching pants that Woolrich marketed as its Big Game Hunter's Suit. In the deep backcountry woods, though, people knew the set as the Pennsylvania Tuxedo.

EXTERNAL AND INTERNAL COLLABORATION

As our approach to identifying and developing new projects continues to evolve, we are discovering that the projects that include both internal and external collaboration are exponentially rich when executed right. A current project we are working on internally at Dogfish with two external partners exemplifies this. Our company's ties to music run deep—from the beers we have produced in collaboration with certain music releases to our focus on live music at our pub every weekend for over 20 years. At the pub, this means celebrating bands who play their own music instead of cover songs—which is typically what you get when you go to pubs in small towns or resort areas. We took our commitment to supporting the music community and the indie retailers who sell great music to a new level last year when we became the official beer of Record Store Day.

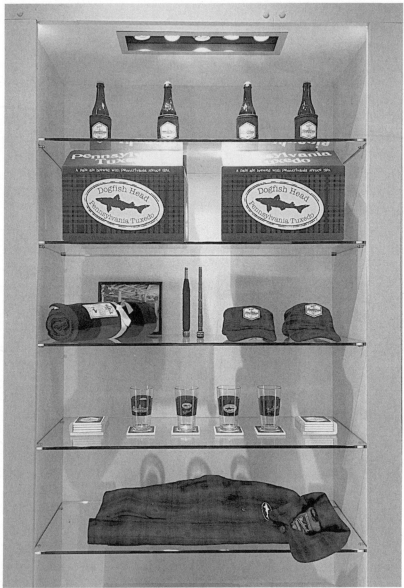

The Pennsylvania Tuxedo Collaboration

RECORD STORE DAY

Record Store Day was created in 2007 to celebrate the spirit at the heart of independently owned record stores, as well as artists and music fans. While there are participating record stores on every continent except Antarctica, in America alone there are almost 500 independent record stores that participate in Record Store Day each year. Each year there are special CD and vinyl albums released on Record Store Day and hundreds of artists perform in stores around the country. There are so many similarities between the challenges indie small record stores face competing against global online and bricks-and-mortar retail conglomerates and the challenges small indie craft breweries around the world face that the good karma coming from overlapping these communities is well worth the significant effort and financial commitment needed to execute this complex program.

In addition to promoting the day and donating beer, we've also developed custom Dogfish record players and a collectable Record Store Day poster that is given away to music lovers at the stores that carry our beers. We even co-curated a limited-release Record Store Day album with our friends at Sony/Legacy called *Music to Drink Beer To*.

My friend Adam Block is the president of Sony/Legacy and he is as big of a beer geek as I am a music geek. We have worked together on projects like Bitches Brew and Hellhound on my Ale—the beer we did to commemorate the Robert Johnson Centennial.

To curate the album I met with Adam (armed with a cooler of special beers) in his NYC office packed floor to ceiling with great vinyl. We spent an afternoon sipping beers and spinning tunes, trying to create the best experience combining a set of great songs with a beer drinking session. Here's what Adam has to say about our work together and his collaboration philosophy.

The *Music to Drink Beer To* collaborations are in many ways a perfect reflection of the broader relationship Legacy Recordings enjoys with Sam and Dogfish Head. That relationship begins with a couple of crucial ingredients: establishing a clear vision for what can we do together that would be mutually beneficial and complementary to both of our businesses and then determining how can we have some fun doing it. Then, through texts, e-mails, calls, voice messages, and the occasional shared beverage—a free-form, no-holds-barred, no boundaries, no shame exchange of ideas—the basis for the next collaboration takes shape. The spirit of adventure, exploration, risk-taking—the essence of great art (and something we have in abundance at Legacy)—is always fundamental to our endeavor.

But if there's one thing I appreciate above all else about working with Sam and the team at Dogfish Head, it's their unwavering commitment to their vision—to their art. The principles of authenticity and integrity are absolutely at the center of what we do at Legacy on behalf of the artists and music we're charged with looking after—and I know that in their beautifully off-centered way, those principles are at the heart of everything Dogfish Head does too. As a leader, Sam's always been crystal clear about those principles. And a partner, it's easy to proceed with confidence when that's understood.

Very kind words from my good friend Adam. For the 2016 Record Store Day, we are adding another component that will accompany the new album, *Music to Drink Beer To, Volume 2*. We are coming out with a beer called "Beer to Drink Music To" that is designed to pair well with the mix of songs. This beer was an internal collaboration between our VP of Marketing Neal Stewart and our Brewmaster Tim Hawn. Tim loves to brew Belgian-style beers that can marry tradition with experimentation—something we do well at Dogfish with beers like Namaste and Noble Rot. For our Beer to Drink Music To brew, we started experimenting with a Belgian dubbel base in test batches at our pub and landed on a Belgian tripel base style to build our off-centered recipe around. Neal decided it would be fun to find a great mix of ingredients that reference some classic rock song lyrics. These would be different songs and artists from those featured on the *Music to Drink Beer To* album to add another layer of diversity to our Record Store Day project. Tim, Neal, and I narrowed down the song-and-ingredient references to those that would work in harmony with each other in this recipe and they are:

Peppercorn: "Sgt. Pepper's Lonely Hearts Club Band," The Beatles
Orange Peel: "Orange Crush," REM
Candi Sugar: "Sugar Baby," Bob Dylan
Cardamom: "Mock Song," Phish

Our goal is that both music lovers and beer lovers will seek out the album and the beer to try them together on Record Store Day. Dogfish Head, Sony/Legacy Records, and Record Store Day all have sizable online presences and media reach so we are confident this story will touch and resonate with both existing Dogfish Head fans and those hearing about our brewery for the first time as a result of this project. This is a great example of the exponential reach and potential that can be realized by embarking on collaborative projects with people and organizations aligned with your values and goals.

GIVING BACK

A successful collaboration has to be aligned with your company's mission. That's true even with the collaborative beers that we release and it's also true with Beer & Benevolence, the philanthropic branch of Dogfish Head. Its mission is to support nonprofits that foster community, nourish artistic advancement, and cultivate environmental stewardship. We give back to the community that gives Dogfish Head its livelihood. So most of our philanthropic work happens in coastal Delaware, which is where most of our coworkers work and live. We take environmental stewardship seriously because Dogfish Head only brews with all-natural ingredients: water, yeast, and ingredients that grow in the wild and agricultural products are our raw materials.

Our philanthropic contributions are focused on causes that are important to us and to our business. We're spending money with organizations whose work we believe in. At the same time, by celebrating our philanthropic activities with our coworkers, customers, and on social media, the people who choose our brand are likely to celebrate it along with us and want to share the details with their friends. We are using our powers for good, as I would tell my children. But it isn't one-sided altruism. What we give out in time, attention, and dollars through our philanthropic endeavors comes back to us in brand awareness and brand loyalty from the consumers who care about the same causes we do.

MAKING THE MOST OF OUR MOST PRECIOUS RESOURCES

Here are a few of the things we're doing to tread lightly on the environment:

Irrigation: We don't just let our wastewater go down the drain. It's all recaptured and sent to local farms. At the farms, the water is used in spray irrigation, where it soaks into the soil and recharges groundwater.

Rain Barrels: Instead of trashing the dozens and dozens of giant plastic ingredient barrels we go through, we donate them to organizations to make rain barrels. A house that sees an inch of rain in 24 hours can produce more than 700 gallons of runoff, and rain barrels help collect and store that water. It can be used to water lawns, wash cars, and clean gardening tools. Meanwhile, water bills are lowered and streams and rivers are protected from litter, fertilizer, pet waste, and motor oil.

Native Plants: Dogfish coworkers and their friends have partnered with the Delaware chapter of the Nature Conservancy to plant 500 shortleaf pine trees at the nearby Ponders Tract. Once used by a lumber company for pine timber production, this plantation is being transformed into a native coastal forest of native oak, hickory, tulip poplar, sassafras, and red maple. It will dramatically cut storm water runoff, prevent evaporation, encourage soil stabilization, and help clean water before it makes it to local streams and rivers.

As the company has grown, so has our concept of collaboration.

Coastal Delaware and the surrounding areas in the Mid-Atlantic are the core commitment areas because this is where we do most of our business. Contributing to the local quality of life is an investment in our future. Not only is this where we live and play, but it's also where potential coworkers will relocate; when we recruit key hires, we bring in their entire family for a weekend to make sure the whole family is going to like living in our part of the world.

In 2013, we asked area nonprofits "Could you use $4,000?" Those that qualified submitted a short video for a chance to win a $3,000 grant and a shot at another $1,000 in our first-ever Beer & Benevolence awards. Those first grants went to Downtown Milford to support its public art project, Art on the Riverwalk. Another went to the Milton Historical Society for educational programs and exhibitions that showcase the town's rich history (it was first settled in 1672). The Delaware Center for the Inland Bays (our regional watershed) won the environmental grant to support its efforts to protect coastal habitats and promote water quality.

The single biggest benefactor of Dogfish Head philanthropy is the Delaware Nature Conservancy. Our biggest effort of the year is our Dogfish Dash—a slightly off-centered 5K and 10K race. Over the years, the Dogfish Dash has raised more than $350,000 for the Delaware chapter of the Nature Conservancy. This collaboration, though, is about so much more than just money: the mission is centered around preserving the natural spaces where we play outdoors and where our ingredients grow.

OUR COMMUNITY

Here is a particularly powerful example of how, through an act of volunteerism, well-executed collaboration helps all parties involved.

One weekday a year, in what's become an annual tradition, we shut the company down. During that day, we use all of our company's hand tools, power tools, engineering skill, and awesome craftsmanship to help build homes with Sussex County Habitat for Humanity. Dogfish Head, in effect, donates a day's worth of company wages and equipment to enable our coworkers to participate (last year the number was around 200). That's the "giving to others" half of the equation. There's also a "giving to ourselves" part. We separate into groups where a person who's good with power tools is paired with others who aren't. This has proven to be a fantastic team-building exercise. Coworkers who would ordinarily never interact—a pub waiter with an accountant with a brewer with someone from marketing or sales—are in the same group and all reporting, say, to a maintenance man. (I'm one of those guys reporting up since I'm lots better at operating a smart phone than a band saw.)

The positive impact of this day is huge and yields benefits long afterward for both Habitat for Humanity and Dogfish Head. There are other stories like these, less elaborate and more along the lines of straightforward contributions of beer or Dogfish gift baskets to charities and events, but they generally follow the same theme. Whenever possible, we like to spend our good will in ways that come back to us with accrued karmic interest that makes our company stronger and our customers more appreciative for the priority of what our brand stands for.

Indeed, our beers—even our concept of brewing itself—are infused with layers of collaboration. Some of this is because of how we started out—a small, scrappy operation that had to make every speck of capital work overtime. With Dogfish the size it is now, we have the luxury of choosing to be collaborative; in the beginning, there was little option. For us, it's always been a way of life. Looking back, I appreciate even more how important it is that bootstrapping entrepreneurs always be on the lookout for potential collaborators with whom to pool creativity, especially in unlikely places. At Dogfish, we believe that synthesizing something collectively with another entity is a catalyst that brings out the best in us as we continue to explore goodness internally and externally together.

INTERVIEW

Nick Brayton, President, Woolrich

Nick Brayton, president of Woolrich, is a family member of the seventh generation of this family-owned company. The oldest manufacturer of outdoor wear in the United States, Woolrich began in the 1830s. Known for its red-and-black-checkered hunting jackets and blankets, the brand is expanding its upscale retail profile with company stores in hip urban locations like New York City and Boston.

The brand Woolrich was revered in my boyhood home because my dad and uncles were big hunters and wore the red-and-black-check iconic Woolrich suits into the woods for their deer and bear hunts. As a mom-and-pop company, Woolrich impressed me even more once I learned that it had managed to stay family owned for seven generations. Through Dogfish Head's multiple collaborations with Woolrich, I have gotten to know the current generation of family leaders very well and have learned a lot from these interactions.

Treating the Brand the Right Way

SAM: In terms of heritage and stature, you guys are mentors and a guiding light for us. We're both family companies in industries dominated by global players who are mostly public companies more focused on maximizing quarterly shareholder return than building a sustainable company culture and a community.

NICK: That's a good way of putting it. We're always thinking about what Woolrich is required to do as a brand versus its shareholders versus its employees. That dynamic is ever evolving. It is not an easy situation. There have been many, many ancestors and generations who have worked here and have created this brand that I am now lucky enough to work for. Hopefully I'll be able to successfully steward it for the future.

Also featured in color photo insert

Traditional Woolrich Suit

SAM: But then what does that responsibility mean?

NICK: Truth. Really, more than anything it means being true to the brand, holding it up, and treating it with the respect that it deserves to have. With that comes a very interesting political landscape because there are employees, some of whom are shareholders, some of whom are nonfamily, outside people who came to work for the brand, and then there are employees who are shareholders that are part of family, and then there are shareholders who don't work for the company.

It gets really stressful at times because we want to treat the brand like it should be treated in every way. We want to pay it back to the shareholders and increase shareholder value as much as possible by making sure the gas tank is full in terms of financial considerations but also in ways that enhance the brand upward and not dilute its integrity.

I will say that to me the message is very clear. If you treat the brand the right way and you treat your employees the right way, you will get what you want long term. Meaning you will be able to give back to the shareholders what they deserve, what they want, what they expect but also sustain and grow a strong brand with a bigger sense of purpose than maximizing quarterly profits.

SAM: Were there eras when revenue growth was more important than brand stature?

NICK: The brand has seen a lot of ebbs and flows over the years. We've seen years where we were the most premium outdoor brand in the world, when we were outfitting people like Admiral Peary, who was the first explorer to reach the North Pole. Then there were times when we were selling to lower-priced retailers like Walmart only to make a sale, not thinking about whether that was positioning the brand best for the future.

SAM: Do you think that your predecessors, the generation that was selling to Walmart, was making a mistake? Were they making the wrong choice?

NICK: I can't say that was the wrong decision back then. It very well may have been the right decision. Unless you are in their environment, you don't know. The brand had been so pristine over so many years that maybe it didn't really matter at the time. In today's market, though, the distribution channel you are in makes a big statement. In building our business, at this moment in our industry I am not afforded the option to sell to certain retailers where I could do a lot of volume because it's not right for the brand.

It's an ever-evolving market but I think we have done a very good job making sure the brand is tapping into the company DNA and being treated with the right respect and authenticity. You can't make up your story, and there is no better outdoor apparel brand than Woolrich. Other brands aspire to have the story that we do.

SAM: I imagine if you were a public company, some of your choices would have been different. Like when you decided a while back not to shut down manufacturing in America. If all you cared about was maximizing shareholder value, that decision probably couldn't have happened.

NICK: I agree with that statement. We like to think beforehand about what's best for shareholders, but in most cases our shareholders would probably prefer that we did things the right way for the brand versus making sure shareholders always see the biggest short-term monetary value growth. They care about where we came from, our heritage, our Pennsylvania roots, and what that means to the brand.

SAM: I am curious about passing on that respect for history. When you're acclimating a new hire in a leadership role or someone who is on a leadership-trajectory track, is there any training about the history of the brand?

NICK: More and more we're talking about the family heritage at the senior level. We're doing that to a much greater degree than we've done in a long time. There has always been family at the helm for the most part, but now it's probably more condensed than it used to be, which makes us think harder about our story. We'll often ask ourselves if we're doing something properly, are we making sure that this is exactly how it should be.

SAM: Did any of the ancestors actually write down their hope for Woolrich to keep on for generations as a family-owned company, or is it up to every generation to assume that family continuity is a valuable expectation?

NICK: I am not sure I actually ever read anything formal about responsibility passing from generation to generation. But at the same time, there is almost an unwritten rule that if you are going to be part of management and working for this company, it is your job to pay for it by sustaining the brand. That's the way that I look at it at least, if only because I am seventh generation and wouldn't be here if it weren't for the six generations before me.

SAM: And with every subsequent generation there is probably more expectation that you will keep going. It is one thing for a first generation to pass something to a second generation—that happens with more frequency since most companies are only a few years or decades old—but when you keep a company going in this direction, with a third or fourth or sixth generation, I imagine the stakes get higher, right?

NICK: Yup, it's usually in the third generation of family ownership that cousins and not just siblings get into the mix. As multiple branches of a family get intertwined within the company over time, there's more tentacles. There are some family members who have no involvement with the company and some who have a lot of involvement. Even my own siblings are a testament to that. I have three siblings; all of them had the opportunity to work for Woolrich, but I am the only one who currently does. Some family members just choose not to, whether because of where they want to live or other professional interests or whatever. But I will say that, even the family members who don't work at Woolrich definitely recognize that family values is what has borne this brand and what has allowed this brand to maintain its integrity for so many generations.

I definitely believe employees are drawn to this feeling as well. We instill that idea here. One of our biggest pillars is making sure people feel like hey, when you work for Woolrich, you are part of the family. On your first day you are going to hear that. That breeds communication. It breeds a commitment to quality. It breeds trust.

SAM: Giving back to the community.

NICK: Giving back, respect, sustainability. Melding all of those different things together is what creates such a cool story.

SAM: It makes people feel like working here is more than punching a clock; they treat it as more than just a paycheck.

NICK: You got it. We have people at Woolrich who have been here over 40 years.

They take a lot of pride in what they do and the goods that we put out on the market. Once they are here, they typically don't leave.

SAM: You are seventh generation. You have children. Are you trying to navigate educational opportunities so your kids consider being eighth-generation leaders at this company?

NICK: I know for myself that if I'm sort of pushed into something, I don't want to do it. If I do a good job, hopefully they are going to have every opportunity they want to be able to work for Woolrich someday. At the same time, if you sort of force them into that lane, they are going to want to go to another lane. I think it is kind of like teaching them about alcohol. You don't want to tell them they can have a 24-pack, but you can say, hey, you can taste a beer or two if you want. And then hopefully they respect the opportunity. But if you push it too far, they might go the other direction.

SAM: Shifting a little bit to the brand side. You know, we are in very similar positions where our goal is to be the premium craft beer and celebrate the stories of our recipes and ingredients that rationalize and justify our premium price. What we are doing here together to make this collaborative beer called Pennsylvania Tuxedo, for example, with literally dozens of people in Pennsylvania who work at Woolrich spending two full workdays in the woods harvesting the spruce tips that will go in this beer instead of running the woolen mill, this massive resource commitment and direct from-the-forest-to-bottle approach means this is not going to be an inexpensive beer, but we are going to celebrate how handmade and unique it is.

At a moment when the H&Ms and Targets are making fashion more commoditized and cheaper, how do you navigate the pricing-pressure challenges?

NICK: There's a couple of different ways to answer that; I will give the middle line answer. Woolrich has a certain expectation for its consumer. Our brand says that we're serious about satisfying that expectation with our range of products—whether it is outerwear, sportswear, accessories, blankets. If we stick to who we are as a brand and that consistency runs through and through, people will respect us for that.

However, I also think that the market in itself is changing. What I mean is that the United States and maybe North America is becoming less of a disposable economy than before. I've got 30 jackets in my closet; a typical European might have 10. I actually believe, though, that in the United States people are becoming less inclined toward disposability and buying a jacket for a season or because of the way it looks versus the quality. So we would rather focus on someone who is going to buy that jacket to wear for several years, a jacket that will last for many years; we want it to be a Woolrich jacket.

Sixty years ago, when people had only one jacket they wore every day, they looked to us because they knew that our commitment to quality construction translated to durability. That is what I want us to continue to be. If we can make people understand and respect that, then they will want to come buy a Woolrich jacket because they know that it is going to last.

SAM: Today, to get them to wear that jacket for three, four, five years, it has to be superior quality so it doesn't fall apart after four months and not succumb to the whims of a season's fashion trend.

NICK: It has to hold up against any other brand, against weather conditions, and stand up to what it was bought for. It has got to have the right down fill, the right fill count, the right accessories, whether it is zippers and pulls or trims. Woolrich is going to make sure that jacket will be there for you for more than a couple of seasons. This is where we stand alone, in my opinion, versus the competition.

SAM: When people buy a Woolrich product, what are they buying?

NICK: They are buying a brand they believe in. They are buying a store. But they also know they are buying quality. We inspect every single garment that comes in. A lot of brands inspect maybe 10 percent or 20 percent of their garments. We look at every single one.

SAM: As a leader, what kind of hard choices do you have to make to sustain the brand?

NICK: Honestly that is the easy part. We've always stood by quality. I didn't have to change any policies about that. All I've had to do is instill the fact that we still believe in who we are and the fact that Woolrich is going to be better than it has been in a long time because of who we are. People get behind that. They see we have a strategic plan and are actually meeting it. We are going to continue to push and push and push and become the quality-oriented brand we think we should be because that is who we are and that is who we deserve to be. And that is what people who care about Woolrich believe in.

SAM: Do you ever have to say "No, we can't do this product because we can't afford to make it up to our standards and sell it where we need to price it?"

NICK: Yes, those decisions are made. We try to have a certain margin; if we can't make the goods at that margin percentage then we will walk away. We offer a lot of styles at different prices but they all bear our brand and must deliver on what it stands for. Parkas, for example; parkas are huge for Woolrich. We will have at least 15 different parka styles in different types of variations whether it is the type of fill or goose or duck or whether it is a long or short length or hooded or not hooded. But at the end of the day, line them up together and they all look Woolrich. And that's what we want, to make sure we are consistent. Does it look like a Woolrich garment? Will it actually stand up in the weather the way it's supposed to do? Would someone be proud to wear that garment? That is what we care about.

SAM: I'd like to know about how you do strategic planning. We are just embarking on our first holistic three-year strategic plan for our company, so it is a loaded question for me to ask of you guys.

NICK: For starters you can always do more. We are not perfect that way. I am not the first to sit here and say we have had enough strategic planning to be successful. I think we will always want to do more.

I think having a three- to five-year plan is critical. Succession planning is one of the most critical things you could ever put in place for the company. Whether you are 35 years old or 70, you need to have a plan for what happens in case of disaster.

Strategic planning comes from a place of passion, too. You've got to have people who truly will die to make sure that what they want is going to happen the right way. Josh Rich, the company executive vice president, who is my cousin, and I fight all the time. We'll each tell the other, "I don't agree with you; here's fricking why!" Then we hear each other out and there is good give-and-take, so at the end of the day we both believe we're doing the right thing and our decisions are stronger as a result of our discussions. This family dynamic helps infuse the rest of the team with passion because they see it in us.

Also featured in color photo insert

Sam (right) and Josh

SAM: Does the long-term strategy mostly start across the table with you and Josh having those discussions? Or does it mostly start at the board level? Where does it begin?

NICK: There is not one answer to that. I think it is filtered throughout. It is a unification of many different discussions, whether it is he and I or whether it is with management, whether it is just the board. It is really a holistic fusion of things that sort of come together.

SAM: Do you formulate an actual operational plan with metrics that you check in with every year? Every few years?

NICK: What we typically do is have a three-year plan that we modify every year. And we have a five-year plan that we check and balance every year. But, as you know, things have changed here over the last couple of years. So the existing three-year plan of 2012 wasn't being executed exactly how we wanted it to by 2015.

SAM: Leadership went through fairly big shifts in the midst of one of these five-year plans.

NICK: Right. Things sort of realigned themselves. The three-year plan as of 2014 is now much more aligned with our five-year plan.

SAM: And the board, how do they figure in planning?

NICK: They want the best for this brand. But we constantly look back as a board; we talk a lot about how well we are doing so far—up to the present. My feeling is that's okay, but is it helping me as much as possible now? Are you guys really sitting here helping give us direction for the future? And the board is getting more attuned to this need. Because what we need to talk about is the future and how we are progressing toward it. Can you give us strategic input about that? What are we going to do moving forward to make this a billion-dollar brand in the next 10 years? Honestly, the answer to that is, in different ways, more of a retail model. We are a wholesale company today, 70-30 wholesale to retail, from a mix perspective. The brand we aspire to be is more retail oriented.

SAM: Because you are always under margin pressure particularly if you are the middleman, selling your brands to the end retailer.

NICK: Exactly. You are under margin pressure. Wholesale profit margins are half of what they are compared to retail margins. That makes for a lot of attrition, companies that just don't make it through the tough times. You are dealing with the multilevel challenges of sell-through as a wholesaler; a lot of personalities and discounts can come into play between you, the retailer, and the end customer. Who knows what you have to give away. Whereas, when you are dealing with your own branded and owned retail stores, you only have to answer to yourself.

SAM: You are controlling your own destiny.

NICK: Right. You're controlling your brand. You control everything else, too.

SAM: You get your brand and your logo on to the facade of the building and more directly into the consumer headspace with your own brick-and-mortar outlets.

NICK: There are brands we believe have done a good job at building out a retail model. Globally. A retail platform online can have the look of thousands of stores. And that is one of the key things that builds equity into that brand. We don't care about going public, but when you look back at any apparel brand that has an IPO, you see that they did it by going direct—online and their own retail portals. That is the model that is going to lead to success.

SAM: Would you describe your leadership as a collaborative model?

NICK: Yes. Very much so. I am the last person to say it is all about my decision. The more I lean on my team and the whole team, the more I want their input, but—and it is the same with Josh—everything we do is collaborative. We almost have a lattice approach to things. I expect input from lower level management as much as I do from a higher level person. I want everybody's input because they are not here to just sell a garment today and only care about today; I want them to realize and think like one of the people deciding what is best for Woolrich for the long haul.

SAM: My last question would be about the balance you strike between things you wholly owned yourself—like the mill, like the store—versus the really dynamic relationships you have with licensing partners. As you develop that long-term strategy to be a billion-dollar brand someday, how do you think about these different kinds of business models?

NICK: Good question. Of course, instinctually we would love to have everything to ourselves and make everything ourselves. But we also have to remember that we don't have core competency in every category. Like footwear. Like headwear. We have some really good partners now that know those businesses better than we do. In certain cases and clothing segments, you are better off trying to find the right partner, making sure it is done the right way. You may end up becoming one with them or buying that business; that could be a great win. We would love for it to all be under one black-and-red-checked umbrella. But in the meantime, just do it the right way. With every decision we make—keep trying to make the right little decisions for the sake of the brand at every step. If we have the right partners, we are just as happy if they are a licensee as long as the product is done the right way and we are intimately involved in its management.

SAM: A really good partner that respects that you are trying to go more upscale in your business and that you want every decision that affects your brand to be for long-term brand health, not short-term dollars.

NICK: Exactly!

chapter 8

COLLABORATIVE CREATIVITY

Passion and Patience

I consider myself blessed to have a career where I can be creative. As I described in *Brewing Up a Business*, I moved to New York to be a writer. The first batch of home brew I ever concocted was in my Manhattan apartment, and the pure joy I experienced in the process—conceiving the recipe, physically making the beer, and then sharing it with my friends—convinced me I had found my calling. I can honestly say I've never looked back nor doubted that decision to commit myself to the beer business. But the urge, maybe even the need, to be creative still runs deep inside me and continually stirs my passions. I've always been able to find satisfying outlets for that ambition at Dogfish Head. For me, inventing a recipe for a beer that never existed before is like writing a poem.

"Off-centered" has served as my paradigm for creativity, and Dogfish Head has always provided a platform to play it out. With this guiding principle it only makes sense that I launched an initiative that is outside the mainstream and appeals to an adventurous, eccentric audience, a little outside the mainstream. My personal sensibility and creative whims are what passed for our company's R&D program for almost two decades. I'd have a flash of insight about the next big unique thing we should do; inspiration would typically come while paddleboarding or riding my bike through the oceanside state park down the road from my house. I pretty much chose these two physical activities, which I toggle between every morning, based on three criteria: (1) Can I do it year-round in the midst of the beauty of coastal Delaware? (2) Can I wear headphones and rock out while doing it?

(3) Can I quickly stop in the middle of the activity and whip out my smart phone and write down an idea for a beer name or Dogfish art project or beer recipe? An hour after these morning-exercise/creative-roaming sessions, I would be at my desk at work sharing the recipe idea I had thought of earlier with our brewmaster, and within a few weeks or months there would be a trial batch of that recipe, which he and I or he and our pub brewer would brew together at our brewpub.

But as our company has grown and become more complex, taking this more spontaneous, accelerated, and personal approach to launching new products is no longer always in our best interest. I agree with our leadership team that it isn't even in our best interest most of the time. We have agreed to be more methodical, strategic, and internally collaborative on bringing new products and projects to life. But I also know, for me to enjoy my work, I still want occasional projects where I take the creative lead as I used to do in almost all these sorts of the decisions. I know now it's best that I take a support role or communal role in many of the creative or strategic decisions our company will make. But I know who I am and what I love to do. I don't care if it sounds pretentious for me to say it, but I consider myself a brewer and an artist before I consider myself a businessperson or a business manager. I will have to work hard with my fellow leaders to prove to them that I can reduce the frequency of projects I want to take creative lead on and use more of my talents supporting and adding to ideas that come from different people in our company. But they also need to give me occasional opportunities to take the lead on creative projects and products, as long as I do them within the scope of our strategic plan and they are in harmony with our brand identity. Projects like Pennsylvania Tuxedo, where I took the lead on the initial beer recipe and clothing design from our side of the collaboration. I'm looking forward to spending more of my time evangelizing not just for my own ideas but also for those of the talented people around me. I see examples of creative and operation decisions being made by other talented people at Dogfish Head every week that blow me away and make me proud to work with the people I work with. I am looking forward to this personal evolution I have embarked on and the challenge: to see if I can spend more time focused on what our company is doing today in the context of a forward-looking strategic plan instead of spending so much time conjuring up the next big thing to move forward with sometime in the future.

INTERVIEW

Neal Stewart, VP of Marketing, Dogfish Head;
Tim Hawn, Brewmaster, Dogfish Head

SAM: I'd like to introduce the readers to Neal Stewart and Tim Hawn. Neal is VP of marketing at Dogfish Head and Tim Hawn is the brewmaster. Today I would like to talk about what staying off-centered means in the context of a growing company, as it relates to marketing, sales, and production. I'd like to start by discussing the process of creating the beer calendar. In earlier chapters of this book, I mentioned that this is the first year that I was not involved in the first draft of a beer calendar, and obviously, it caused me some anxiety since I love staying so close to things. I am trying to grow as a leader, to be more inclusive and add support to the process, instead of trying to direct the process. Neal and Tim, can you explain the beer calendar process, who was involved in different departments, and what that process looked like?

NEAL: The process was basically managed by the heads of a triangle of departments: sales, marketing, and production. Tim, Amy—who is our sales operations manager—and I worked together on creating the beer calendar.

SAM: A beer calendar, in the context of other businesses, is basically us talking about our sales budget for the upcoming year. It's where we decide which products work for us, which beers we are going to sell, and what the costs, revenue structure, and timing of our products are.

NEAL: Exactly. In the future, we'll challenge ourselves to think about the process much earlier each year, to give ourselves more time to consider industry trends, reflect on our intuition, talk with outside experts, and use data to guide our decisions. For this particular year, we were on a very accelerated time line. We probably crammed three or four months' worth of work into one month to meet our deadline. So, for me, one of the really important things was that each person involved in the process, at each point of the triangle, had very clearly defined roles and responsibilities. We tried to establish that early on: I was the hub of the information gathering, Tim brought in market experience, and Amy managed the tentative schedule. When Amy and I shared our thoughts or suggested a beer to throw into the mix, Tim would give us a gut reaction. Amy owned the process of plotting all the different brands on the spreadsheet and starting to plot them on the calendar. Essentially, we plot the brands and beers onto the calendar and assign numbers to each beer, so that we can reference the changes we made throughout the year, and how they affected our revenue per barrel goal versus our volume goal.

TIM: From an operations side, I think it's important to frame it with some history and context about Dogfish. How did we get to where we are today, which I think helped in some of our decision making. The difficult part of the process is trying not to bite off so much that we cannot do high-quality, super-innovative work. We have to stay balanced so that we can do new things with a twist, but not do so much that we cannot get it done on the production side on time while maintaining our standards. A lot of it came down to discussing the data, talking to our sales folks, and getting a feel for what is really out there. We explored what they think will help them versus what we believe will help them, and tried to find some way to combine both points of view. The process should keep us at the forefront of being very creative and innovative as we go forward.

SAM: What we are learning, and what I have come to accept and now to start championing especially with my own actions, is that we should focus on a strategy that clearly defines about 80 percent of what we plan to do. But we will also allow room and resources for the 20 percent of spontaneous inspiration in the best way we can accommodate it, but are moving away from a world where 80 percent of what we did was spontaneous and took us down a whimsical path that was always veering and was unknown to the majority of the company. We're tightening up our work flow in a way that will still allow us to be on brand and authentic to our off-centered creative value, but also give more structure to our processes.

NEAL: I think something that is kind of important here is that as the team grows, as the number of coworkers we have here at the brewery grows but then also our senior management team grows, it is important for us to embark on these big projects and look at them from a variety of different angles. My vision of Dogfish 20 years ago, when you started the company, was that you would just walk into the kitchen and say, "Oh, what can I put into this next batch of beer?" That is total intuition. That's intuition in its purest form, but now that we have more members of the team, you have to consider the decisions you make not only from an intuitive side, but also from a creative side and an analytical side. We work in a democracy now, where different people bring different things to the table, and it's essential to get everyone in a place where they feel comfortable about the path forward. Our new CEO is much more analytical; he's the kind of person who needs to manage the business using the hard numbers, whereas you, Sam, are more of a gut-feeling kind of person. Bringing those different elements to the table every time we make that decision is more and more important as we go.

SAM: As we are moving into our strategic retreat next week, things like having our beer filters on the wall will help remind us that we need to be united, not in our exact beliefs in each particular idea, but united in the way we consider each idea through the same filter, through the same lens. We have to be respectful of each other's opinions, as we are discussing what we should be moving toward.

NEAL: Exactly.

SAM: Neal, you've been with us for a year and a half, and Tim, you've been with us for more than four years. So Tim, as the brewmaster, how do you balance needing to be the person responsible both for real budgets and hitting costs, but also for incorporating, into the operational approach, the opportunity to be off-centered and creative from the highest level on the production side?

TIM: From the production side, one of the things that has evolved in the past four years has been the addition of more structure to the process. That structure is what allows us to have more time to be creative; without that structure, being creative feels like something that you are trying to manage versus something that you can devote time to pursuing. Purely adding structure throughout the process lets us work better by having specifications and better procedures. Our real creativity, the real off-centeredness, is really about that initial recipe development, and how we get to where we want to go. There have been times when I have heard brewers ask, "Why are we doing this?" when something is really difficult, but the funny part is almost all of them say that why they came here is to create something original and authentic—and from scratch—which means do it the hard way at times.

But when you're doing it every day the hard way, you start to find simpler ways to do it while still being true to your standards and goals. Other people would rather use added flavors, but we're using real fruits, we're using real honey, and we're pumping it in huge quantities; but they can do that with flavoring. Other people are doing that, but that's not okay for us. Doing things differently, sometimes the hard way, is part of what being off-centered means.

SAM: We are blissfully inefficient in some things.

TIM: It is part of us being off-centered, but we are also implementing more structure from an engineering standpoint, to allow us to do what we do much more efficiently. That's why I have a great team of people who can manage the day-to-day operations, and can also find a balance between efficiently managing those operations while also thinking creatively outside of the box. And what that means to each member of the team is different: off-centered to an engineer might translate into finding a new creative way to do something. It is not finding something unique, and creating a ground place where nobody else is really doing it. For our brewers, on the other hand, who want to be highly creative, we've created programs like a small batch brewing facility where they can go do it. Right now, we are getting brewers down to the pub to do a few of their own recipes.

SAM: Right. So Dogfish Head has four brewing systems. Two are relatively big (200 barrel) and big (100 barrel) brewery systems; those are the production ones. Then, we also have a two-barrel brewery, which is human scale, up to your shoulder, and a half-barrel system, a glorified little home-brewing system that our coworkers—any coworker in any department—can make a decision with other coworkers to brew whatever they want.

TIM: One of our teams using the two-barrel brewery was the accounting team. So the accounting team is down there making a different beer. They made a thyme beer with lemon in it and blueberries. If you think about how we make beer, you know that it is also to encourage a creative off-centeredness throughout our many groups. It's not just a theory residing with us at the leadership level. We want everyone in our organization to be creative and do something different.

SAM: It ties every department at Dogfish Head to what this company is all about. The heart of this company's financial engine and creative engine is off-centered beers. So when a team from accounting can make a beer so beloved by the rest of the coworkers that they vote it to be made on a bigger scale at our pub, the Summer Thyme, they become evangelists for off-centered brewing. It demystifies the brewing process, and they get more respect for the brewing department, quality control, and all the more technical people who touched the beer.

Neal, what about developing our marketing plans? As you know, before you arrived here about two years ago, Mariah and I did all the marketing. I still love designing promotional stuff, and sometimes I still want to go deep on those, but I see that much like brewing, I have to pick and choose which projects to go deep on, and allow you to oversee the whole marketing plan. As you oversee a marketing plan that is growing, what is your approach, and your philosophy, on allocating those huge new spends in a way that lets us be off-centered and doesn't reek of a traditional monologue that large companies do, from billboards to TV ads and that kind of stuff?

NEAL: Two things. Number one would be that I honestly do not think about our budget, hardly at all. In past lives and past jobs, the overall budget has been the guide for the entire year. When you were talking about the filters earlier, the filter at previous jobs when an opportunity came up, or we created an opportunity, would be if we had the money to execute that. That is not the filter here; the filter here is time and if we have the time to do this.

SAM: We have more money than time.

NEAL: In a way, yes.

SAM: We did not before, but it is pretty cool that we do now.

NEAL: Yeah, so when an opportunity comes to us, the first filter we look at is whether it fits the brand from a marketing perspective. Then we look at a second filter of whether we can execute it at the level that fits our standards. From there, we give it a hard look of whether we do it or not.

The second thing you mentioned was the difference between traditional marketing and advertising versus our off-centered way of doing things. The way that I think of it is that we always try to go for marketing strategies or campaigns that, in reality, you cannot pay for. It goes back to the budget not being the guiding principle. If you ever hear someone say, when there is a great piece of publicity in a magazine or just a great viral marketing campaign, "That is the kind of marketing you cannot pay for," that's how I think about the way that we do things. That oftentimes means it's harder. We know that whatever we do is going to take up more time than just placing an ad.

SAM: Just placing an ad?

NEAL: Just placing an ad in a magazine, and designing an 8½ by 11 full-page ad. I am sure there are a lot of companies that spend a lot of time on creating the right messaging, creating a great photo shoot with the best-looking product photography and all that, but for us, marketing and advertising are an investment of time across several different people. Rarely is there a project that we work on that is just our event coordinator or just our social media team. Almost always, those events come together and have a thread through all of those people who worked on it. Going back to the principle of a campaign that you cannot pay for, we did a Beer for Breakfast brew, a beer made with maple syrup and pork products that was available only at our brewpub in a very limited supply, but still that got national publicity. Even though a lot of people may not be able to find that beer or get to drink it, they still walk away with a very favorable opinion of the brew, and hopefully a favorable opinion of Dogfish that we are pushing the boundaries and doing things in an off-centered way. We couldn't have bought the publicity that came out of those articles. We couldn't have bought editorial coverage in print publications or online magazines about a tiny, limited-supply beer.

SAM: We approach projects like that authentically, so that it allows us to brew something so exciting and unique that it makes our fan base excited. We, as creative brewers, as marketers, and as people who work here, get excited about doing unique things. If we do a good job at it, we get the media attention and that of their readership. It's likely that most small business people do not have the budget for huge editorial spends, so the most important thing is to come from this unique place that is David among Goliaths. You know that you are not going to outspend them or make a product that is going to dominate market share in whatever industry you are in, so have fun with it. Do something really distinctive and creative; the process won't be easy, because you don't have the world-class resources or world-class dollars of the Under Armour or Nike, but it leads to really creative opportunities when you approach it that way.

NEAL: One of the big things that brought me to Dogfish is that I have no desire to work for a brand or a company where $100,000 becomes a rounding area, where the marketing vision is driven by money and not time, because that ultimately takes away from our creativity. We are truly more creative with just people.

SAM: With limited dollars.

NEAL: With limited dollars, yes. The limitations on money force people to be more creative and force them to think about things that end up being more authentic and connecting with people in a stronger way.

SAM: Well said. Tim, what were the parts of Dogfish Head that attracted you to the company that brought you here, and how do you make sure you stay connected with them now that you are in a leadership position and as the company grows and evolves?

TIM: One of the biggest things that brought me here is that when I was working in a massive corporate structure, any idea that you wanted to implement took two to three years. One of the things that I love about being here is that process is faster. Our ideas are bigger, ideas flow quickly, they can be heard, and they can be decided and acted upon. There are really three different responses we hear when we present new ideas: One, it is a great idea—why haven't we thought about it? Or two, it's a great idea but this isn't the right time. Or three, what the hell are you really thinking? That's top to bottom, and it is nice to be a lot more hands-on here than at other places where there's only a little bit of actual doing. At a big company, it is a lot of bureaucracy. At Dogfish, a nice-sized company that is still fairly flat, things happen quicker. The things that need to get done are the right things to do and often just happen naturally. We make them happen even if it's a new brand idea or new engineering. We quickly go down this list, which makes it much easier to get things done relative to other places or other companies where I have worked.

SAM: The last question for each of you would be this: the company is growing, and we are bringing in new team members. We have a relatively flat structure. Looking at our offices, we all, no matter what our title is, have the same size work spaces at Dogfish. We all share the same few conference rooms, and do not have special parking spaces for senior people. In that way, we are a very flat company, but we do understand the need for different layers of leadership. Tim, in production, you have a layer of management below you, now in charge of running the day-to-day operations. Neal, just recently we hired a marketing manager. What do you both notice as these other layers of leadership have come into your respective departments? How has that changed your roles here? Starting with Neal, where do you see the changes to Dogfish impacting your life, your average workday, and the kind of stuff that you focused on six months ago? Where do you spend your time on the VP level so that you're working on what's most important and adds the most value to Dogfish?

NEAL: One of my favorite phrases that we constantly hear in our management meetings is that our job now is to plan, and then when we are done planning, we plan some more. We plan for the next cycle. If we are mapping out a very sound plan that is clear, makes sense, and delivers on our business objectives, we can hand that off to our management team, our management layer, and they will be able to execute it. Our work during the planning period should allow the management team to fully flesh out the plan, have more ownership of it, stick to the time lines from start to finish, and in the end, create a better end result.

The way my role is changing is in the planning, the thinking ahead. I'm going from thinking about today or tomorrow, and instead thinking about a few months in advance or a year in advance, and eventually a few years in advance, all simultaneously. That's what I feel like my role will be. The other thing that has changed is that now we are constantly looking for ways we can work more efficiently. Whether that means within our department or with projects that are interdepartmental, I want to make sure that we have great communication internally, so that everyone is on the same page. Marketing will play a role with all of our departments in the future. It is the hub of communication, not that it dictates what people should be doing within their departments, but more to make sure that the communication across those teams is very sound.

SAM: Internally, as well as the market externally.

NEAL: Exactly.

SAM: Tim, you have the last word. Neal mentioned his excitement about having more time to lift his head up and look years in advance, look down the path for Dogfish. We are embarking on our first-ever strategic retreat, and we've built in the days to create a multiyear company-wide strategic plan. Personally, how is your job changing and also what are you most excited about as we go toward our first multiyear company-wide strategic plan?

TIM: My role is changing as we have grown just as a brewery, and there are significantly more people in my department than when I got here four-plus years ago. At that time I could go out and spend more time with coworkers. Given the time constraints and the bigger team, I have to focus on a few; so there is a lot more development that is going into my direct reports, to make sure we are moving the right way. The other big piece of my job is making sure that we maintain the quality of our products going out the door. To do that, I have to work with people, set up an initial plan, and then take a step back and let them go develop, flesh out, and refine those ideas. I have to ensure that I don't get caught anymore in the very deep trenches, but try to manage a little bit higher. What makes me excited about these multiyear plans is the raw ingredient strategies that are out there. Our market is so competitive in profit; we have to have and to continue to develop a better, longer-term raw material strategy to allow us to grow. My job is also evolving to focus more externally, to ensure that Dogfish is a leader in brewing. We are talking to farmers about why they should grow certain hops, and why we need them to grow those hops that not only affect us but also affect the crop-growing industry. It cements Dogfish's position, but it's not only that we're pushing to become an industry leader; we are also trying to help guide and influence other things that go out there when it comes to raw materials, like barley for malt or even hops.

SAM: Part of your role is thinking about how many pounds of barley and hops we are going to need two years from now, and the ordering of those now.

TIM: Yes, there's a lot of planning and structure required for that. There are a lot of elements to consider and one is watching the weather. What does the weather forecast look like? What are farmers saying? It is an interesting dynamic as we've grown. We're still fairly small. We don't have a massive purchasing department or research arm to study agronomic trends. So I still get to do a little bit of both. To Neal's point, it is about planning. It is about leading and guiding what is going on, not only at Dogfish today, but what will be going on in the market in the future.

SAM: More planning, guiding, and a little less physical doing is what is needed from the highest level of leadership.

NEAL: I would say that is a challenge for us, because I think part of the reason why we are at Dogfish is because we enjoy doing.

SAM: We get to pick our projects.

NEAL: Tim often says that his favorite days are going down to the brewpub and brewing beer.

SAM: Mine too.

NEAL: Marketing is a little bit different, but I love getting out and talking to consumers and working events. It is a challenge to us to break away from that. I think it is good to have that connection, but day to day the challenge is to think ahead and not get caught up in what's going on today.

TIM: I brew on my days off. When you still love doing so much of what you love, and you are willing to do it on your day off, that's a good thing.

SAM: Thanks, guys.

When I wrote the first business plan for Dogfish Head, I was excited to explore the outer edges of beer. Helping to redefine the ingredients, concepts, and historical antecedents that we think of as beer has been a central, rewarding component of my career. As I type this today, there is a front-page story in the *Wall Street Journal* calling me the pioneer of the extreme brewing movement. When I read that story in the paper, I thought of all of my coworkers, and I know that I will sometimes take the recognition for the risks we take in the beer world, but the execution and success of our beers is owned by all of us. I also know how lucky I am to have operational and people management leaders at this company who are much stronger in their areas of expertise than I will ever be. This has allowed me to venture out of our facilities more and more to help sell our beer and drive awareness of all of our businesses while I am on the road. What was not in my business plan, and what I didn't realize at the time, was the extent to which my quest to open a creative brewery would become a catalyst for travel.

THE BIRRERIA STORY

The exploration that comes with creating experimental beers has led me to meet and make beer with amazing brewers in over a dozen countries. When you break bread with someone, you get to know them and learn from them. Beer is liquid bread, and I've broken that liquid bread around the world. On my life list of interactions that give me creative fulfillment, these relationships with brewers in different parts of the world rank among the top.

My experiences with the craft brewing community in Italy and the wonderful ways these experiences have influenced numerous projects at Dogfish Head are examples of the goodness that can come out of creative roaming and collaboration. I don't speak Italian at all but I suppose it isn't entirely surprising that Italy is the country that I have most often traveled to and worked with. I'm a Calagione; my mom's maiden name is Mastroianni; and my grandfather was born in Calabria. So you might say I was genetically programmed to find this endeavor a good fit.

How did it happen? A dozen years ago, when Dogfish was barely profitable, I was invited on a trip subsidized by the U.S. Department of Agriculture to have American brewers set up a booth at the Salone del Gusto in Turin. The event is the largest food fair in the world, a festival of traditional cuisine and local produce from all over in celebration of Slow Food.

SLOW FOOD MOVEMENT

McDonald's announced plans in 1986 to open a franchise adjacent to the historic Spanish Steps in the center of Rome. The news outraged Italian journalist Carlo Petrini, who launched a public outcry against the global industrialization of food. His original protest has since grown into an international gastro-economic movement, Slow Food, with some 150,000 members in chapters worldwide. At its core is a commitment to preserving alternative food choices that protect small growers and artisanal producers, safeguard the environment, and promote biodiversity.

"We are enslaved by speed and have all succumbed to the same insidious virus: Fast Life, which disrupts our habits, pervades the privacy of our homes and forces us to eat Fast Foods. . . . A firm defense of quiet material pleasure is the only way to oppose the universal folly of Fast Life. . . . May suitable doses of guaranteed sensual pleasure and slow, long-lasting enjoyment preserve us from the contagion of the multitude who mistake frenzy for efficiency. Our defense should begin at the table with Slow Food. Let us rediscover the flavors and savors of regional cooking and banish the degrading effects of Fast Food." (*The Official Slow Food Manifesto*, 2001)

The craft beer renaissance could itself be included in the Slow Food movement, although it evolved independently. The constructs of our communities' philosophies are very much aligned. We, too, celebrate the authenticity and pleasures of artisan craftsmanship and the relationship between the earth, the growers, and the consumers—rather than focusing on accelerating a return on investment through continually increasing industrial scale and efficiency.

At the time of my first visit to Italy, the country's craft beer culture was in its infancy and at least a decade behind the U.S. scene's trajectory. But they were so welcoming. I was invited with open arms to come to their breweries, do beer dinners with them, visit their homes, and drink many pints together.

It was in Turin (which is the home of the Slow Food movement) that I got to know my two best Italian beer buddies, Leonardo DiVincenzo and Teo Musso. Birra del Borgo in Borgorose is Leo's company, known for its India pale ale inspirations with citrusy and pepper notes and also for brewing with exotic ingredients like chestnuts and tobacco. Teo Musso started Baladin Brewery as a brewpub in his tiny hometown of Piozzo, a most unlikely place to become one of the temples of modern Italian beer making. Through them I got to know their friend, Nicola Farinetti.

Nicola's family business has evolved from his grandfather's small local grocery store to the retail chain Eataly, as in "Eat Italy." The *New York Times* describes Eataly as a combination of "a bustling European open market, a high end food court, and a New Age learning center."[1] I think of them as

---

[1]Alan Tardi, "Spacious Food Bazaar in Turin Plans Manhattan Branch," *New York Times*, October 24, 2007, www.nytimes.com/2007/10/24/dining/24eata.html?pagewanted=print &_r=1&.

Whole Foods on steroids centered entirely on Italian cuisine, with restaurants in the store, music playing, educational lectures going on, and tasting bars offering beer and wine so the shopping experience feels festive.

Patriarch Oscar Farinetti, Nicola's father, is an amazing entrepreneur who wants to celebrate and educate the world about the diversity of all-natural Italian food. The mix he has assembled ranges from some of the country's biggest food-and-beverage makers to small farmers offering mushrooms from the Alps or homemade fig jams. They don't just throw stuff on the shelves and hope it sells itself. They have knowledgeable, well-trained people on the floor to educate consumers about the products. There are now over 30 Eataly stores on four continents, testimony to the wisdom of Oscar's business model: passion first, money second.

The first Eataly opened in 2007 in Turin, fittingly in the hometown of Slow Food. I was invited to host an event at that store and learned that the family was thinking about opening a Manhattan location, the first in the United States. I suggested that it would be a great business move to install a brewery on the premises. They liked the concept, which was all the encouragement I needed. Teo, Leo, and I formed a consortium, the Birreria Brothers. Several years later, in 2010, we opened a rooftop brewery pub at Eataly's 50,000-square-foot operation located at 200 Fifth Avenue, with views of the top of the Chrysler Building. Now there are additional Birreria Brewpubs within the Eataly locations in Chicago and Rome with our three brewery logos above the brewing equipment. We may work with Eataly as they consider opening additional Birrerias in other cities as well.

The relationship the three Birreria Brothers breweries have with Eataly is very unique and trusting. The three distinct brewery logos hang above the brewing equipment but none of the three breweries own any equity in Eataly. No contract says our beers have to be sold in the Eataly stores and restaurants. Instead, we are operating on the good faith premise that if we contribute our beer knowledge, brewing experience, and brand reputations and reach, and add to that our skill to do special recipes and the time to promote events, Eataly stores and restaurants will sell a lot of our beer.

When I proposed this opportunity to the Monday Team, it didn't encounter much resistance. I did the initial outreach to brewery equipment companies and worked with Eataly architects and designers to lay out the brewery floor plan. We made plans to send our brewmaster up to New York to set up the equipment and train brewers, and began scheduling events where I could promote the venture.

Mariah and I attended the grand opening. Famous Italian singers were performing on the rooftop; everybody was toasting everybody with lots of dancing and hugging and drinking; the beautiful copper-clad brewery behind glass displayed our logo. I was thrilled, all the more so because I could imagine my immigrant grandfather arriving by boat in nearby New York harbor two generations earlier, dreaming that this land of opportunity would be fruitful for his family if he worked hard. I was proud we got to do this Italy-centric project in the U.S. city my ancestors first arrived in.

Three years later another Birreria location opened in Chicago with an on-site brewhouse capable of producing 450 barrels annually. All three Birreria locations are doing well today. "The second-floor craft beer bar holds its own among the wine-dominated aisles," wrote *Chicago* magazine's critic. "Sunlight bathes the sectioned-off corner space; the high-top tables hold Alpine-inspired bar snacks and pints, including 14 drafts and dozens of bottled varieties. . . . The beers made on-site will stun you."[2]

As the Birreria Brothers brewers, Dogfish, Baladin, and Birra del Borgo breweries have used the Birreria locations in Italy and America as collaboration workshops. We have each taken turns taking the lead on certain recipes that have sold well (Panna Cotta Porter—a beer with a similar ingredient list to that eponymous Italian dessert) and those that didn't sell quite as well (Garlic Breadth—a big dark brew made with the most savory roasted black garlic . . . perhaps this beer was ahead of its time . . . I loved it but it didn't sell as well as Panna Cotta Porter). Whether the risky experiments we incorporated into our creative and collective approach to brewing at Birreria came out great or came out polarizing, the fun was in the journey. As Lindsay Nohl, a professor at Minneapolis College of Art and Design, writes in the book *Design School Wisdom*, "Be generous with your appreciation, conversation, and collaboration. (Support the creative cause, critique and discuss freely, and collaborate often.) This is about the importance of connecting with other creatives while helping to foster a positive art and design community." Her words may have been directed at design students

---

[2]Carly Bowers and Emmet Sullivan, "Chicago's 20 Best New Bars," *Chicago* magazine, January 20, 2014.

Also featured in color photo insert

The Brewpub Birreria at Eataly New York.

but any entrepreneur or businessperson working to build a brand is a student of design.

My most comprehensive and elaborate brewing project with the Birreria Brothers brewers was Birra Etrusca—the resurrection of an ancient ale we worked on not only with each other but also with the scientific and academic communities in both Italy and the United States.

BIRRA ETRUSCA

This ancient ale proves that beside the wine on every proud Italian's dinner table there should also be a place for beer. To develop the recipe for Birra Etrusca Bronze, I traveled to Rome with University of Pennsylvania–based molecular archaeologist Dr. Pat McGovern. With the help of Birreria Brothers brewers Leo DiVincenzo of Birra del Borgo and Teo Musso of Baladin, we spent a few days meeting with archaeologists and scientists and we analyzed drinking vessels found in 2,800-year-old Etruscan tombs.

Although Italian historians were a little reluctant to admit it, the team clearly found that the Etruscans had a taste for ale.

"In every part of the process, we go for as much authenticity as we can," Calagione says. "Ingredients are often tough to track down and there can be financial and logistical challenges. But we really love embracing these risks to bring these beers to market."

The backbone of Birra Etrusca comes from two-row malted barley and heirloom Italian wheat. Specialty ingredients we resurrected from the ancient recipes we learned about in our research in the Eutruscan hillsides outside Rome include hazelnut flour, pomegranates, Italian chestnut honey, Delaware wildflower honey, and clover honey. A handful of whole-flower hops are added, but the bulk of the bitterness comes from gentian root and the sarsaparilla-like Ethiopian myrrh resin found by Teo from Baladin.

To bring another layer of depth to the richness of this project, Birra del Borgo and Baladin will brew their own very different versions of Birra Etrusca; to add complexity and variety, each brewery will ferment its batches with different traditional materials. Dogfish will use bronze; Baladin will use wood; and Birra del Borgo will use terra cotta.

For the storytelling component of this brew, we had a Scandinavian filmmaker follow us and interview us as we researched and brewed this beer. All three versions of this beer have been brewed multiple times and found receptive audiences in the beer communities in both Italy and the United States.

From Dogfish Head Birra Etrusca press release.

Our most recent collaborative project using Eataly/Birreria as a creative hub centered around the WastED concept that was initiated by NYC-based celebrity chef Dan Barber. The project is described on their website (http://wastedny.com) this way: "WastED is a community of chefs, farmers, fishermen, distributors, processors, producers, designers, and retailers working together to reconceive 'waste' that occurs at every link in the food chain. Our goal is to celebrate what chefs do every day on their menus; creating something delicious out of the ignored or uncoveted and inspiring new applications for the overlooked byproducts of our food system."

Inspired by the WastED movement to reduce food waste in America, I reached out to the legendary chef Mario Batali, a partner in the Eataly/Birreria restaurants and markets, and I worked with him to create an exclu-

sive Birreria ale that utilizes bruised fruit, overripe tomatoes, and other produce from within the Eataly produce section that may have been past their
prime to sell to customers, but still perfect perfectly delicious for pureeing
and adding to a brew.

Mario and I captured the story of this WastED brew in an episode of
That's Odd, Let's Drink It!, the web series joint venture between Dogfish
Head and *Complex* magazine.

The reason that the collaborative projects we have embarked on as the
Birreria Brothers have been successful is that we each bring considerable
resources, passion, and inspiration to the project. We listen to each other, we
have conversations to make sure each other's creative and economic priorities
are considered, and then we do the fun work of bringing the project to life,
incorporating the skills and the perspective of each other and our respective
coworkers. In this way we learn a lot from each other. This new knowledge
doesn't just inform the projects the Birreria Brothers work on together. It
informs the future work of our individual companies as well.

INTERVIEW

Will Oldham, Renaissance Man

Will Oldham is a true Renaissance man: a photographer, actor, musician, and beyond.
Better known as Bonnie "Prince" Billy, he is a celebrated indie singer-songwriter, once
described by a music journalist as "the underground artist most likely to work his way
into the Rock and Roll Hall of Fame."

Our brewpub in Rehoboth features all original music and, as a big Bonnie
"Prince" Billy fan, it was a proud moment for me when Will first played our stage.
He stayed at my house that night and we've been talking about our shared love for
artistic creativity and collaboration ever since.

"The Communal Exploration of Goodness"

SAM: There's this phenomenon called founder's syndrome that affects
entrepreneurs at the helm of growing companies. Because a somewhat
different set of skills is required to start a business as compared to leading
and growing a business, an entrepreneur must make the shift to leader for
a business to be successful. I own up to the fact that I suffer from found-

er's syndrome. I think I've been great at appreciating my coworkers and acknowledging that they contribute to Dogfish Head in ways that I cannot, but I can also acknowledge that I have not been so great at allowing them into the creative and strategic processes at Dogfish. I was hoping to chat with you about your experiences in the collaborative process within the music industry.

WILL: My wheels started spinning immediately with—what'd you call it? founder's syndrome? I think I've always identified with—in the back of my mind—whatever the parallel would be for me. When I see people in music evolve to another level of whatever it is they do, I just think "I wouldn't want to do that," in terms of not wanting to play certain kinds of shows or have to do certain kinds of things. It would take time away from me being able to do the things that I'm actually good at or interested in.

SAM: The things that matter to you—given the finite amount of time we have—you don't want to be doings things that you aren't fully 100 percent excited about?

WILL: Right. Here's an example from the record business: a year or so back, I self-released a record. The reason why demonstrates what we're talking about—making choices to do things you like to do.

Drag City was the record label we started with, way back in the early 1990s. Like every label, they had the process of releasing an album down to a science. Every step of it. As an artist, you turn in the record, you turn in the artwork, and then they'd get it all assembled. The label would inform their staff, they'd inform their distributors, they'd communicate with the record production plants, they'd communicate with the printing companies, they'd make promos. Back in the day, I'd be on the phone once or twice a day, talking with Dan, Dan (there are two Dans at DC), or Rian, the label guys, about all those things. I loved the process. Then Drag City got pretty streamlined, and the headaches of running a label in the newer age got intense. By 2012 it was no fun making records anymore because I wasn't having that depth of collaboration; I wasn't involved in the different steps.

SAM: You felt disconnected from the holistic approach you used to be a part of?

WILL: Yeah. I make records because I like to make records. There are a lot of musicians who aren't like that; they say, "I just want to create," and let the label take care of all the other stuff. But I don't want to do that. I value the interaction with the record label and I value the interaction with the stores and with the audience. But my relationship with them was eventually reduced to just giving Drag City the tracks and they would then put it out.

SAM: But you've always been very close to the physical presentation of your music as well, right?

WILL: I need that: putting out the records. Getting the vinyl plant to ship me my records here to this house and have that room stacked with boxes and boxes of records and then calling record stores, asking, "Do you want to buy my record?"

SAM: That's funny. They must wonder, "Who are you representing?"

WILL: It felt absolutely natural and great. It was like the best I'd felt about putting out a record in years. For most people, that's not logical. The record store people who would answer the phone didn't think it was logical. They were very excited, but they didn't think it was logical.

But I don't want to build an organization around putting out records. You need a staff that has to have salaries and you need a building and the building has overhead, and the building has a mortgage and these things. I don't want to ever grow my organization to where I'd have to think I should do these shows because I need to pay the bills.

SAM: Because other people are relying on you.

WILL: Yeah, in order to keep this aspect of the thing going. It's not that I'm bad at playing a show, but just playing a show to play a show and then playing another show and just showing up, that's not what I'm good at.

SAM: Right.

WILL: You know, I'm better at thinking, assembling the musicians to play a show or to record a record, and communicating with them and creating something from the beginning, than I am being on the road and coordinating all those details.

SAM: Like putting the album out in 2012 or 2013?

WILL: Yeah. It's kind of strange, but I like the idea that everything I do is kind of reinventing the wheel. Each project is reinventing the wheel and that's the fun thing for me.

SAM: I get it. At Dogfish Head we've now got more than 230 workers, so I'm driving a bus with 230 people on board. At this scale, I've had to accept that they need more certainty about where we're going: a strategic plan. Which means trading creative spontaneity for predictability and forecasting.

This is my challenge: I understand that as a company we've moved to where a forecasted or future-looking strategic plan has to exist for the sake of all these people. But at the same time, where can I find opportunities to be creative within that process?

It sounds like what you do is choose some projects that are kind of within the structure, and some projects that are not. Are you more motivated to prioritize the projects that don't have to have as much structure?

WILL: Right now, I'm more motivated to prioritize the things that don't have as much structure. I've recognized that I never thought about writing songs just for the sake of writing songs. In my brain, writing a song is all about establishing something upon which you can begin the collaboration with other people.

SAM: It's not just an end in itself. It's the first stage of a project.

WILL: Absolutely. The only reason to make a song is to begin communicating and collaborating with musicians and visual artists and the record label and audience. That's what I love the best. That's my work. But today that's not financially viable. People don't make money selling records, not enough to live off unless they license them to commercials, TV shows, movies.

SAM: Would you ever write for things like that?

WILL: Sure. I love it when someone asks, "Would you write a song for this commercial or would you write a song for this movie?" That sounds really exciting.

SAM: Instead of them asking for something you've already written that has nothing to do with their project and trying to force it into that hole?

WILL: Yeah. I feel like if you helped a song get written and recorded and released and then somebody's paid for it, that's a binding contract. You can't then sell the song to Chrysler. You have to say, "No, I already sold it to the audience. I don't own it anymore. You can't buy it from me."

SAM: I never thought about it like that. It's not like a legal definition of your rights to those songs but a kind of ethical, personal contract with your collaborators.

WILL: I sort of wish audiences could band together and say, you know, "You can't sell that song to Volkswagen, because we already bought it and we own it collectively. We're invested in it. We invested our time, our emotion, and our money in this."

SAM: A class-action emotional suit.

WILL: I like that. It might even have some legal bearing.

SAM: What we're saying here is that connecting all these different people to the products makes the product that much more exciting and real.

WILL: Yeah. I think so, yeah. I get thrilled by thinking that any song that begins here has to go through all of these steps and that each of these steps should have some sort of attention given to it, some sort of quality associated with it. I like the idea of thinking that even at the record-pressing plant someone might say, "I'm glad I worked on that record."

SAM: You're talking about all those people who touched it in the process and the magic that comes from all those passionate, interested fingerprints that are on it, regardless of the specific artist's name on the front of the album.

WILL: That's right.

SAM: What you're talking about sounds sort of like a Karmic ledger book.
    That leads us to another subject I'd like to discuss with you. At Dogfish Head we've got a kind of purpose statement: it's a long quote from Ralph Waldo Emerson that, to make it simple, comes down to this concept that the route to virtue is to cut your own path, outside the status quo. Even if it's a tiny path, if it's worthy and other people join you, then that becomes a communal exploration of goodness. For me, the heart of this is collaboration.

WILL: I'm a huge Golden Rule person. It's an inherent concept in what is arguably my most popular song, "I See a Darkness." In the chorus, it says that my loving you is hoping that you, in turn, will love me, and that together we buoy each other up. I wake up every day and think about working with people or collaborating with people or in hopes that tomorrow they will wake up and think about collaborating with me and call me and say, "Would you come and sing this song? Would you come and eat this meal? Would you come and do this thing?"

SAM: You're not going to stop hoping if it doesn't happen tomorrow. Inevitably it starts enriching your life, because all the goodness you sent out starts returning. And it's awesome not knowing when and where and how it's coming back, but trusting that at some point, in some way, it will.

WILL: Absolutely.

SAM: That brings up the notion of time and mortality, which are things I'm thinking about now in respect to the changes we're going through at Dogfish Head. You and I are now in our mid-forties. I've got aches and pains; I need glasses to read. I feel time is almost accelerating, and I find myself thinking, "Holy shit, that year went by so much faster." Is that happening with you? Are you starting to look at your future as more precious than you thought of your future 10 years ago?

WILL: My dad died out of the blue at 63 years old. Totally unexpectedly. He just had a heart attack, even though he was healthy and he exercised. He was on his bike. I turned 45 this year and I thought to myself, "I'm more than two-thirds of the way through this life." I have certain behavioral traits like him; we look alike; so it's not stupid to think that I could die out of the blue at 63.

SAM: What I feel sometimes is that too often there's so much going on that I'm not enjoying each individual thing. I'm not going as deep into each project to get as much out of it. I'm kind of going two-thirds deep on too many projects.

WILL: Right.

SAM: I don't know if you've had that feeling and how you navigate it.

WILL: I try to give absolute, equal significance to different things that I do every day. The first thing I do in the morning when I get up is make coffee and sit down and put two records on the stack record player and read. I have to read at least through two sides of the records. That's as important to me as any work thing, any family thing, anything else.

Now I have a dog and the dog has to be walked. So I'm healthier, but I also get these times of being alone, exploring my neighborhood and my community, experiencing this animal thing. If someone says, "Can you . . . whatever . . . come sing this song right now or have this work-related phone call?" I'll say, "No, I have a commitment to reading this morning or walking the dog. I can't be there at that time."

SAM: Sounds like you're doing a really good job with being clear about protecting things that you need to do for yourself every day. I've got to get better at that. I do my workout, my yoga every day, and I get up and do coffee and check websites and e-mails but it's still kind of work-related when I'm doing that. I've got to get a little better at that balance moving forward because I'm feeling the compression of time now. Part of that means getting to this place where, instead of trying to be the sole creative and strategic driver of Dogfish, I'm okay with being a creative driver.

When you're making an album, early in the process, do you decide you're going to really drive the creative process or do you plan for a collaboration?

WILL: A crucial part of the identity of anything we do—whether it be Bonnie Prince Billy and the Cairo Gang tour or projects—is knowing that we're going to make every decision pretty much together. We're going to talk about microphones and what room and what time of day we're going to work, and all of that is going to be something that they want to hear from me and I want to hear from them.

SAM: 100 percent democratic.

WILL: Yeah. But then when I'm working with Dawn McCarthy [singer/musician], I know that she doesn't think about some of those things. She doesn't care that much about which studio or which microphone or how the CD packages end up getting assembled. So then I have to think that this is collaborative and I'm doing it as a presentation of us. So when she doesn't provide input, I have to bend my brain in order for this thing to be *our* thing.

If you initiate a lot of projects and you ask somebody in, you have to be super attuned to their input because they're not even aware of the potential for their input.

SAM: Can you think of an example?

WILL: I'll keep thinking of things like what the record's going to look like or which songs we're going to record. I'll create an idea, either specific or loose, of what it's going to be like once it's done and she's not thinking necessarily along those lines.

Then, she'll come up with other ideas and I'll have to recognize that her ideas are absolutely crucial to the eventual identity of the project and so I have to change everything I was imagining. But I do this without saying "I was thinking like this, your idea's not a part of that." It's more understanding that the reason to work with someone as great and powerful as Dawn McCarthy is that she is going to significantly change everything with her creative energies and forces and decisions. But she doesn't even know that it's happening, so if you go into a project and you invite somebody into the process, when they contribute, you have to listen twice as hard.

When they say, "Let's do this song; let's not; I don't like that song," or, "Let's mix the drums low," they're affecting the whole thing even if they're not thinking about it.

SAM: It's like they have different super powers. Everyone has different super powers. Your super power might be seeing nine steps in advance but the other's is adding something amazing to this moment. You've got to respect each other's super powers if you're in collaboration. I'm trying to get better at that and be more sensitive to recognizing when to step back. The collaborator brings something different than I do but that doesn't necessarily mean mine is better. I suppose that's a version of wisdom.

WILL: But it also means you have to be so careful about who you work with.

If somebody else has an idea, I love to help bring it to life. I don't have to start everything myself and keep track of everything. I don't want to worry about keeping ownership of the creative process, of keeping it mine. I know that I have certain skills at this point in life and in work, and that other people are aware of those things that I have to offer, and that they might now be able to envision how to incorporate my things into their things.

At this point I'm not hand-to-mouth or anything like that. So, I'm starting to think, well, how many things can I do that don't make any money?

SAM: Might as well do as many of those as possible.

WILL: It's sort of stupid to try to do something because it makes money if you don't need to make that money anymore. It's kind of insulting to the work that you're doing and to the people that you're trying to work with and the audience that you're trying to reach. It's like saying to them, "I want you to give me some more money."

You could do a bunch of volunteer work, but that's not necessarily what you're good at. You know what you're good at, so you've got to figure out how to do those things and not have it taken for granted, not feel like you're working your ass off and not getting anything back. You have to get something back.

SAM: But it might not be money.

WILL: No, it might not be money.

SAM: Big companies have budgets and financial goals but those don't have to be my personal goals.

WILL: It would make more sense, more karmic sense, if they spent their money trying to repair what they'd done specifically related to their industry. It makes more sense to say "Now I want to make this industry better for all," instead of "I want to create a museum." What the heck does a museum or a foundation to feed the poor have to do with railroads or oil or finance?

So, by that logic, you would probably pursue things that are related to craft beer and craft distilling because that's what you do. You're good at it and you want to continue to do it. I hate it when people become successful and say "Now I'm going to do what I really want to do."

SAM: It's like saying every day you were doing something you didn't like to make money.

WILL: Like the betrayals of the Jim Carreys and the Steve Martins of the world, or the Eddie Murphys, who say I made all this money being funny and now I'm going to do something else. And make more money. That's not fair to the audience. That's not why I gave them money. I gave you money because I thought you were funny. I thought you wanted to be funny.

SAM: Maybe a good way to say it is now that we've established our careers and the industries that we're pretty good at, how do we give back to the other people that are good in those industries?

WILL: I have a problem with the people who have success and then are confused in thinking that their success is based only on themselves. It never is. It's based on everything and everyone who helped them do what they did. I just think it's wrong to believe if somebody gives you a pile of money for something that you did, that you alone actually deserve it.

SAM: Amen.

chapter 9

OFF-CENTERED CAPITAL

partnering for the future

The craft brewing community is in the midst of a dramatic, turbulent transformation. We're still in a relatively early stage of this transition (think of it as the eerie quiet that precedes a violent summer thunderstorm), but I see the storm clouds gathering. As I described in Chapter 3, the beer business today is very different from when Dogfish Head started or even from the first craft marketplace shakeout in the late 1990s. What I didn't quite expect, though, was how fast the structure of and competitive-set within the beer industry would be changing, even during the course of writing this book.

Greg Koch, who founded Stone Brewing in 1996 and is one of the leaders of our industry, likens this zeitgeist moment to one of those colorful, packed-to-the-gills ancient buses you see in developing countries. With so many craft brewers now on the scene—on average, two new breweries are opening every day—the market is becoming oversaturated with supply. Greg describes the situation this way: "I've got a seat inside this bouncy bus, with a lot of other great brewers. But there's also many, many others precariously hanging out the door or perched on the roof. And the bus is about to hit a huge, jolting bump in the road!"

Another of my craft brothers, Larry Bell of Bell's Brewery in Michigan, which began selling beer in 1985, says, "Right now we are in the middle of the end of the beginning of the craft beer renaissance." What I believe he's referencing is the growing number of family-owned beer-centric breweries selling out control, or in some cases, entirely to foreign partners, venture capital groups, and the Budweiser/Miller/Etc. international conglomerates. At least when you look at the top-30 list of sizable American brewing companies, where the majority of the indie craft sales volume exists, the era when the craft industry was dominated by beer-passionate founder-entrepreneurs is coming to an end. Thank goodness there are thousands of smaller indie craft breweries who will adamantly stay indie.

Don't get me wrong. Craft beer isn't going to disappear. *Au contraire.* The more people taste it, the more its popularity will grow. But the structure of the industry is not going to be the same, and, as a consequence, that warm inviting brotherhood/sisterhood of craft brewers and drinkers that we all so treasure is at risk.

Profit is certainly not an ugly word; without it you don't get to hang around to make great beer for long. But the ugly undercurrent in this wave of change is that many of the new owners and entities are unabashedly, proudly, money-first-beer-second-oriented. Whether they directly acquire a brewery to contribute to the parent-company corporate balance sheet or are rolling up several breweries together for an eventual sale or IPO, financial engineering and return on capital are driving the process. While making great beer and building a community of great beer fans may still be on the radar screen somewhere down the priority list for some of these groups, when the rubber hits the road it's not the top priority.

Of the top 30 American craft breweries, we are now on a path where more than half will have completed some deal that took them from founder/entrepreneur control into something else. Some have gone the ESOP route—employee stock ownership—where the entrepreneur sells some or all of the company to employees. New Belgium, Deschuttes, Harpoon, and Odell have done this to varying extents. Typically, there are good things and bad things that can come from going the ESOP route. It can be great for internal culture—making everyone within the company aligned and entrepreneurial as they work together to hit goals that help the company and each of them personally as stockholders—but an ESOP can also saddle the company with substantial debt that eventually must be paid off to investors and can strangle cash flow and profitability. Other craft brewers have sold partial or total control to larger strategic partners. Founders Brewing Company sold 30 percent ownership to the Spanish brewer Mahou San Miguel. Firestone Walker, Ommegang, and Boulevard have all combined with Duvell Moortgat, a major publicly traded Belgian company. Fireman Capital Partners, which raised $132.8 million in private equity to create an entity called United Craft Brewing, proceeded two weeks after its Securities and Exchange Commission (SEC) filing to buy a majority stake in Oskar Blues, which then, in turn, bought Perrin Brewing. Meanwhile, A-B InBev owns Shock Top, Goose Island, Elysian, 10 Barrel Brewing, Golden Road, and part of Redhook. And Blue Moon is a wholly developed product of MillerCoors, which also bought 100 percent of Saint Archers Brewery in California. Heineken owns 50 percent of Lagunitas. And Constellation (Corona) owns 100 percent of Ballast Point Brewery.

As a brewer-entrepreneur who is hoping to keep his company family-controlled, this trend makes me uncomfortable but I understand its inevitability. Such is capitalism. And such is the desire for hardworking, successful people to monetize their success and find a clear pathway to stepping away from control and operations within the companies they founded. Let me be clear, I have great respect for many of the founders and employees of many of the companies who have made these transactions. And most of them wouldn't give a crap for my opinion of their business decisions anyway. Totally understandable and totally cool.

I understand that some founders don't want to consider keeping their companies family-owned for the second generation, or they have adult children who lack the desire or ability to carry on their interest. Founders need an exit to transfer out.

The coming shakeout will be unlike the first one we lived through in the late 1990s. This time we are no longer a bunch of friendly beer entrepreneurs, a group of peers rooting for each other and working together to grow the segment. Back then, we all looked and thought mostly the same way. The new order is hardly warm and cuddly. Some of the world's biggest corporations and money-motivated entities, corporate suits, and Wall Street denizens are now very much part of the scene, all facing considerable pressure to pay off debt associated with their acquisitions.

In many instances that translates into forcing fast growth, aggressive cost cutting (think premium ingredients), dumbing down brands, and ruthless "bugger-thy-neighbor" practices.

My commitment to Dogfish Head's independence and integrity, however, remains undiminished. If anything, the corporate character of the competition has heightened my passion for our beer, our coworkers, our customers, and our community. However, to thrive in this new landscape, to protect what Dogfish stands for, and to preserve our capabilities for remaining a family-controlled company, I knew we could benefit from bringing on external advisors and resources who could help us navigate this challenging moment.

I came to the realization about a year ago. Mariah, Nick, and I were doing a good job working together as executive leadership at Dogfish Head. Our three areas of strength are complementary, and during our formative years directing the company, we had demonstrated that we had all the brain capacity required to handle any situation or event confronting us; Mariah and I in the first decade of our explosive growth and Mariah, Nick, and I in the next decade. What became clear to me, though, was that what Dogfish had needed when it was a smaller company of 40 people managing smaller levels of production and distribution, with the leadership contributions of our talented internal team of managers, VPs, and coworkers, was no longer everything we needed as a company of 230 people and a large production and distribution system, with current volumes and growth plans. If we were to continue on our path of growth as a brand known for innovation, we would also need to become more capable at planning and execution, and we recognized that, in many ways, our organization was becoming unwieldy. Much of this growing unwieldiness was at my personal direction as I have driven the company to be dynamic with a spectrum of off-centered projects and business units. It was unrealistic to believe that the three of us could continue to figure out everything by ourselves. Internally, in managing the company, we needed help from people with knowledge and expertise that we didn't have. We needed to create a more comprehensive strategy internally ourselves, but we could also benefit from outside perspective and advice.

Meanwhile, the external competitive scene, as I noted, was quickly heating up. Predatory discounting had come to our world. Innovative products from indie craft breweries were being copied and pushed into the market by bigger breweries at a lower price and a faster clip. I have often said that Dogfish Head is not a discount brand, that consumers understand that our beer is worth what it costs in terms of ingredients, craftsmanship, and satisfaction. Having to compete on price instead of quality and distinction is a line in the sand I hope never to cross. It's contrary to everything I believe in. But if this is the way the business is heading, with big-company economies of scale enabling huge competitors to sell the beer they market as indie craft labels cheaply, Dogfish would need a more robust strategy and network of resources to stay as strong a brand as possible.

As I contemplated these challenges, an image of the best way forward frequently popped into my head. On the wall of our main conference room at the brewery in Milton is a magnetic wall with photos of each of our coworkers, every one of us (as up-to-date as possible), organized in clusters by departments. One reason they're there on that wall is so the leadership team (as well as anybody else who wants to look) gets to know the names and associate the faces of our coworkers with what they do at the company. There's also a second reason, which for me is even more important. When we gather there, for a Monday leadership meeting or for some special big-picture strategy discussion, the faces of the Dogfish Head family are there smiling down on us, as if to say, "Don't fuck up and make bad decisions—my livelihood is at stake." Truly, that feeling of responsibility is humbling and inspiring and stays at the forefront of my mind.

This decision to potentially work with more business-focused external advisers beyond the great board members and leaders we already had helping us grow strong would be a big leap forward into uncharted waters. With increasingly sophisticated, sometimes ruthless, competitors circling, Mariah, Nick, and I agreed that we needed to have more great business minds, who had helped companies navigate similar moments in other industries, advising us. Advising but not directing us. The Calagione family would keep control of the company. That was nonnegotiable.

The prompt to action came in the form of a call from an investment banker in late fall of 2015. Over the last 10 years investment bankers had contacted me many times, and I'm usually polite but get off the phone as quickly as I can, telling them that I want to keep Dogfish family-owned. This guy, Vann Russell, seemed different. He spoke knowledgeably about the industry. He was smart enough to say right off the bat that he knew that maintaining the Brewers Association definition of an indie craft brewery and retaining family control were critical to me. He mentioned that he had done other deals in the beer industry where Dogfish Head had come up in the conversation as a highly respected brand that seasoned successful companies wanted to work with, knowing we wanted to stay family-controlled. He got very specific, telling me that a much larger family-controlled brewery in Europe was interested in partnering with us.

After a couple of long phone calls discussing Dogfish and the changing landscape of the beer world, I talked through the options and opportunities with Nick and Mariah, to get their input and make sure that they agreed with me that we should at least start exploring the different options and deals that were out there, if only for the sake of being fully informed about what was going on. They did agree. Vann came to Delaware for a face-to-face meeting; we liked him. An agreement was structured in which he would set up meetings with all sorts of potential partners, help us navigate through those meetings, negotiate a deal if it got that far, and, should we accept an offer, get a percentage of the total. If there were no deal, we'd pay him for his time.

We continually reiterated, Dogfish Head wasn't in play; the company was not on the market, but we were open to hearing propositions about new external resources we could bring on board for a finite amount of time. One other thing I was emphatic about was that there was zero chance that we'd consider the Miller-Budweiser duopoly if we ever sought a minority partner.

The bath is always frothiest before the bubbles burst, and myriad rumors of pending deals were flying on the eve of the annual Craft Brewers Convention in Portland, Oregon. For the first time in my 20 years attending, the conference felt foreign to me. Instead of the social, friendly, altruistic hookup of beer geeks that I have always loved, this time the talk was about valuations. Breweries were being discussed as if they were merely kindling for deals. My description of the scene was quoted in an online beer industry blog: "There's a ridiculous amount of flirting going on between money people, big breweries, and foreign breweries. The Craft Brewers Convention is supposed to be about camaraderie, getting together with old friends, collaboration. Not the equivalent of the hookup app Tinder for bankers and brewers."

I returned from Portland more convinced than ever that defining winners and losers in the craft brewing community was going to become more challenging and nuanced. Within the coming half-dozen years, some of the breweries that are being fueled by the expectations of aggressive investors were going to have awesome growth trajectories. The public would likely see this popularity as confirmation of the brand's virtues. What they wouldn't know, though, was the extent to which these breweries were putting their destinies in the hands of people who don't necessarily care about long-term brand sustainability. Rather, in some cases, in their quest for short-term financial gains, they would be using these brands as strategic pawns in a game to disrupt the playing field and drive out true craft brewers.

We began to explore two basic scenarios. One option was to partner with a strategic partner, most likely another large craft brewer, domestic or overseas, whose strengths complemented ours. In this model, the tandem of Dogfish and Brand X ideally would be enormously attractive to distributors throughout the country, giving us considerable leverage to get in more stores and on more taps. The other route was to take on a more purely financial partner who would bring experience, knowledge, and resources to our board and as an external resource. These were mostly private equity groups, entities that organize funds using other people's money to invest in a company, intending to cash out with a premium on their investment within a fixed time frame of about 5 to 10 years. The exit strategies would usually be the sale of the company or a public offering. A family office is a variation of this, where the investors are not looking for a quick return, but are in for the long term.

As more of our craft brethren began taking these paths, we wanted to understand how things worked and what the effect of these deals would be on the commercial brewing landscape. From our perspective at Dogfish, taking on a minority equity partner needn't be innately evil, as long as we structured the deal to remain a true indie craft brewery, according to our association definition, and they understood our primary goal was to buy them out after a finite number of years and stay on our family-controlled course. Under the right circumstances, a partnership could offer Dogfish awesome opportunities for exporting, buying ingredients, and acquiring institutional knowledge. Certain partners even brought super powers in the form of expert analysts who could help us with sales distribution, branding, and operational efficiencies. But everything depended on the deal and the people.

Over the course of several months, we met with about 20 different groups. Some of these meetings were with other craft brewers where we explored how we might be able to pool resources and work together in interesting ways; some were with European and Asian brewers where we discussed international distribution; and some were with financial types and potential thought partners. The other side often came armed with binders full of data and analysis and presentations that they had done with consultants and focus groups about Dogfish Head. We learned a lot about how outsiders viewed our company and brand. What they thought we were especially good at and areas where they saw more opportunity for us. It was flattering to hear that we consistently ranked among the three or four strongest craft brewery brands in the country....We always made it clear in these meetings that our goal was to be the most off-centered high-end craft brewing company, not the biggest. Sure, we intended to grow, but we would do it in a controlled, conscious manner and never put the pedal to the metal to ramp up, chasing top line growth and market share to position the company for a future sale.

Of all the meetings we had, I am particularly pleased about one that *didn't* take place. An e-mail showed up in June, totally out of the blue. It was from the mergers and acquisitions head honcho at A-B InBev, telling me he was the guy who put together the Goose Island and Elysian deals and was currently scouting out craft beers in the mid-Atlantic region. He was in nearby Philadelphia; and he let me know he wanted to drive down to Milton to chat about domestic and international opportunities because he believed Dogfish Head was the right mid-Atlantic brewery to go under the ABI umbrella. My first reaction was disbelief. Not that they would consider Dogfish Head a target, as I'm sure they're targeting many craft breweries in the top 100. What shocked me was that he would think that I, after having been so outspoken about how bad it was for the indie craft beer community each time a global conglomerate non-craft brewery bought out another brewery, would possibly be interested. I called Nick over to my cubicle (we have open-space offices) to let him read the e-mail and then, in the fastest reply I've ever sent, responded, "I appreciate your interest in Dogfish but the Brewers Association definition of a craft brewery is dear to us so I am afraid there is no opportunity for a fit." I wanted to make sure they knew that no amount of their money could make me sell out Dogfish Head. With that, I deleted his e-mail.

The reason most of our meetings with private equity groups were short and we didn't meet with most of them a second time is that almost all of them had the same philosophy of why they wanted to invest in Dogfish Head and what their expectations would be. They wanted to help Dogfish grow as big as we could get as fast as we could get there. Most of them really didn't bring much added value to the table. Concurrently we discussed equity propositions that entailed aligning Dogfish with one or several other indie craft companies. A few private equity firms are in the middle of their plans for buying up as many as a half-dozen breweries and rolling them into a single entity in the hopes of bringing this combined entity toward an IPO. One group offered to make me the biggest single brewery shareholder and president of their roll-up. It was quite an honor. But I told them I wanted to focus my limited amount of time and energy on Dogfish Head and I knew our internal leadership team felt the same way. I like to collaborate and invent recipes with other craft brewers, but I don't want to wake up in the morning having to think about the coworkers' needs and the financial success of another brewery.

Months into the process, we were still leaning toward going it alone, with our existing internal team of leaders and external team of advisors and board members, which at the start we had all sort of assumed was what we'd end up deciding after hearing all the options. If we chose this status quo path, we could still arm ourselves by paying a big consulting firm to access their expertise on a fee basis with no need for an equity play, particularly in the expertise areas of strategy and operations. We'd have to pay a lot of money for this engagement, but wouldn't have to give up equity in our company. I called around to other company presidents and CEOs who had gone that route, but found that in general they didn't have a lot of positive things to say about the experience. The consulting people were bright, there was no doubt about that, but they had no incentive to deliver anything beyond the tightly focused, per-project work you asked of them. Their business model means they're financially disadvantaged if they give you even one more hour of access to their resources than their contractual obligation specifies.

We ultimately decided the right decision was to move forward and work with an organization that had great external resources but understood our plan for prioritizing strong brand growth over fast top-line growth: a group that would believe in and support our intention to stay family-controlled. We'd sell them a minority equity stake at the front end, but, in return, we'd have access to their organization's strong full-time resources, strategic insights, and experience in similar industries. We'd have aligned incentives to succeed. The better we did in terms of growing the brand strength organically instead of emphasizing top-line growth, the better the investor would do.

We were in a luxurious position when it came to picking and choosing. Some prospects in those early meetings wanted faster growth than we were comfortable with, or a primary path to an IPO, or an ultimate sale to an international conglomerate. They weren't for us.

By midsummer, the options were down to two thought partner oriented private equity groups who fit our specs. Nick, Mariah, and I spent a lot of time meeting and chatting with the leadership teams of both groups. On paper, there wasn't much difference between the two groups—both had great track records of helping high-end companies in industries similar to our own achieve their internally set growth goals, but in personal interactions we had a clear preference.

After many meetings and many long interviews with the CEOs and presidents of the private companies each of these two groups had invested in—to get their perspective—we decided to work with LNK because the firm brought considerable investment experience in areas relevant to Dogfish, like food and beverage consumer products companies and restaurants. LNK cofounder David Landau and his leadership team came to our meetings with Mariah, Nick, and I having clearly studied the beer industry. But he didn't try to impress us with his knowledge; he didn't come on like he was smarter than we were about where Dogfish Head could go in the marketplace. He was candid about his firm's strengths and weaknesses, which set the mood for spirited, informal conversations. We fell right into a friendly mode, exchanging ideas and discussing obstacles. Vann, our adviser on the deal, said that of all the meetings he had sat in between craft brewers and potential investors, he had never seen such a robust, positive, mutually respectful session between potential investor and company.

During subsequent meetings, we continued to be pleased by the LNK participants' knowledge and enthusiasm. They made specific suggestions about ways to expand and build our brand strength, and our distributing and retailing sales acumen—never telling us what we should do but rather making suggestions for us to consider. What most struck us, though, was how often, unprompted, their talk focused on values and principles. "Genuine," "ethical," and "honest" were words we used among ourselves to describe them. When Nick and I conducted due diligence interviews with the CEOs of other companies LNK had invested in, I heard the same comments: they were great business resources but they were also ethical, trustworthy people. LNK "got" Dogfish Head. They understood and agreed with our priority to grow strong rather than fast. They made it clear they didn't want to run our business but rather wanted to help us, the internal leadership team, run our business better. Our culture and their culture were in sync.

We were also excited about the quality of guidance LNK could put at our disposal. I'm a big believer that everybody has some special super power, and, in the case of LNK's people, they had super powers complementary to ours that would help us not only survive the increasingly competitive reality of the craft brewing industry but emerge as a considerably more potent company. With their guidance and added input, alongside our board members, we could put internal strategies in place that would, for example, enable Brewmaster Tim Hawn to more methodically connect production schedules to sales plans. Marketing Director Neal Stewart and our sales and marketing leaders would have LNK's knowledgeable consumer insights analysts ready to help.

Internally at Dogfish Head we were doing the hard and important work of getting our internal departments more in sync with each other. We knew we had to prioritize internal synchronicity before we could focus on syncing up with an external partner like LNK.

Mariah, the kids, and I took a vacation trip to Maine at this point, although I spent much of the vacation talking to different leaders who had worked with LNK. When we returned to Delaware, I knew the moment had come to fish or cut bait. I was sitting by myself in the conference room I mentioned earlier, pondering the right course of action, when I looked up at the pictures of all my coworkers who seemed to be saying, "Don't fuck up." I appreciated the uncertainty in taking on a private equity partner for a company whose whole history has been about being off-centered doing nontraditional things.

But as I scanned the faces on the wall, I understood that it would be a bigger fuck-up for us to just maintain the status quo. I was sure Dogfish Head would continue to grow and convert new fans even without an influx of private equity, but if we tried to do that, it would be more risky for all those people whose livelihoods were at stake. My mind was made up. We would do the deal.

So I'm going into this thing with my eyes wide open and thinking about what's best for Dogfish Head—the company, our leadership team, and all of our coworkers. I'm proud to say that we left no stone unturned in figuring out the best way to preserve our independence and strengthen our resources.

INTERVIEW

David Landau, Cofounder, LNK Partners

David Landau cofounded the private equity firm LNK Partners in 2005, and has more than 23 years' experience focused on investing in the consumer and retail sectors. LNK's founding partners have invested in, operated, or served on the boards of such premier companies as Staples, Inc., Phillips–Van Heusen Corporation, Panera Bread Company, Life Time Fitness, Inc., Au Bon Pain, and Levi Strauss & Co.

We chose LNK in large part because they presented themselves very differently from the stereotypical private equity firm. David Landau personifies that difference in his candor and recognition that treating people right, fairly, and with dignity is the first priority. Profit making is number two.

"You Have Taken on a Small Minority Investor Who Is Not Going to Tell You How to Make the Beer"

SAM: This book is aimed, not so much at the aspiring start-up entrepreneur, but rather at a leader who has already launched his or her business and is more focused on growing a sustainable business than surviving the start-up gauntlet. How would you and entities in the financial world define the difference between a small company and a mid-sized company?

DAVID: I would compare them in two dimensions. The first is the extent to which the business model is proven. How profitable is the company? Are the core economics demonstrated? An early-phase, small company is one that is still proving that it is going to survive amidst competition and find a niche that is sustainable. Most companies can't break through that ceiling. But those that can break through, that can go on to the next level, I consider those mid-sized companies. Survival is no longer the issue. At this stage, the questions are: How big can it get? How big do you want it to get? How profitable is it going to be?

The second dimension is to what extent the company is really surviving around an individual entrepreneur, and to what extent has it gone beyond that. Most mid-sized companies are still very influenced and driven by the founder, but he or she has also surrounded themselves with a team.

SAM: What is your definition of a viable company to invest in? Every industry, every investment is different, but what are the overarching factors?

DAVID: By far, the number one factor is the strength of the management team. Ultimately, it does come down to the person we are backing. The founder tends to be the lifeblood of the business, the DNA of the business, and, in mid-sized companies, a huge contributor to the business. At this size, the founder charts out the mission and tracks the team.

The second factor is if the company's core value proposition is strong, as manifested by a strong brand, or an emerging brand. Is the brand not only something we can be proud of, but also something that will create a lasting experience for the consumer? The brand must offer a strong value proposition that will withstand the buffeting of the economy. The brand has to withstand competition.

We also look at the core economics of the business when evaluating companies. Is the company financially viable? Can you make money in this industry? Does the business offer other significant growth opportunities?

SAM: I know that what gets you excited to get up every morning is the prospect of growing brands. That is a big reason that we decided to work together. We like that you spend more time on the people side than the brand side. Of course, in going from the start-up phase to the sustainable mid-size phase, brand strength and financial strength are what allow a viable business to stay viable. You can be a very busy mom-and-pop shop, but being busy isn't what makes it viable. It also has to be profitable and capable of long-term growth. That is just the nature of business.

What are the most important financial metrics when you look at a company? Is it cash flow? Is it liquidity? Is it a product-by-product analysis?

DAVID: The overarching macro question is "What creates economic value?" What will be the measurable value of the company down the road? Some companies go public, some companies are sold. However a company is going to be valued, how is the company performing and how will it eventually perform against those metrics? That's the macro take.

Usually, for us, companies are valued by EBITDA, as it approximates cash flows. We are also looking at sales growth, and the underlying economics of the business. A lot of the businesses we invest in will make a conscious decision to significantly invest in growth, which can depress earnings for a period of time. We look to invest anticipating increased earnings over the long term.

SAM: It is our primary intention to keep Dogfish a family-owned, family-controlled company for decades to come. How was your decision to invest in us affected by our plan to stay a family-owned company, as opposed to a company that is heading for an IPO or is particularly interested in monetizing our Calagione family majority-stake investment?

DAVID: Most private equity firms say they don't have a formula, but they have an implicit formula in their minds. There is an understanding that when the firm makes an investment, the company is getting on a train to maximize value as quickly as possible. It is almost an assumed language. We never had that. Not because we are better than other firms, but because every company we've chosen to invest in has a very special situation with a unique, outstanding entrepreneur. We want to back the best people, and the best people have many options and are smart enough to realize that. So for us, it has never been about assuming that there is an implicit path. We know that these unique founders are where much of the company's value comes from, and so we spend time with the people that we're backing, in order to fully understand what it is they really want to do and how we can help them get there.

Now, we are not doing this philanthropically. If the path that they want to take is one that won't result in us making money, we will simply shake hands, say thanks, it has been great getting to know you, make no investment, and move on. That happens a lot.

SAM: Most of the time? Most of the companies that you talk with?

DAVID: The vast majority of companies that we talk to. In fact, people who introduce us to companies are amazed how quickly we say "no." We are probably the quickest no and we are probably one of the groups who say no the most. We have a very clear view of what we want and what we don't want. We set a very high bar in terms of management, a very high bar in terms of value proposition and brand. We also are very focused on creating quality partnerships. If a company is selling out, we have no interest.

With Dogfish, the more that you and the people around you said, "We are not selling out. We are doing this differently," the more we were interested. It probably would have scared most equity firms, but we kept saying, "Great, this is our kind of guy!"

From the beginning, you said, "Look, we have to assume we are not going to ever go public, and we are not ever going to sell" and that is how we have gone into the situation. It focused the mind. We had to make a single decision: is there a way to do this where we can all win? If there is not, we will step away. Given the uniqueness of the team and the uniqueness of you, Sam, and the uniqueness of the brand, we decided it is worth trying.

In a lot of ways, actually, we use the process as an indicator of what the partnership would be like. One thing we know is that when you enter into a partnership, it never goes exactly as planned, but if you're with the right people, you never look backwards. You are in there together, figuring it out together, and in our experience over 20 years, there has always been kind of a right way to deal with anything that comes up.

We don't want to work with wrong or incompatible partners. So we used our conversations with the Dogfish team as an opportunity to learn, and our experience was the more we talked about the issues, the more we felt comfortable. For us the key is not the formula. The key is finding a fit that makes sense.

SAM: You've said that the issues at Dogfish are predictable for companies of our size with engaged management. What are the most common issues?

DAVID: I would say young, growing companies express it in different ways, but they tend to lay the railroad tracks right before the railroad gets there. They are just trying to keep up. To keep up the infrastructure and the systems and the processes of the company with the growth of the business. I would say this applies to nearly every business we have partnered with. Not every company, but almost every one. It's the key issue most mid-sized companies face.

Dogfish is a great example. You guys know how to make beer, how to sell beer. Marketing, sales, and product development is terrific. That said, there are increasing challenges along the way. The world is getting more competitive. In every industry, people are facing that, and it's a big reason that we're brought into companies. Management teams want another group at the table who has experience with competition and growth. It's not that we have all the answers, but we're a thought partner in figuring this out.

In almost every case, the company recognizes that they have grown so much, their back end needs to catch up, or at least continue to evolve. With Dogfish, we've talked with you and your leadership team about tying all the elements together, from sales planning and demand forecasting, all the way back through production, and managing distributors and retail relationships through to producing and the supply chain.

We see that regularly. It is not always to the same extent that Dogfish has been fortunate to be supply constrained, but we have seen a number of companies that have been supply constrained. In almost all cases, it is just when you are going from a small company to a mid-sized company to a larger mid-sized company. That is the transition that companies go through. None of the companies we've worked with are asking us to sell their core product. That's not our value add. One of the things we see often is companies with too many opportunities, who need our help to focus and prioritize. That is clearly a theme with Dogfish, and is clearly a theme with most of the companies we invest in.

Another common issue that we see is difficulties with the management transition; in early phases, companies typically depend heavily on the entrepreneur. By the time we get involved, most companies have built out a solid team around the entrepreneur, but they still recognize that the team needs to continue to evolve.

SAM: At Dogfish, our situation is unique because I find the most joy in contributing to the creative process and being out there as the analog representative of Dogfish: a leader in innovation and customer and retailer engagement more than an internal leader of management teams. In this context, what is your recommendation for me as the entrepreneur, the founder? What do you see as the value I bring to Dogfish and how do we make sure that works with the value Nick and Cindy and our other leaders bring to Dogfish?

DAVID: For a company at Dogfish's size, there needs to be a heart and soul of the business, a whole culture, and a whole group of people who buy into that. Somebody has to be the core leader of that business, in terms of culture and in terms of the DNA. As strong as Dogfish is financially, and in sales and branding, it's a competitive marketplace and brands are fragile. We chose to partner with Dogfish because you, Sam, were completely committed to playing a massive role in the company's future. That role can evolve, but we wouldn't do it without you. As you know, we asked the question several different ways, several different times to help us understand your commitment. Having you out there. as the face of the brand, is critical.

You have navigated from zero to here, in terms of finding your way and building Dogfish. Undoubtedly, you made mistakes along the way, as every entrepreneur does. But through passion and commitment, humility and hard work, you figured it out, and we're betting that you'll continue to do so.

Frankly, if we were to consider the biggest risks of this investment, we could talk about competition, but really, when push comes to shove, we would say the biggest blow to this company would be if Sam left. Of course, everyone else in the company is essential, as is the brand. But you, Sam, are a huge upside for us.

SAM: I appreciate that. We discussed my commitment that my level of engagement is not going to go down. That said, we all recognize that, in terms of long-term brand equity, it is also important that this company lives beyond me. I have to be conscious of taking Dogfish in that direction, while still knowing my value as the brand ambassador. It is an interesting line for me to walk. I have to give more responsibility and autonomy to the other leaders on my team now, if there is going to be a smooth transition between this generation of the Calagione family and the next generation of family leadership and management leadership. At the same time, this baton will be more authentically and smoothly passed if Mariah and I are the face of the company while we pass it to the next generation (assuming either or both of our children are willing and capable).

DAVID: Exactly, and at the scale you're at, you can't transition the company by yourself; it just won't work, and you don't necessarily have all of the skills to do so. So having a great team is part of the art of building a business. You have to figure out how to give more autonomy, and get the right pieces in place, while also making sure the culture remains strong enough. There is no formula to that process. I am sure you, like all entrepreneurs, have made mistakes, and will continue to make mistakes.

One of the ways that LNK can support Dogfish is in helping you see around corners. We can say, "Hey, have you thought about this? Would it be helpful if you had another person in here? You think that person is cool, but are they really going to be a fit?" Of course, you already spend a lot of time thinking about these things, but it's another area that we can help.

SAM: As you are helping entrepreneurs and founders flesh out strong leadership teams, are there filters or priorities that can apply across industries in regard to hiring? Who are the key people with whom founders should surround themselves, to get from the entrepreneurial phase into the mid-size strategic growth phase? In your experience, are there patterns to the positions needed to support that entrepreneur?

DAVID: Ninety percent of my answer is that it is situation specific. But I think there are a couple of themes. One macro theme is that the people who get the company to a certain level sometimes aren't the people to take it to the next level. This isn't something we're seeing at Dogfish, but at other companies, often the people who launched the business don't have the experience base or an ability to expand beyond a certain level. Bringing in a new team member, in addition to them or on top of them, can be important. Changing the team can be a difficult and painful experience for most entrepreneurs because they tend to be fiercely loyal to those original folks. It is a tough thing to work through.

Breakthroughs tend to happen when the entrepreneur can find people who can take them to another level, who are a cultural fit and can be trusted. In other businesses we've been involved in, that person is often the CFO; a strong, experienced CFO that the entrepreneur can trust to open their eyes to things that they never thought of can be very important. I am not sure that is the case here.

SAM: Just to interject and give due credit to Nick, we are very lucky that we have a CEO who was our CFO. Nick has a brilliant financial mind and a great team. I agree with you; that is not our situation.

DAVID: Operationally, most of the entrepreneurs that we have seen are, at their core, marketing-sales-product development people who have made sure the operations work because they need to. But that is not really their thing. Having a team member strong in operations has been very helpful to them. Often by the time we get involved, the operations strategy, from the founder's standpoint, is "We are going to create value by selling a great, innovative product, so just make it work. Just make it work without mistakes."

SAM: Without drama.

DAVID: Right. Without drama. They say to themselves, "At the end of the day, it is going to cost us more because we are inefficient operationally, but I can create a new product line so I am not going to sweat that." I think that is the theme we have seen. But as you grow you get to a point where the numbers get bigger and the risks get bigger. Increasing the operational prowess, which I know Dogfish has invested in, becomes even more important.

SAM: Besides making sure, on behalf of the investors, that you are checking every box, studying a company from the financial end, and auditing our numbers, you're also getting to know our leadership team. What was your goal in our first meeting, not just with Nick and Mariah and myself, but with the leadership team as a whole?

DAVID: The number one goal was to get to know them. We wanted to ensure that the strength of that next layer was what we hoped it would be to support and grow the business.

We also wanted to see how they interacted with each other. Frankly, seeing their level of candor with us and each other was very important, because we are not going to be here in the same building or state with you most of the time.

We asked them not only about what they do, but also about the things that worry them, the challenges, the opportunities. We spent the most time on the challenges. Not from a negative perspective, but instead from a very practical, positive, forward-looking viewpoint. Although many firms in our shoes may have felt nervous about that, we were actually comforted. One, because they didn't bullshit us. They didn't try to put on a happy face, which is really important. Two, they weren't bullshitting themselves, in making believe that things were better than they were. Three, they weren't saying it from the perspective of anxiety or pessimism. Instead, they expressed thoughtful concerns that let us know they think about the business, see great things for it, and know what needs to be done to ensure growth and success in the future. It was great and is exactly how we talk to our investors.

We walked away knowing that your team had a sense of urgency, particularly on the operations side, as well as with the marketplace stuff. That is, in our view, a good dynamic. In our experience, many things that the next layer of management will push top leadership to do are dead on. In fact, I can't think of a circumstance where they have not been done right. Of course, the timing and the calibration of how it happens is really up to the top leadership; prioritizing those things is what you guys get paid to do.

Although there was urgency, there was no panic from the team. Their thinking was that if we don't develop the process from sales planning all the way through, there will be negative repercussions sooner rather than later. Not tomorrow, but sooner rather than later. That has a dramatic impact on the business, as lead times really matter.

SAM: Communication also really matters, in every phase from raw ingredients through retail marketing. We want the way that we communicate to be consistent and robust. We need to focus on more harmonic and better articulated communication both internally with coworkers and externally with retailers, distributors, and beer-loving consumers.

DAVID: We recognize that over the next phase, over five or ten years, as the business grows and the industry changes, Dogfish will evolve and may go through large changes. There may be turbulence in the business. So the ability to handle the operational side of things before any shift is a move that will really benefit the company.

SAM: Our goal is to look further ahead down the track, so that we can build a bridge over that abyss in advance, instead of building the track rail-by-rail and then suddenly getting to the edge. That is really why we want a thought partner who is also a minority equity holder, to help us accelerate our ability to look beyond that abyss. A partner who is aligned with our goals and feels the rewards when we hit our goals.

DAVID: Companies are making telling decisions in the craft beer industry right now. It seems that a number of entrepreneurs who have taken on private equity are pumping up growth and have decided to move rapidly toward an exit.

SAM: Growth that is not necessarily healthy. It's often top-line revenue growth.

DAVID: Exactly. In the short term, top-line revenue growth will reward them handsomely, assuming the financial markets continue as they are. But those markets are not going to continue forever and I would argue that some companies are not laying the tracks appropriately. A lot of breweries have sold out to the big guys and they will be solidified operationally, but likely, that will be at the cost of the authenticity that got them there. I think Dogfish is taking a really courageous and intelligent path.

SAM: We don't want to sell. It's a perfectly valid option for companies with other goals, but for us, it's important to pass Dogfish down to the next generation, and maintain the off-centered philosophy that got us here.

DAVID: Absolutely. You have chosen family ownership. You have taken on a very small minority investor, who is not going to tell you how to make the beer. You are maintaining your authenticity, but seeking outside council and resources.

By the way, LNK shouldn't take full credit for the evolution that the company undergoes when we are investors, because they have gone through the process themselves of identifying that they need to evolve. Are we helpful in that evolution? Yes, I think we are. We are there to help and to ask questions. But I don't know there is as much causality there as we are given credit for. The founders and their teams are really the ones doing it. The fact that you are willing to go through this whole process, and the soul-searching involved, says to me you are committed to this evolution. We will be helpful, but we are not going to drag you into it. We are there to support you, along the ride.

SAM: We spent a ton of time talking with CEOs and leaders of companies that you have invested in. The common themes that we talked about were not focused on contributions to that company's financial growth or bottom line. Instead, they usually revolved around their pleasant surprise to the ethics, the principles, and the humility that LNK brings to the table.

I know you are a man of faith. For me, there is no real difference between goodness and godliness. We have a respectful separation of church and state at our company. If you treat people the way you want to be treated, goodness comes of that, in business and in life. Can you talk about how you apply that goodness?

DAVID: We definitely don't bring our specific faith directly into the business world. But our principles, we do bring. We seek out partners that have impeccable integrity, impeccable values, and are just good people. We don't want to put ourselves at risk by being with people that we don't trust in that regard. We are not at the extreme of sacrificing all financial considerations just to be good guys, but we are willing to make trade-offs to do the right thing. We are not going to ask our partners or our investors to spend their money for causes that we like. We are a for-profit business. But there are ethical ways in our view to operate. If you have to part ways with someone, there is a way to do that in a care-full manner that respects them as a human being and doesn't put their reputation or family at risk.

SAM: These practices may not be financially savvy or legally mandated, but that's the least that you do for those folks.

DAVID: That's right. We want to do the right thing and we want our partners to do the right thing. We are very open with our own investors about how we do business, and they may choose to look at it in one of two ways. They could think that is not short-term greedy, that is long-term greedy. We are going to get a great reputation and people are going to want to work with you, and you are going to have good karma and you are going to make more money. If that is how they want to view it, that is fine. But that is not why we do it. We do it because we firmly believe that you get one trip around in this life, and we are not only here to maximize the last nickel. If anything about us surprises people, it will be in a boardroom when we talk about doing what's fair, and they're expecting us to make a purely financial argument.

We're not trying to give away free money. We are trying to do the right thing. We want to put our heads on the pillow at night and know we contributed to goodness in the world that day.

SAM: Thanks, David.

chapter 10

DECADE THREE AS AN OFF-CENTERED LEADER

While writing this book, Dogfish Head celebrated its twentieth anniversary. When I think about where we've come since I concocted my first batch of home brew in a cramped New York City apartment, I sometimes shake my head in disbelief. And pride. And humility. What an incredible life journey this has been. But as the company begins its third decade, I'm well aware of how much more there is for me to learn and experience if I am to continue developing as a leader.

As I often repeat, my mission is to see Dogfish Head go forward as a family-owned company, assuming my son, Sammy, and/or daughter, Grier, are interested in grabbing the torch from Mariah and me. Like any parent, we want them to have happy and exciting lives, regardless of what they choose to do when they grow up. Even if they are not interested in continuing in the business, Mariah and I are in our mid-forties and have many years in front of us to contribute to this company. Either way, the next 10 years represent the critical decade to set up Dogfish Head for the best opportunity to transition from a first-generation to a second-generation company.

I believe this family-owned/family of coworkers stance is deeply woven into our company's DNA and thus, during the next phase of our history, it's going to be critical that Mariah and I retain our roles as the voices and faces of the company. A big reason for our success is that the beer community and the local community see us as a team. She's very strong in the community-building (online and real world) and nonprofit initiatives, and I focus on innovating off-centered projects and events. We see how much people appreciate the husband-and-wife leaders and the team of leaders we have built around us, keeping this not-so-little-anymore company going. Should the moment come for us to phase out our mom-and-pop worklife in favor of the next generation, it will be critical that our coworkers and the marketplace understand that our kids have been well mentored in their preparation for growing roles. Were Mariah and I to step away from personifying the brand and put somebody else in that outward-facing position, the changing of the guard would be a lot more awkward and difficult. It will feel more authentic if we can carry this baton all the way through our leg of the race and then hand it to Sammy and/or Grier. And if they choose career paths outside of Dogfish Head, we will hand this baton to whatever group we think is best capable of shepherding our brand and community most gracefully.

I'll stay very active as the public face of the company for more personal reasons, too. Our fans and customers expect me to be in that role, and serving them and building these relationships is important to me. I truly enjoy hanging out with folks who love Dogfish Head, be they customers, distributors, or retailers. Making off-centered ales with off-centered people and sharing off-centered ales with off-centered people are my favorite things to do.

With the business becoming more competitive, our customers expect higher levels of performance from us. Nick, as CEO, is the guy most responsible for making sure we deliver on those expectations and grow sales volume. He has to reassure them that we're up to any challenge. Nick understands that, as CEO, he has to go deeper into our sales and distribution business than he did as COO. And I understand that his way of doing this will be different from mine. He's making great steps analyzing data and trends that I never looked at, and giving more guidance and input to our sales planning and execution as well.

This past year, 2015, has been especially challenging because we have been without a vice president of sales for most of it. Our outgoing sales VP left Dogfish to follow his heart, moving to the Midwest to be with his love. We had certain "must have" credentials in our search for his successor: national leadership experience in a past role at a brand bigger than ours so that the new VP would bring experience grander than ours; great cultural fit; and somebody who would love to live on the rural Delaware coast. None of us ever expected it would take eight months to hire that person, and, frankly, that was too long for a company of our scale to go without a sales VP. I'm glad that we held out for the ideal candidate, but the long wait cost us some momentum and attention with certain distributors. Our direct customers are our distributors.

The experience, though, has taught me much about the evolving shift in responsibility on my personal leadership journey. One lesson learned is that helping the other leaders at Dogfish find and hire the right person for an empty key position goes straight to the top of my to-do list until it's filled. It's a top priority just behind our work on strategic planning and our need to stay innovative. My responsibility as a leader is to make sure that in the future we don't get distracted when we have a similar situation with an open position and that we put everything we have into getting the right person into that job as quickly as possible.

The second big lesson I've learned from this experience is what my role must be while that key position is unfilled. If you have a vacant leadership position that is critical to your company's business execution, you have to make sure the other leaders keep communicating well with each other about who is filling in which gaps. We kind of coasted on the momentum of the past 10 years while the sales VP job was vacant, and I, as leader, didn't do a great job holding my coleaders accountable for still hitting what we had budgeted to achieve in sales. The damage wasn't insurmountable; we're still growing revenue and unit sales over last year, which is testimony to the strength of our brand. But we as a team and I as a leader have to realize that we underperformed in terms of communicating with each other during this period about how critical it was that we move fast to fill the position and also cover the gaps until we filled it, and that hurt the company.

My new leadership role is a work in progress for me. I'm learning along the way. Sometimes I do well, sometimes less well.

Our newest restaurant, Chesapeake & Maine, has long been a dream for me. In the same way we look for unexplored niches in beer and spirits, I saw an unexplored niche for a restaurant theme that would combine my loves of the bounty of the Maine coastal waters and those of the Chesapeake region. Most readers familiar with the East Coast can probably visualize what an awesome indigenous menu would look like at a lobster shack in Maine, with fried clams and New England white chowder, and the quintessential Chesapeake crab shack with Old Bay–infused crab cakes and hush puppies. But nobody has combined these two regional cuisines with an off-centered flair under one roof.

From my house in Lewes, Delaware, I look out at a harbor that is an estuary to the same Atlantic Ocean that I see from the window of my house in Maine. And when I am not working, I am my happiest with family and friends on the water and at the beach. Many who buy our beer think that Dogfish Head is a whimsical, fun, but kind of random name. They don't know it's also a real place where I spent my summers growing up in Maine, near Boothbay Harbor. I love the intensity of nature up there. Dogfish Head is a jut of land on a rocky island with steep cliffs so that in many areas, literally within feet, you go from bracing, cold water into pine forest. There is no town on the whole island, just a store and a few restaurants. During the day the air is intensely clear and clean and smells of nature and trees and salt; at night the sky is brilliant with stars. I identify Dogfish Head as a brand with an intense and palpable immersion in the rawest forms of nature: the sea, the woods, and the wilderness.

My goal in conceptualizing Chesapeake & Maine was to connect these two loves of mine, to connect the origin story of Dogfish Head with the locale of our brewery. I wanted a project that allowed people coming to coastal Delaware to experience the home of Dogfish Head the brand. This was the vision.

I had never heard of a restaurant that specifically combined these two regional cuisines, one centered around a creative take on a menu of Maine and Chesapeake classics. What a perfect concept, thought I, to complement the traditional wood-grilled food we serve at our existing Rehoboth Brewpub. And then a building became available right next door to Dogfish Head Brewings & Eats, and it was game on.

I knew we had a built-in audience for seafood: our location is literally blocks from the Atlantic ocean in our state's biggest vacation town and we had been losing customers at the pub all summer long who didn't want to wait an hour and a half for a table. I'm delighted that Dogfish Head lovers are checking out other restaurants in Rehoboth, but if every busy night we're turning away 100 people because our brewpub is too full, it would be nice to give them another Dogfish experience. I also saw that Chesapeake & Maine would neatly fit into our business strategy, with a bar outfitted to be the main stage for a world-class cocktail business to highlight our emerging line of scratch-distilled spirits.

So far, so good. I proposed the idea: Chesapeake & Maine would be a concept driven directly by me that combined our two Dogfish Head brand home geographies. I should have left my conceptual direction at that high-level concept when I brought the proposal to our leadership team. That's what the new Sam is going to try to do in situations like this. But I didn't. Instead, I had meetings with my friends who fish for lobsters and oysters. I told the fishermen around Southport Island, where Dogfish Head is, that we were going to buy their seafood for the restaurant, whatever was of the highest quality and consistency available. There was a good reason I did this. I envisioned that a critical component in a compelling story about C&M would be that the lobsters were coming from traps within sight of the actual Dogfish Head piece of land and my summer home and that I felt a personal connection with the food being served. Similarly, I chose some of the Chesapeake oystermen and fishermen we would buy from based on my personal connections to them.

By imposing my plan to provision the restaurant with seafood caught by personal friends, I ended up throwing a monkey wrench into the start-up process. Other company leaders admitted that my heavy-handedness made it hard for them to get excited about the project. Rather than asking them to help create a cool way into a menu, I had simply told them what we would serve. Had I sought their input, we would have tried to figure out which existing distribution businesses are out there specializing in high-quality seafood from Maine and Chesapeake, and then let the leaders at Dogfish Head who would oversee that business unit develop our plans accordingly. Instead, I told them, "I expect you to buy from specific lobstermen and oystermen." I learned that there was some coworker frustration around having to spend a considerable amount of time figuring out seafood shipping logistics from Sam's boyhood friend's lobster pound.

I don't regret standing up for this option, and I am hopeful that it will prove to bring a level of differentiation and distinction to C&M. The seafood we are sourcing is truly world-class. Still, I could have done a better job internally on being more inclusive with fleshing out the key components of this project and involved coworkers earlier in the conceptualization process. I was frustrated that the other leaders didn't see why this direct connection to specific fishermen was so critical for me and made C&M different from just another seafood restaurant using the same seafood suppliers as the restaurant down the street. But I had myself to blame for not doing a better job of selling the importance of this point of differentiation to the rest of our team.

What do I now wish I had done in keeping with my commitment to prioritize collaborative leadership? The right thing would have been to request that the business unit leaders choose the right purveyors on the right two-region-specific criteria and ask them to explore the viability of working with some of my fishermen friends and other fishermen-direct entities they would identify for themselves.

Now I'm involved in the menu development of Chesapeake & Maine only as a sounding board. I still share ideas with the chef and general manager, like "How about beer-infused oyster sauces or chocolate lobster beer to help tie into the opening?" Or I'll read a story about a grilled fish dish and suggest we might be able to adapt it to an off-centered version with a beer reduction sauce. When I had an idea in the old days, I'd make it clear I expected it on the menu by a specific date. Now I ask them to simply explore it. If they want it, okay. If they don't want it, I'm okay with that, too. I got a lot of enjoyment out of participating in the menu development component of Chesapeake & Maine in a creative supporting role instead of a lead role. I enjoyed taking the lead creative role on less complicated project components like creating the jazz-and-old-school-country playlist and selecting all the artwork and commissioning artists who did original sculptures and paintings for Chesapeake & Maine. I know I am making small steps in the right direction when I get as much joy out of participating in creative projects in a support role as I do in a lead role. It's not easy for an entrepreneur to give up some of these brand-oriented decisions, but surrounding yourself with talented people and letting them take the lead with guidance, one project at a time, is the best way to go.

I have done a better job of playing a support role from the start of a project with our new distillery than I did with Chesapeake & Maine. In the past few years small batch distilled spirits have emerged as a growing market, attracting the same kinds of passionate loyalty as craft beer. Craft distilling as a broad market is still pretty new. The spirits business, much like the beer industry, continues to be dominated by corporate giants. In that world, the difference between two kinds of Big Company gin, for example, has less to do with flavor or ingredients and more to do with image, packaging, and marketing. Small, independent distillers, who now number over 800, are responsible for much of the innovation and growth in the sector. Demand for craft spirits, like that of indie craft beer, continues to dramatically grow year to year.

Experts have various explanations for why craft spirits are gaining market share. One theory is that federal government advertising restrictions for spirits have loosened in the last decade, allowing spirits brands to compete head-to-head with hyper-marketed beer brands. Another theory is the *Mad Men* effect, the popular cable series about advertising executives set in the 1960s that made it look retro cool to drink spirits. Pop stars and celebrities are now willing to partner with spirits brands, something they didn't previously do, as television now permits distilled alcohol advertisements. Another theory is that the flavor preferences of millennials are diverging from those of their elders; having grown up with Snapple, a myriad of sports drinks, and flavored vodka, they have a palate for diversity. As is true with beer, younger spirits drinkers want authentic products made by real people. If it's local, so much the better (although the *terroir* benefit is less than with beer). Craft drinkers are willing to pay a premium when they believe in a brand; they'll spend more for it even when the Big Company competition costs less. All these factors together have opened up an expanding market for a new generation of independent, entrepreneurial distillers.

About 13 years ago, back when it was just Mariah and me as the leadership team of Dogfish Head, I decided to open a small craft distillery within our existing brewpub in Rehoboth. Just as we had to change the laws in Delaware to open the first brewery, we also had to change the laws to be able to distill. I saw early on that, in the same way we had established our own version with beer, we could do it with spirits. It was a complementary industry where we could get in early and be an innovator.

Unlike beer, though, we were much more physically restricted in growing the distillery business because I made the decision early on to house it in a small upstairs room within the restaurant's dining room space. I walled the distillery off with a big plate glass widow facing the dining room. Even though we started super tiny, during the past two decades we have become really good distillers. When we started this project I worked on everything—initial recipes, buying and helping to design the distilling equipment, concepts for our spirits, packaging—while my coworkers were becoming acclimated to taking more day-to-day operational roles in our distilling business.

The company is in a position now to launch one or two big new projects every year or so. The entire Monday Team was involved in deciding what we wanted to do in 2015. This was before the Nick meeting where my "founder's syndrome" was discussed, but even then I was conscious of not wanting to force the choice in any direction but rather leave it up to the group's discretion. They collectively committed to expanding the distillery outside of the restaurant. We made the decision to build a nice distillery on the campus of our Milton production brewery and hire the right people to run it.

Dogfish Head has been distilling spirits since 2002. Dogfish Head was the second brewery in the United States to open a distillery. We created rums with nontraditional ingredients like honey, orange, and coriander; our rums have always been made from scratch from house-fermented molasses. We also made our Blue Hen vodka with infused flavors that varied by the season and my whim; and Jin (as in gin), distilled with botanicals, including juniper berries, cucumbers, and whole-leaf hops. I'm pretty sure our Jin was the first hop-forward spirit commercially brewed in America. Unlike our from-scratch rums, when we first began doing gins and vodkas, we skipped a step in the distilling process because we didn't have enough space for all of the necessary fermenting equipment. Rather than start at the first stage, we, like many other distillers, bought grain neutral spirits in 55 gallon drums for our gin and vodka, and then added flavors and bottled it. I was never excited enough to promote these spirits outside our walls, because, while we got to experiment and make them our own, starting with an existing product rather than starting from scratch meant they were not as authentically homemade as our beers, food, and rum. Now, however, we're putting in the people, staff, and resources to do a distillery the right way—where every liquid we produce will be done from scratch.

We've decided to launch the distillery business with a brand-new take on vodka. Vodka is an awesome challenge because, by definition, it's supposed to be odorless and flavorless or with very subtle fruit flavors. So how do we make a spirit that is off-centered when it is supposed to be odorless and flavorless? Our creative approach is to use a flavor-forward blend of beer brewer's grains to make our wash (the pre-distilled fermentable liquid that is the base for our vodka and gin), which will give it a rich earthy sweetness in the taste. By fermenting the wash for our vodka with our proprietary Doggie ale yeast, the aroma of the vodka will have subtle fruit and pepper notes. This delicate sweetness will make it distinctive from odorless and flavorless competitors.

If I were taking the lead on our 2.0 distillery project, I would have likely been inclined to launch this new business with something intensely flavorful and exotic, but the other leaders and business managers agreed it would be best to launch with a more off-centered take on the conventional spirit classes of vodka and gin and then release some more experimental spirits a year or so later. Walk before we run and put our storytelling powers around how great these from-scratch spirits taste instead of around stories of spirits so exotic they wouldn't fit into categories like vodka and gin. The Monday Team has a solid collective rationale for starting with a more approachable product first; I listened and learned and bought in.

The process of coming to market has taken longer than we expected and, in truth, longer that I might have liked. Part of the reason for this delay is inherent in the collaboration process itself. Consensus is slow moving. We have spent months in preparation, endless meetings to decide things like packaging and the verbiage on labels. In the old days, this would have taken a day or two of me sitting in a room working on the design and verbiage either by myself or with a designer. This time there have been lots of checkpoint steps in the launch process.

It's easy for me to contrast this methodical, time-intensive development with the more manic, resource-intensive process of launching the beer-centric food projects we released a few years ago. In the new distillery project the big difference is that, unlike with food, there's now a sense of ownership from everybody involved. Getting buy-in when we go into operation mode won't be a problem because the right people were brought into the process at the right moments of the evolution of the project, from concept to launch.

This whole episode of my journey, which I've been fortunate enough to explore in a more analytical way by writing this book as it unfolds, is providing me with the opportunity to intensely engage in self-appraisal. I'm known as an outgoing, super-social extrovert. As I once told a friend who was just discovering the pleasure of 60-Minute IPA, "There's a lot of fun in that beer!" That phrase could make a pretty good tagline for my public life. When I host events or do beer education films or projects, I always try to inject some humor and levity to show that although we take beer and spirits very seriously at Dogfish Head, we don't take ourselves too seriously. There's a more critical and serious side to my personality as well, one that few coworkers or beer lovers ever see. It's an introspective mode that slips through the cracks of my hyperactivity, stuff that I think about in the middle of the night: concerns about whether I'm doing right by the people I love, by my coworkers, by the communities I'm part of. I don't see myself as a selfish guy, but I have come to accept that I am often so lost in Dogfish Head obsession that I am inattentive to the needs and concerns of those around me. Not insensitive, just oblivious.

Here's a telling example of what I'm talking about. When my daughter Grier was a lot younger, I'd suggest sometimes that it would be a fun thing for us to paint together. We'd get out the brushes and jars and gather the art supplies and arrange ourselves around the kitchen table. She'd paint dolls or flowers or rainbows. And I'd paint sketches for Dogfish Head beer labels or T-shirt designs. She's now 13, and recently I proposed we again paint together. She answered, with the painful honesty of a teenage girl, "You mean I can just sit there and watch you work? If you're asking me to do that, no thanks." It was funny. And it wasn't.

So in the next stage of my development as an off-centered leader, I'm looking to prioritize those non-Dogfish aspects of my life that I've too often put on the back burner. I'm forcing myself to go outside the comfort zone I've inhabited for the past two decades, where nearly every waking hour of my day has been filled with Dogfish-centric thoughts and activities. Pretty much every summer I make it a point, with Mariah and Sammy and Grier, to take a few days and go up to Dogfish Head, the jut of land near Boothbay Harbor in Maine. As part of my new commitment to personal and family life, I've started making it a goal to spend a few weeks there in the summer, instead of a few days. When I'm there, I get to spend time with my boyhood friends who are lobstermen and fishermen. Although I don't love fishing myself, I'm happy when I'm on a boat or paddleboard on the water.

Until recently I would still spend a few hours on each of my "vacation days" checking e-mail, making a couple work calls, and taking notes on Dogfish-related ideas. I am now making a conscious effort to stop thinking about work, to stop thinking about the future, and to be fully focused on the present, the moment I am in—with family and friends. I can't turn my work brain off completely so I do allow myself exactly one hour on each of these days to think or write about work. And I am also trying to use half of that time thinking about existing projects, products, and challenges at the company and half thinking about potential new projects or products.

I am trying not to call, e-mail, or text my coworkers as much as I used to. While I am on the road, I am trying to have more of my interactions with the Monday leadership team be less about emergencies du jour, micromanaging, and injecting myself in the tactics their teams are engaged in relating to current projects and objectives. I am trying to be more of a sounding board for them for big-picture, forward-looking goals and strategic discussions. Growing from the entrepreneurial mode to the team-oriented more democratic and holistic approach isn't easy for me but it gets a little easier every month. Thankfully I am not learning my lessons on how to evolve as a leader in a vacuum. Besides Mariah at home and Tammy at work, I have found it helpful to spend time discussing these existential questions of shifting leadership roles with other businesspeople who have navigated similar transitions.

INTERVIEW

Terri Kelly, CEO, W. L. Gore & Associates

Terri Kelly is president and CEO of W. L. Gore & Associates, a multibillion-dollar global enterprise based in Delaware with plants around the world. Best known for waterproof, breathable Gore-Tex fabric, its portfolio of advanced materials products is diverse and inventive. The company is widely recognized for its unique managerial culture. Instead of rigid hierarchies, it functions as a "latticework," interconnected teams of diverse talent organized as equal-ranking "associates" without titles or bosses.

Having the home base for Dogfish Head in Delaware has allowed us to rub up against some of the greatest, most revered companies in the world that just happen to be in our backyard, whether learning about result-oriented ways to reinvest in our local community from the DuPont company or the innovative approach to management and leadership pioneered by W. L. Gore.

"Horizons of Growth"

SAM: I wonder what this is like for you and this company. When it comes to what I should do and what Dogfish Head should do next I feel like there are more choices to be made, good or bad, at the size that we're getting to versus where we were. Up until now, it has been mostly me coming up with what we're going to do next—the new beer, the new product, the new project. I love the creative opportunity that this job has given me, but we've gotten to a scale where it's unwieldy and also selfish, I think, to try to drive creativity and strategy unilaterally if I'm trying to attract these amazing, autonomous leaders to join our team.

TERRI: The question I'm hearing is: Now that your company has reached a level of maturity, how do you build organizational capacity versus the direction of a single leader? We have a lot of parallels if you think about starting with Bill Gore. He was the entrepreneur . . .

SAM: Entrepreneurial founder.

TERRI: He had the vision that started the company, and I would say that carried over to his son, Bob Gore, who was our CEO for several decades, and got dispersed more into the divisions. We've had to evolve from our early days, and it's even more important now that we are sure we're embedding the vision into the organization so multiple folks are thinking about how the vision applies to their function and asking themselves, "What does the enterprise want?"

One of the challenges you'll have is that everyone will have a different vision of where they want to take the company, so I think what you still need to own is that anchoring thing that defines Dogfish Head.

Our vision of who we are is very fundamental. We were put on this planet to be an advanced materials company, focused on our core technology, which we keep expanding, looking for attractive markets where we can apply creative business models and creative approaches. That's what everyone understands. So, when someone comes in and wants to go somewhere else, this touchstone defines who we are. There's this kind of overlay of what the company stands for that you want to be very clear about with your leadership team and confident they can play within that framework.

SAM: But there's still room for ideas to go in any direction?

TERRI: Oh, my God, talk about creativity! But without that overlay, not everyone, especially those without the rich internal history, will have that understanding of the subtleties that really differentiate the company.

SAM: For us, we have our purpose statement, which is super general but kind of evergreen. It's from an Emerson quote that basically we shortened to "Off-centered ales for off-centered people." It not only talks about what we do and what we make but also talks about who we're making it for: off-centered people. The word "ales" in there is a dynamic placeholder. It can be off-centered spirits, a beer-themed hotel. But that's the purpose statement we want to stay with.

We are now for the first time deeply engaged in the challenge of drilling down from this overarching purpose to a clear, concise number of actionable strategic position statements. With the company being so big compared to where we came from and our purpose statement being generic and nebulous, making it practical in terms of where we go next is the goal for this phase of our company's journey.

TERRI: I think we went through a similar journey here at Gore. When we were smaller, folks didn't need a narrative to go with our high-level principles and values. We avoided doing a narrative for many, many years. What I have found more recently, though, as we've hired lots of new associates who come from other companies that may have a different way of thinking about organization, is that we've actually had to write down the narrative.

SAM: Like rules of thumb about how your company works?

TERRI: About how we compete. It's really the statement about how we take that high-level purpose and then use it to compete. Why we made the choices we have made. In your case, it would be something like what you would expect to come from Dogfish Head and what you would not expect to come from it. The more deliberate you can be about choices you made, and it can be choices like why you have chosen to work in certain geographical boundaries or why you have chosen to focus on certain kinds of recipes—whatever it may be—the more you write that down, the easier it is for folks to understand. That doesn't mean the choices don't change over time, but it really helps folks to not go on wild goose chases that are well off the mark.

We call the boundaries within which people can operate the "invisible fence." If they don't know where the invisible fence is, they'll go over it and then you have to say, "Wrong, wrong." That's so demotivating because they didn't know it was there. The more you can kind of show them where the invisible fence is, the better for everybody. And I have to say, in our history it started feeling like we had a lot of those invisible fences, but we weren't teaching the organization to know the boundaries. . . .

SAM: Can you also communicate that in less formal ways?

TERRI: We grew up as a fairly intact and geographically connected team, so the travel of knowledge would be shared naturally. Then, as we've grown, you can't rely on that tribal knowledge to be passed along because of the sheer global scale and number of plans.

SAM: You've talked about the challenge of creating environments where creative, adventurous people feel safe because you need folks who implement creative ideas. You need product and project innovators just as you need operational and managerial leaders. But inevitably as the organizations become bigger and more responsible to the shareholders or their coworkers, it tends to be the more pragmatic folks who get stuff done and have a louder voice and win out instead of the creative types. They bring in more and more structure to the point where you're left wondering, "Well, where did the creativity go as a priority?"

TERRI: We're facing that right now. In our history, we weren't as disciplined, and I think that comes with the territory of having a very entrepreneurial spirit. Our approach was sort of "Just keep trying stuff." But we also need to be effective, and I think our entrepreneurial gene kind of trumped the effectiveness discipline gene. About 15 years ago, we realized we've got to put more structure around making choices because, again, you're always limited on resources; you're always trying to make these calls that you're going to invest in this and not that. So, we did a ton of work on things like portfolio management, which we had not done before, making hard choices and teaching the organization that we've got to be really disciplined around our investments.

SAM: Identifying the ones that weren't working and having the courage to kill them or put them into hiatus for a while?

TERRI: And doing it in a way that the teams made those decisions. This is where you can put discipline in, but it's more empowering to the team if they make the call versus when someone from leadership comes down and says, "Guess what? Your project was killed." So how do you put the tools in front of the team so they can decide why this opportunity would be more attractive than that opportunity? We call it a bull's-eye tool, and it's a pretty simplistic concept. It looks at financial attractiveness, market attractiveness, and then the product differentiation to provide a set of criteria with which they look at each individual opportunity. You need some objective view in the mix as well. Which ones are attractive from all three perspectives? Which ones are less attractive?

This is different from what a lot of companies do where the top-down leader would come and show you what your road map looks like. In our approach, you want the team to learn and have a little bit of the peer pressure from above but then to be educated so the next time they're going to know themselves what to look for that makes one opportunity more attractive than another. We did a lot of work to help teams understand selection process, prioritization, and so forth. That was all good stuff.

What happened to us was that the folks started to value the executors—the folks who really were disciplined around meeting the numbers and hitting the forecast. And lo and behold, even though we always talked about exploring the frontier and all the entrepreneurship, it became less attractive for folks because the time lines are longer; the risk is more fully assessed and articulated.

SAM: Because they knew they'd run the gauntlet of this bull's-eye plus its filters. It has to get through these filters.

TERRI: Exactly. What we've done just in the last year is we've really embraced this concept of what's called "horizons of growth," where you bucket things and you have very different people, very different metrics, and very different disciplines involved together. The Horizon 1s are your executors; they crank out the business plan and are very clear about execution. They're generating all the cash to fund the rest of the operation. They're very important, but you've got to be very careful. On the other side is what we call Horizon 3s. These are the pie-in-the-sky "what if" folks. We've actually had to do some work to help identify and champion the kinds of skills and attributes of individuals who naturally gravitate to that. And guess what? They usually drive the H1 folks nuts.

SAM: Polar opposites.

TERRI: Polar opposites. So we've started to reward them differently. We've started to say we need both of those worlds to be operating with excellence.

A mistake we've made is when we've been really committed to explore the frontier. An idea can get too big and too fleshed out, too fast, to the point where so many people are invested in it that it can't fail and it takes on a life of its own. You've got a whole single team now versus what we've been really embracing, this idea of a tandem between H1 and H3, someone who is more business market savvy and then someone who is more technical. It takes this tandem to determine how something aligns with our capabilities.

SAM: Is the Horizon 2 between them?

TERRI: Yes. Horizon 2 enters once you have these great ideas and you've proven the initial concept.

SAM: Less risk.

TERRI: What we're trying to build now is a clearinghouse for these tandem teams using a common approach across the enterprise. We had pockets of folks doing that in Gore, but everyone did it differently; each had a different language, and now we're saying we want to use a common approach.

So we embrace what's called the "lean start-up." There is a guy named Steve Blank out from Silicon Valley; he was a venture capitalist who built a couple of companies of his own. His whole concept is: How do you make a start-up work in an established company? How do you create that structure within an established structure? We've really shamelessly stolen from him and the concept of how you set up these teams. His big mantra is: "You've got to get out of the building." Because what happens in big organizations is that everyone spends more time internally on the execution even though most of the answers are not inside. They're outside, because you don't have the knowledge within your organization you need to be successful out in the marketplace.

I'll give you a live example of what happens once a concept looks promising. In our protected fabrics, we created a new flame-retardant technology that replaces Nomex, which is basically a fiber that DuPont invented that makes textiles to solve flame-retardant needs. But it comes with lots of trade-offs: cost, functionality, durability, and it's heavy. We've been able to impart a technology where you can take any textile and impart flame-retardant capability. A wonderful concept. The next step in our analysis was what we call product concepts, an exact example of an application—maybe a military application for a battle dress uniform. Now that we've proven the concept, you want to scale some of these things.

This is where the H2 organization comes in; they're the springboard for your execution. We've found that you don't want to just throw the idea over to the execution folks, because they still might kill it in working through the details of how to go to scale. There are all sorts of issues early in the production process that have to be figured out. So at this point there is a handoff to H2 folks, who are maybe not your most creative, exploratory folks but they're really good at building and scaling and addressing those scale problems in advance.

SAM: Getting it out to market viability.

TERRI: Right. You've almost proven viability with the tandem, but now you've got to get the critical mass of building a team. How do you get them established? How do you organize? The Horizon 2 folks start from an exploratory basis and then work through to being an established business, which are the machines running the organization.

So, I would say the cautionary moment for you comes when you get that execution machine humming. Maybe one of your jobs as leader, Sam, will be to ask, "How do I make sure we're really supporting that group of very creative, front-end folks with an environment that can help them think through organizational questions about scale and make sure they're protected from the folks who are really just about profitability and execution?"

SAM: It is sort of like that for us. We have a pretty unique organizational chart—not the lattice scenario that you guys do so well, but a pretty unique org chart in that I'm founder, president, and majority vote for the company. But I've given an opportunity to a really talented guy who is now CEO and rose from a CFO to COO. Last year as chairman of the board I appointed him CEO. His skills are very strong in financial, operational, executional realms, also with people leadership—with all of the VPs reporting to him. My skills are more "What are we going to do next? Let's do an exotic beer. Let's keep pushing the envelope." We generally have very complementary skills, and Mariah is the keeper of our communities and the bullshit meter between Nick and me. . . .

TERRI: Mediates between the two. I can see her doing that.

SAM: It works pretty well, but we're getting to a scale that we have to let him have more autonomy to run what is a sizable org chart but still be sensitive to keeping Dogfish Head known as an innovative, off-centered company. That's one of the challenges that we're facing.

TERRI: The Horizon arrangement might be a framework to look at, because what I'm finding is that if you blur that line between creative and execution, the company will unfortunately gravitate to what is certain, what is known, what is on a surer time horizon. These are typically not the things that are pie-in-the-sky creative.

Many of those execution folks actually get agitated by the creative folks because they don't think the same way. You and your CEO need to value all those activities and consistently be messaging that the execution machine is what is going to allow us to fund the future, and, equally, the folks on the entrepreneurial side have to understand that they would not exist if not for the people funding and executing today. But both sides have to contribute to their rightful roles to make the whole work. I don't think you're going to get every leader to straddle the middle—that's something we call the ambidextrous organization—but your most senior leadership has to do that. They have to be able to recognize and value both sides of the organization, even though they may have a natural inclination . . .

SAM: Toward one or the other.

TERRI: Toward one or the other.

SAM: To shift topics, how do you hire senior executives? Our process is rigorous and exhausting. It took us eight months to hire a VP of sales because we're really hiring a person who fits our senior leadership group first instead of hiring them primarily for their capabilities to run the specific department. We say we have an obligation to each other as leaders to care about each other's departments before we have to care about our own department. We expect our senior folks to be leaders of the whole company, not just individual departments.

TERRI: To have more than just functional expertise.

SAM: How do you navigate that approach in hires? Is it similar for you guys?

TERRI: One of the challenges we have is we also value the deep smarts. We've got some really deep, technical folks who are developing the next polymer. . . .

SAM: I imagine they're very much hard-core technical engineering minds where they don't really care so much about what's happening, say, in HR.

TERRI: Exactly, and what we've tried not to message is that one role is more important than the other. We do a grid and call it a "potential development matrix" where we examine deep leadership versus broad leadership. What you've described, people who consider the whole company, are the folks who can span breadth, people with broad leadership. That's one axis. But it's equally important that you have some deep smarts who are high performers in their field. You want to continue to value them in the organization, so there's an axis to measure deep knowledge performance, as well.

We have a lot of conversations about where we think folks are on that grid. That helps inform who you would be looking at to take on new initiatives and who you would be targeting for more responsibility. Folks with breadth can be stretched into a different function, a different region, versus the deep smarts where you're just . . .

SAM: Keeping making that good beer. Keeping that bottling running.

TERRI: I think what every strong organization is recognizing is the need to find leaders who can look across functions or divisions and not be just one-dimensional. You want a leadership team that is really looking at the whole. They're not there to represent their function.

SAM: You have had more success expanding and growing by grooming internal coworkers toward leadership positions versus finding outside people who have awesome high-level experience elsewhere to come in at a high level. Why is that?

TERRI: What we've found is because we're such a value-based, principle-based organization, with some very strong cultural underpinnings, that bringing someone in to lead right out of the gate, even if they've got all the requisite talent, is a high risk for them and a high risk for the organization. What we typically do, if we know we've got a gap somewhere, is have them fulfill some other role to kind of prove their capability and then they naturally grow.

We've told ourselves that 75 percent of our senior leadership should come from within, meaning we have developed them within the past five years. That still leaves that 25 percent where we need new expertise, and we do better right now to give them time to get acculturated to Gore. For instance, we have a gap in IT security. Every company is worried about cyber security, and we really need to bring in some external talent. We actually have high confidence in that regard because they're coming with the requisite knowledge that we don't have. But if I were to look at our forward division, our market-facing group where all the action happens, to bring in someone from the outside and then have them slot directly into leadership would be really a stretch. If we did that, I would almost feel like we were remiss in doing our job of developing internal talent.

I think that's the problem with a strong culture; it is really hard for someone to come into that environment, especially if they've come from other organizations. They're going to have a different language and a different approach. It has worked in some cases, but we've had probably as many failures.

SAM: When someone is one of the newer slotted people, how do you integrate them?

TERRI: We've had to do that because you don't always have the right person already in the organization and the right timing and so forth. When we bring in an external leader, we have a really frank discussion with the team where they are on board about why we need to bring in an external person, and hopefully they understand it. We explain why. And then we explain that their job is to support that person being successful. You don't want them sitting back on the sidelines.

SAM: Are they involved in the interview process?

TERRI: Typically, they're involved in the interview. But you don't want to run amok; it can't be 20 people.

I'd love to tell you that you can screen everyone who espouses they have your values and they're a team player. But results can be amazing sometimes, especially with experienced hires brought in from the outside. They think they know themselves in terms of how they got there and how they lead, but then when you strip out the power they were accustomed to having by virtue of title and authority and they have to lead through influence, sometimes you get a different reaction in terms of what they're really like.

SAM: For us, we have a liquid truth serum component to hiring a certain level of folks at Dogfish. They spend a whole day with different departments, and we get the feedback from people at different levels and different departments. Then, at night we take them out for beers. How someone acts after three or four beers, after a day of more traditional interactions, can be quite revealing.

TERRI: It's probably a great idea.

SAM: We're a brewery, so we have an excuse.

TERRI: That's awesome.

SAM: We're about to face this shakeout moment in the craft beer community where demand is going to get eclipsed by supply. The best run and differentiated breweries, regardless of scale, will make it through but not every brewery will. I know you wrote in an interview recently about embracing the chaos that is coming. How are you guys navigating that?

TERRI: Right. I always joked that I used to say, "We're in an uncertain period," and then you start to realize that you've basically got to get the organization to understand that it's always going to be volatile. We talk about the VUCA world of volatile, uncertain, complex, and ambiguous. Have you heard that?

SAM: No.

TERRI: Okay. They call VUCA the world's new norm: volatile, uncertain, complex, and ambiguous. It's always going to be in constant flux. . . .

SAM: And stop trying to create a path out of that and instead create a plan through it?

TERRI: And try not to oversimplify that you've got it under control. Now as leaders, you've got to be very careful of what messages you send to not panic the organization, but it really has helped play into our leadership of really getting leaders who are more comfortable in that environment. It's not about having the 10-year plan and just marching to it. I think what they used to teach people in business school is you've got to have that well-articulated plan, you've got to have step one, step two, step three, but step one might be out the window before you start. How do you get folks to have the vision of where they want to go but lots of flexibility in how to get there? That's a different mind-set. We call it the agility to move. Don't get locked into a plan; don't oversimplify messages to your organization that convey an oversimplified view of the world.

One of our other philosophies is some leaders will try to spoon-feed it to the organization and not give them the big picture. They say, "This is what we need to focus on today." As a leader, you're actually thinking of lots of things you need to focus on. How do you paint that there are all these tensions—we call them polarities—that you're always managing? I like teaching the organization to understand these polarities; the more they understand these tensions, the more likely it is that they are going to understand and appreciate that we can't predict the future.

SAM: And not be anxious about it.

TERRI: And not be anxious. Okay, we have to make choices. On the one hand we want to innovate over here, but on the other hand we've got to execute. I think business is a bunch of tensions. We've got to manage short-term and we need to manage long-term.

SAM: As a private company, you're not faced with quarterly Wall Street analyst updates, but internally is there some set communication on all these polarities to maintain the calm within the chaos? How do you do that internally?

TERRI: We are not public. We have quarterly evaluation from an independent stock evaluator so folks can see how we're doing. We publish our monthly financials so every associate can see how we're doing financially. In our team meetings, we're really trying to paint the big picture of how we're doing, what we are trying to accomplish. There is a ton of communication, and I think because we have just been coming out of this strategy refreshed, it has been a great opportunity to put that in the broader context of some of the gaps in our performance.

We've got three gaps that we've identified. One is around this balance of innovation we just talked about.

The second for us, and maybe you'll face this as well, is that when you have a very entrepreneurial company, every team wants to do it their way and so the creative juices can run amok. They'll come up with their own language, their own process, their own system they want to use, and we've allowed that to proliferate over 50-some years, so can you imagine the mess that we've created when you're trying to hook all that together.

So, the second big initiative for us is how do we continue to value those autonomous teams but then also have a common IT backbone. We want creativity in certain areas. In other areas, it's just waste. I've been messaging that differentiation for the past 10 years, but it took a structural shift to say, "This is what we're going to do" in terms of core processes at Gore.

SAM: How does the rubber hit the road there? Did you find one format that is a good way in to the first step, of saying, "Keep your creativity in terms of your work, but we need more uniformity in terms of communicating your work"?

TERRI: We probably have been lax in thinking of everything as a business process. We think about how to get our arms around manufacturing as a process of steps, but there is a whole process for how to do product development; there is a whole process for how you screen new ideas or how you pay your bills. We are trying to get folks to think more about what are the core processes that we need as a company. We do not need 20,000 different ways to ship product out the door.

It's a huge project for us because we've allowed it to grow up to now 10,000 associates with many teams having done things in a different way.

SAM: That's basically the head count globally of everyone on the Gore payroll?

TERRI: Yes, 10,000 around the world, right.

SAM: Those were the first two gaps. What is the third?

TERRI: The third one is interesting. It is more around the culture and how much folks are really aligning with the strategic intent of our culture and values. How do we get back to what the Gores saw from the beginning about creating an environment that was going to make us more successful? With a very strong value-based organization, if you're not careful, people lose the plot. They understand that we're here to have this great value-based organization, but every day you're thinking about business outcomes. If we don't deliver profits, we're not going to get there. Believe it or not, with 10,000 associates you can lose that connectivity to "What is the environment we want to create?" that allows us to get to that outcome.

So, the third one is really looking at what are the things that are going to challenge our values, our DNA, to make the shifts that I talked about.

SAM: That's timely for us, because we're in the early phases of our first-ever strategic plan. I get it that with 230 coworkers we need some map of where we're going. I really have embraced the concept, though, that we can still be a creative, unique company even with a strategic plan if we do it our way instead of the cookie-cutter way. What recommendations do you have for me and for Dogfish as we embark on our first-ever, holistic sort of company-wide strategic plan?

TERRI: We don't have a strategic plan. We have a destination of what we were put on this planet to do. For us, it is advancing our materials, and we have specific definitions of that—improving lives through advanced materials. How are we applying our materials to make huge impact in the markets we serve? You can go into a lot of material application where you can make a cigarette filter. Well, we're not sure that's improving lives, so we also are making a statement around impact—societal impact. I think we still feel this commitment is as true today as it was 50-some years ago. We start from that point, and then we consider strategic choices of how we choose to compete.

We are, at the heart of Gore, a product leadership company. We've made a strategic choice about markets and product areas that we're really going to compete in; we've also decided what we're not going to do. I think that's different from a plan. In essence, you are kind of giving some guardrails with a lot of flexibility to the relative teams for the broad road they're driving down. You don't want to overprescribe a plan that assumes you can predict the future; instead, we determine the destination and some clear values or parameters that shape our focusing strategies of how we will compete.

SAM: So the consultants who helped you, the Institute for the Future, worked with you on the gap process, not on the strategy?

TERRI: Actually, they worked at the very beginning. We didn't even have a strategy. They worked to understand us and they got to know our DNA, and then they picked hot buttons. They picked, for example, this whole idea of data analytics, and they learned a lot about our dysfunctionality, about how we can't even find our data because of the various silos and just started to paint a picture about how companies are going to be using data to inform decisions and how that is going to be a huge competitive advantage.

Another one they picked was around the Internet of Things and how all products are connected. It is kind of related to the data analytics but more to just smart materials and how they will shape the products of the future. All of our products are pretty passive, so how does that maybe help inform future product ideas?

Another one they picked for us was what they called "New Stories, New Meaning." How do we successfully engage our associates' thinking about changing demographics and how younger demographics work?

SAM: There's one last area I wanted to cover with you if you've got 10 more minutes—this has been awesome! How do you attract great leaders to stay with the company when, since you're a privately held company, there's not a scenario where equity can be considered? What have you found are the greatest performance-based things that you can offer?

TERRI: Fundamentally, we have a different way of rewarding talent for all of our associates. One merit criterion is a peer ranking, based on contribution. Now, for some that's scary, but for many very high-performing leaders who really want to be first, it gives them a chance to rise to the top. It's not the leader assessing the talent. The peers are ranking who is making the greatest contribution to the enterprise. That's scary for some, but for those who are really driven, they feel that they can make a difference based on the impact of what they're able to accomplish.

For senior leaders, we do have opportunities where they can actually get stock. I don't know if you'd ever think of this. We have a stock ownership program, which is our ESOP, which is our retirement that every associate gets.

The idea is that if they really are instrumental in growing the value of the company or, on the other hand, if we're not growing, they should have skin in the game. You could create a stock or whatever you want to call it with an outside evaluator based on performance and data you give them, and then you could issue participating shares to associates who meet certain criteria, which they could cash after it has been vested.

Now, is this as lucrative as what other folks can get? Probably not. But what I have found, and I am sure you have, is that those who are driven purely by the financial and the big plate high risk are going to leave, and it doesn't matter what you pay them. You're going to lose them. But for those who are really passionate, I think you can create a competitive pay mix.

SAM: Thanks so much. I've waterboarded you with questions, and you've been honest.

TERRI: No, it's been fun. I'm curious: What are the things that keep you up at night for Dogfish?

SAM: The biggest thing is not getting enough resources to the company quickly enough to keep making the bold innovative decisions that have made our brand resonate in an increasingly crowded market. We don't have enough resources at our company to manage all these things that are fun and creative that we've done; we're starting to resent new ideas at our company because we don't have enough resources to manage the ideas that are already partially gestated.

TERRI: And that's back to the right mix, to the right level of activity you would expect in each of those buckets. You have to be purposeful, to say "Okay, we can't manage many more of these new ideas." But you want to go in consciously so it doesn't default to only what you have the capacity to handle. Unfortunately, what typically happens is the stuff that you can execute on that is more near-term and more certain takes priority, and then those other ideas never get acted upon.

SAM: They just stay out there.

TERRI: You keep pushing them out and pushing them out. We're guilty as charged. We did do some work on even looking at what are the kinds of attributes of folks who tend to work better on long-term projects, the folks who naturally gravitate to the front-end exploratory phase of a project. One of the misnomers that we found is that some people think the front end doesn't have a discipline. That's not true; it's just a different kind. It's not the same metrics; it's not the same discipline, but you are trying to test things every day and kill things fast. If people have the idea that you kind of unleash the "invisible fence" for these creative types and let them out to roam and do whatever they want, that creates resentment in the folks who are executing. They see these guys as just freelancing; they're not doing anything. You have to have rigor on both sides. Lean start-up requires a lot of rigor.

SAM: Not having the humility to kill things early on is something that, frankly, I've personally suffered from when I was the guy who was doing all the strategic and creative stuff. I was too tied to my ego as the founder. I need to also use my creativity to help move other people's great creative ideas forward while still getting the chance to take the lead on a few manageable and well-communicated innovative projects myself since I know that has been beneficial for the company since the start.

TERRI: We all get very passionate. We're looking at what kind of objective group is best suited to help make those decisions and most qualified to manage the front-end portfolio.

SAM: Amen to that. I want to be conscious of your time. This was wonderful. Thank you.

Afterword

> Do I contradict myself? Very well, then I contradict myself, I am large, I contain multitudes.
>
> —*Walt Whitman*

It may seem strange for me to end a book on leadership by saying that I am still learning how to be a better leader. Perhaps it's a bit of a contradiction to consider myself both a student *and* a teacher in this realm, but I am comfortable with this truth. We have all heard some version of the old adage: life is not about reaching a destination; it's about getting the most out of the journey. For me, the process of writing this book has given me a journal to document the major lessons I am learning as well as a forum through which I can share and teach. It is my hope that readers who are also in leadership roles can find common ground, useful directions, and similar routes that can positively inform their respective journeys.

Good leaders invite the people they lead to influence them—to teach them—to push them—to help them continually improve and evolve. This is the reason I have dedicated this book to the talented and passionate leaders I work with and have worked with in the past at Dogfish Head. *This is not my book.* As its author, it's mostly my voice telling our story, but I have worked hard to be as honest and open as possible and to incorporate the perspectives and contributions of my fellow leaders in the journey documented on these pages.

My evolution as a leader has become more rewarding as I have become more proactive and considerate in sharing the creative and strategic directing opportunities at our company, rather than keeping them for myself. It was a luxury I couldn't afford when Dogfish Head was a tiny company fighting for survival and Mariah and I were the de facto leadership team. It was the right next step but I didn't fully embrace it until a couple of short years ago. I am learning to be more patient, and more intentional in terms of developing the right instincts to know when my creative leadership contributions are most effective and when I am serving the company better by playing a supporting role and allowing others to take the lead. The moments of creativity and trust that come with encouraging and developing rising leaders have to be as rewarding as the moments when the entrepreneur gets to use his or her own creativity—or the organization will never grow beyond the involvement of the founding entrepreneur(s).

For any reader in the most senior leadership position taking steps in the direction of a more inclusive and collaborative leadership journey at your organization, I recommend you begin by sitting down with your leadership team and taking an honest look at where you are today, personally and as a team, where you want to go tomorrow, and how you will help and hold each other accountable to get there. This is the work we are doing at Dogfish Head now: with Tammy our internal Dogfish leadership coach; with Stew Friedman, our external personal leadership coach; and most critically, with each other every day as the fellow leaders and coworkers of Dogfish Head define, execute, and evolve our strategic plan and our off-centered position in the marketplace together.

I have learned that before you can focus on togetherness and creating harmony as a leadership team, you have to focus on yourself. You must first mentor yourself to be open to this growth and positive change before you are truly capable of mentoring others.

If you are already in a leadership role and/or you are a successful entrepreneur, you are obviously the leader you needed to be to get to where you stand today, but—are you the leader you need to be to get your organization moving forward toward the brightest, most rewarding future possible?

To begin to answer this, ask this question: are you doing the creative and leadership work that brings you the most personal happiness *and* the work that brings the most value to your organization? Can you take steps to move these (frequently) different but related goals into a greater overlapping foundation? Review your calendar for the last three months and honestly assess how much of the work you have done is aligned with both of these priorities. Do everything you can to tweak your forward-looking three-month calendar into allocating time to these related value- and happiness-driving priorities with a goal of having them overlap more and more.

I believe you are more likely to find happiness following your passion in your worklife instead of following a paycheck. Each of us as individuals contains talents and preferences that make our personal passions resonate and our individual journeys unique. We contain multitudes. And that is a beautiful thing. I am beginning to understand there is an important trait that all successful leaders share. Those of us who have become successful leaders share a passion for connecting with other people. Whether they are customers or coworkers, or people related to our work in more tangential ways, connecting with other people means listening. Listening to what is important to them, what excites them, and sharing what is important and meaningful to you. Listening and learning and letting the best and most truthful pieces of information we learn from each other inform our respective journeys is at the core of our growth as leaders.

This is why you can get so much further ahead as an organization and as an individual on your continual quest to become a better leader by focusing on collaboration instead of competition. Collaboration is about engaging *with* other people and competition is about working *against* other people. What do we build up when we focus on competing *against* each other? Mistrust, misalignment, separatism, disengagement, and alienation. When we engage *with* other people collaboratively we listen, we learn, we evolve, and we improve. We build communities and commonalities. We build trust and harmony. I am thankful for each of the collaborative-minded talented and passionate people I have encountered on my personal leadership journey so far—many of whom are mentioned or quoted within this book and many of whom are not.

A meaningful life is built on a foundation of concentric circles, from yourself, to your immediate family outward, to your loved ones, coworkers, friends, and customers. Making these connections and continuing to enhance them is what life is mostly about. In addition to family life, at the heart of it, your business—your job—is nothing more nor less than the primary catalyst for interconnectivity between you and other people: as in my relationship with the customers whose support for our company has contributed to the success of Dogfish Head and has brought me much happiness in my life. In addition to my interfamily relationships, it's my relationships with my fellow leaders, my coworkers, the fellow artists, and entrepreneurs I have been lucky enough to work with, that have brought the most meaning to my life. Happiness and meaningfulness are interrelated but not necessarily synonymous. This is just another illustration of how we each contain multitudes.

The excerpt following is from a study conducted at Stanford on finding meaning and happiness in life which succinctly describes what I am talking about. I would include my relationships with fellow leaders and coworkers in the category of deep relationships described here:

> Connections to other people are important both for meaning and happiness. But the nature of those relationships is how they differ. Deep relationships—such as family—increase meaning, while spending time with friends may increase happiness but have little effect on meaning. Time with loved ones involves hashing out problems or challenges, while time with friends may simply foster good feelings without much responsibility.[1]

Keep driving to make new connections to passionate and positive people and keep working to enhance those deep relationships we have already forged. A priority of interconnectivity over one of exclusivity, of status, wealth, and competition, is the most rewarding path we can take.

As an aspiring entrepreneur trying to create a niche in a competitive market, you must focus on creating a product or service that is balanced on three priorities: quality, consistency, and a well-differentiated market position. As a leader who is still learning how to be a *better* leader, I also believe that there are three characteristics all great leaders share: intelligence, creativity, and flexibility. The need for intelligence and creativity as fundamental leadership components is self-explanatory. I believe it's the flexibility component that is more nuanced and more elusive and yet equally necessary to those who understand the importance of working collaboratively. The very definition of flexibility is *the quality of bending easily without breaking*. Great leaders know that they cannot succeed by being militant and rigid and issuing unilateral directives. They always have a sense of balance—trusting that the support given will be reciprocated. Great leaders know that the connections to their direct reports and coworkers in general are bonds that are conduits

[1]http://news.stanford.edu/news/2014/january/meaningful-happy-life-010114.html.

to shared success—not puppet strings implemented for their selfish control. Leaders who try to control everything themselves, who micromanage and undervalue the contributions of others, can never be *great* leaders.

Somewhat unexpectedly, I found a great summary for the need for flexibility, balance, and productive interaction between coworkers in the text of Herman Melville's *Moby Dick*. In this passage Ishmael, the sailor and the book's narrator, is literally tethered by a rope (a monkey rope in the sailing vernacular) to Queequeg, the harpooner, who is dangling precariously off the side of the ship, cutting the precious blubber from the body of a sperm whale:

> So strongly and metaphysically did I conceive of my situation then, that while earnestly watching his motions, I seemed distinctly to perceive that my own individuality was now merged in a joint stock company of two: that my free will had received a mortal wound; and that another's mistake or misfortune might plunge innocent me into unmerited disaster and death. Therefore, I saw that here was a sort of interregnum in Providence; for its even-handed equity never could have sanctioned so gross an injustice. And yet still further pondering—while I jerked him now and then from between the whale and the ship, which would threaten to jam him—still further pondering, I say, I saw that this situation of mine was the precise situation of every mortal that breathes; only, in most cases, he, one way or other, has this Siamese connexion with a plurality of other mortals. If your banker breaks, you snap; if your apothecary by mistake sends you poison pills, you die. True, you may say that, by exceeding caution, you may possibly escape these and the multitudinous other evil chances of life. But handle Queequeg's monkey-rope heedfully as I would, sometimes he jerked it so, that I came very near sliding overboard. Nor could I possibly forget that, do what I would I only had the management of one end of it.

A "Siamese connexion with a plurality of other mortals" is maybe the most beautiful definition of human collaboration I have ever read.

I want to end this book with a shout out and provocation directly to you, the reader: one word that is the most concise rallying cry for collaborative interaction in any language. I wish you much joy, success, and enlightenment as you continue on your own leadership journey. The spirit in me celebrates the spirit in you: NAMASTE!

Index